Organized Skepticism in the Age of Misinformation

Drawing from philosophy, information theory, and network science, *Organized Skepticism in the Age of Misinformation: Surviving the Kingdom of Gossip* offers a novel conceptual framework that views information as a form of gossip.

This book challenges the idea that truthfulness is a necessary, or even a relevant condition, of information. Instead, this book develops a conceptual framework in which information is understood as gossip, which fits within a more general account of information and knowledge as constrained but contingent social practices. Using this framework, this book provides a nuanced understanding of the "grammar" of gossip that permeates both online and real-world environments and sheds light on the often overused and confused terms of our time: information, misinformation, and knowledge.

This book offers a fundamental reconfiguration of the evolving virtual interdependence of humans and information technology. It is a key resource for students and scholars in areas relating to social media, information diffusion, human/computer interface, and computational social science.

Organized Skepticism in the Age of Misinformation
Surviving the Kingdom of Gossip

Brett Bourbon and Renita Murimi

CRC Press
Taylor & Francis Group
Boca Raton London New York

CRC Press is an imprint of the
Taylor & Francis Group, an **informa** business

First edition published 2025
by CRC Press
2385 NW Executive Center Drive, Suite 320, Boca Raton FL 33431

and by CRC Press
4 Park Square, Milton Park, Abingdon, Oxon, OX14 4RN

CRC Press is an imprint of Taylor & Francis Group, LLC

© 2025 Brett Bourbon and Renita Murimi

ISBN: 9781032513218 (hbk)
ISBN: 9781032493473 (pbk)
ISBN: 9781003401674 (ebk)

DOI: 10.1201/9781003401674

Typeset in Minion
by codeMantra

Contents

Preface, vii

Acknowledgments, ix

Authors, xi

Preface

THIS BOOK IS ABOUT misinformation and the internet. Therefore, it is also about information and knowledge, and in the end about gossip and rumor. Authorities, pundits, and academics all shout in panic that we are afflicted by a misinformation pandemic, a plague of data, and a crisis of knowledge. Others say that we are threatened by "Information Disorder" or by the pollution of the information ecosystems. We face problems, but panic is unnecessary. Nevertheless, people continue to panic. They search for cures, magic bullets, and ideological grails. Among these searchers, a faith persists that if only people knew the facts, then they would give up their false notions and reject their misinformed beliefs. Misinformation, people continue to imagine, can be corrected with true information. We do not think this is true. Knowledge, information, and misinformation are all misunderstood and their relationship with gossip and rumor is too often denied and overlooked.

Gossip is the monarch of the internet, and we live in its kingdom. This book is meant to motivate, although not accomplish, a dispossession of the monarchy. Revolt is pointless. Gossip is pervasively human. We dream of replacing the kingdom of gossip with a republic of gossip. Gossip, itself, cannot be defeated. It will remain the master form of information. But if we become citizens of information, responsible for our informing and being informed, then we will more readily live flourishing lives amidst gossip's powerful tides and currents.

The monarchy of gossip has several areas of vulnerability. The area of vulnerability that we want to leverage involves what we call the crisis of knowledge amidst which we live. This will be the lever we use to clarify, describe, and diagnose the economy of information supporting the kingdom of gossip. In response to this crisis, we will delineate a practice of everyday epistemology, or the study and evaluation of everyday modes of knowledge which will include their overlap or impingement on scientific ways of knowing.

People in the land of Oz fear and respect the power of the great Oz, a mysterious figure who rules the land from his castle. But when Dorothy and her friends reach the castle, they discover that Oz is a wizened old man, using technology to make himself appear great and to induce awe in the people around him. But behind the curtain of this projected appearance, he is nothing much at all. Gossip is a king like Oz. It seems all powerful, but its power is parasitic on our own behavior. We need not subject ourselves to its power, if only we can pull back the curtain and see clearly what knowledge, information, misinformation, and gossip really are. We might then lose our awe of the monarchy of gossip, while also renouncing the misguided dream of a theocracy of information.

We began establishing a counter-position to much of the literature on misinformation in computational social science through a series of papers, the first of which was published in 2020 in *Proceedings of the 6th International Conference on Computational Social Science* (IC2S2). As our explorations deepened, so did our conviction that a book about misinformation is necessary. This is that book.

Acknowledgments

We would like to thank Paskalina Bourbon for her editorial care and philosophical acumen. We also owe the title of the book to the good auspices of Felicia Martinez.

- **Brett:** I would also like to thank my electrical engineer father, Bruce Bourbon, for many conversations about computers and the internet. He encouraged my love of physics, which I have nurtured over the many years even as I studied other topics.
- **Renita:** I would like to thank my family for their unwavering support of my writing endeavors. In particular, I thank my husband, Robert, and our three children, my mother Irene, and acknowledge the memory of my father, who have all inspired me to explore and write.

Authors

Brett Bourbon is Professor of English Literature at the University of Dallas. He is also a Visiting Professor in The Program of Literary Theory at the University of Lisbon. He received his PhD from Harvard and was a professor at Stanford. He was awarded a Mellon postdoctoral fellowship and a Fulbright Award. He has published many essays and four books, including *Finding a Replacement for the Soul: Meaning and Mind in Literature and Philosophy* (Harvard UP, 2004), *Everyday Poetics: Ethics, Love, and Logic* (Bloomsbury Academic, 2022), *Jane Austen and the Ethics of Life* (Routledge Press, 2022), and *Thinking with Words: A Literary Groundwork* (with Miguel Tamen) (Routledge Press, 2024).

Renita Murimi is Associate Professor of Cybersecurity at the University of Dallas. She received her PhD and MS in Electrical Engineering from the New Jersey Institute of Technology. Her research interests are in the areas of cybersecurity and network science. She has received the Melinda Gates Foundation's Grand Challenges Exploration grant. Her research has been widely published in journals, book chapters, and conference proceedings. She is also the author of an upcoming book titled *Ten Modern Cryptographic Algorithms* (No Starch Press, forthcoming).

Introduction

In 2021, on average 319.6 billion emails were exchanged worldwide. In 2025, that number is expected to approximate 376.4 billion. Of course, there are many more ways of sharing information, pictures, and other kinds of content than by email. So, the total amount of information exchanged by means of the internet and the World Wide Web, excluding news, magazines, blogs, and other more traditional media, is incredibly high. Online social networks (OSNs), including Facebook, Instagram, and X (Twitter), have become overlapping virtual public spheres. In addition, texting has become the primary means for personal and private communication. This mix of private and public, in conjunction with the immediacy and scope of internet exchanges, undermines and further polarizes public and political discourse and discussion. And it also facilitates the narcissistic vectors in modern culture, encouraging lives of public display. In such a culture, the online influencer becomes the pinnacle of self-fulfillment and public success.

One particularly acute problem corrupting and distorting the virtual public sphere is the prevalence of misinformation. The spread of misinformation and 'fake news' undermines the ability of people to act as responsible citizens, distorting civil society into a volatile mix of polarizing belief and mistrust. If the public sphere is inundated and thus deformed by misinformation and 'fake' news, then, many wonder, how can our societies survive?

The most common response to this threat is to imagine that 'false information' must be countered with 'true information.' Such a solution, however, fails to take into account the motives and mechanisms of information exchange. In *Organized Skepticism in the Age of Misinformation*, we argue that most of what we call information should be understood as gossip. With gossip, truth is secondary to the social value of the gossip

DOI: 10.1201/9781003401674-1

shared. As a consequence, the spread of information online is part of an economy of social exchange that mimics ordinary human gossip, but with some dangerous and critical differences. If we understand the problem of information diffusion as not one about facts, data, or knowledge, but as the consequence of a peculiar form of gossip, we can more clearly determine how to respond to the challenges and dangers of social media.

There have been a few important studies that point to the inappropriateness of current models of misinformation diffusion. An earlier important study by Sharad Goel, Duncan J. Watts, and Daniel G. Goldstein (2012) shows clearly that information diffusion is seldom viral, since it is not self-replicating. While this does not offer direct support for our contention that online information diffusion should be understood as a form of gossip, it does suggest that internet behavior, while facilitated and constrained by network structures, is often more powerfully guided by the personal and social realities of which it is a part. The work of Zeynep Tufekci also shows how the meaning of online behavior is both dynamic and embedded in critical ways within offline human communities.

Similarly, Soroush Vosoughi, Deb Roy, and Sinan Aral (2018) discovered that false information spread more rapidly and more deeply through a network than did true information. This again points to the critical role of social dynamics in information spread, a dynamics that we contend is best modeled as gossip.

Despite our continual intimacy with gossip, or maybe because of that intimacy, accounts of gossip tend to be rich in details but underconceptualized. Information, on the other hand, is overformalized and overgeneralized as a concept, leading to multiple confusions and misunderstandings. One of our primary goals is to provide an adequate conceptual description of gossip (as well as of information and misinformation). A poor understanding of the social dynamics of information exchange, as well as the nature of misinformation and social media, will necessarily encourage beliefs, policies, and laws that will only exacerbate the problems they were intended to ameliorate. Consequently, if we are to mitigate the dangers of OSNs, we must shift our focus from the truth or falsity of information and instead focus on the social dynamics of information exchange. If we are to do that, we must have an adequate understanding and descriptive conceptualization of gossip and misinformation. This is what we provide in *Organized Skepticism in the Age of Misinformation*.

The study of OSNs and information diffusion and uptake involves numerous disciplines. Given the centrality of computers, data, and networks, the initially relevant disciplines are computer science, information sciences, network science, data science, and other related disciplines. Our involvement with OSNs, of course, does not just involve network data; it involves psychological and sociological factors, modes, and patterns. New fields have emerged to explore this mix of computational and network affordances with human behavior. These include computational social science (CSS) and connection science. The latter is described on an MIT website as "Working to revolutionize technology-mediated human networks through analysis, prediction, data-driven design, and evaluation" (http://connection.mit.edu/). This is called a science, but it is really an attempt at social engineering by technological means: attempting to solve social problems using networks, data, computation, and so on.

The development of the social sciences in the 20th century was accompanied by strong critical arguments against the very possibility of such sciences. Controlled and rigorous experiments on social conditions or so-called structures are difficult. The social sciences, particularly sociology, are invariably guided by ideologies. This cannot help but distort the conclusions drawn by social scientists. Statistical descriptions of particular communities and populations have contributed to a greater understanding of various forces and patterns in social life, especially if such descriptions are framed historically. Nevertheless, it is unclear if social behavior and patterns can be explained by the development of law-like generalizations. The social sciences, in general, lack the rigor and precision of physics. And even if society is more like an organism than it is an object, social scientists cannot establish, let alone study the mechanisms of the so-called social organism in the way biologists can study DNA, cells, physiology, anatomy, and so on. In addition, the explanations of human behavior require that we examine what this behavior means for human agents, and such explorations of meaning are interpretative and bound to judgment in ways that explanations in the physical sciences never are.

Nevertheless, the social sciences should retain one of the central constraints and principles of all sciences, what the sociologist Robert Merton called "organized skepticism." This is not all that science is, but it is the key factor that allows it to be self-correcting, suspicious of theory, and focused on evidence.[1] Social science, however, has a very complicated relation to evidence. Recent controversies have shown that over 50% of the findings in the various social sciences, including psychology, cannot be replicated (Ritchie, 2023). More importantly, we are the targets of these sciences, and thus, whatever we take ourselves to be as objects of study is already implicated in our descriptions of ourselves. Social science, therefore, is radically dependent on our self-understanding and on our descriptions and conceptualizations of ourselves as agents and as part of various groups—family, friends, communities, societies, and states.

All of the different sciences involve exploration, questioning, and the determination of the appropriate concepts by which to explain and describe the various phenomena under investigation. In physics, such concepts can be defined mathematically. In earth's gravity field, force is defined in Newtonian physics as the mass of some object times its acceleration. Mass and acceleration are both measurements, as is force. Mass, as a concept, over time has replaced the notion of matter, which has become ill-defined under the pressures of atomic theory and relativity theory. Sociological concepts are not like those developed and used in physics. Concepts like class, structure, identity, and power are difficult or impossible to measure, or their measures are tendentious and ideologically determined. The majority of sociological concepts do not have mathematical definitions and are often a mix of terms developed in everyday culture and those formalized through the study of that culture. Here we see part of the problem. The targets of our study—individual behavior, class, hierarchy—are bound up with ideas that individuals have about themselves and about what they do. Peter Winch recognizes this in his arguments for the development of an interpretative social science to counter the misguided tendency to model the social sciences on the physical sciences. Our goal is not to rehearse and then adjudicate among the various accounts of science. Nor do we want to develop a theory about the role of evidence and concepts in the various sciences. We simply want to motivate the importance of developing, critiquing, and justifying a minimal vocabulary in our analysis and attempts to understand our involvement with the internet and social media. And this vocabulary is not simply a list of vetted words, but rather is a complex of words, ideas, thoughts, descriptions, data, and so on—always grounded in a vast range of examples.

Consequently, our central task will be to clarify and reconceptualize the master terms we use to characterize our complex involvement with online social media. The terms we explore are the ones you would expect: information, misinformation, disinformation, information diffusion (spread), data, content, and fake news. We will also explore important sociological terms: community, groups, crowds, friends, gossip, and rumors. A few other theorists argue that these terms are misleading and encourage us to replace them with others. For example, Claire Wardle suggests that we replace misinformation, disinformation, and mal-informationwith"theumbrellaterm'informationdisorder'"(https://issues.org/misunderstanding-misinformation-wardle/). What is needed, however, are not new labels. All of these terms are what we call *contested*, which means that what they mean is determined as much by our theories about them as from evidence derived from experience. The sense of what is described cannot be separated from our assumptions and theories about what we describe. Our ideas about power and class, for example, are bound up in varying degrees with our theories of these, since what they are and how they are manifest are partly determined by those theories. This does not mean that these terms are nothing more than theoretical constructs, but that arguments about what they are cannot be separated from our arguments about the various theories we hold about such concepts.

In response to such a situation, we must be scrupulous in our descriptions of phenomena and strive for minimal descriptions that diminish the theoretical element in our characterizations. This will allow us to trace how phenomena get absorbed in our theories. Instead of simply further-ing that absorption, we can stay focused on how the phenomena we want to understand are manifest in our everyday lives and interactions. We can then develop an adequate conceptual vocabulary and understanding of the phenomena in a minimal way.

This will allow us to be at least intellectually responsible for the theo-retical (often ideological) additions and elaborations we introject into our minimal descriptions. An ideological science is not science. If ideology is sovereign in the work of scientists and researchers, then evidence and notions of truth become subservient to proper ideology. That is politics and propaganda, and not science. So, either they should pursue minimal descriptions as one of the primary tasks of CSS, or they should give up their pretensions of science. In which case, their arguments would become interpretations within ideological battles. Not only would that be unfortu-nate and debilitating, it would disguise the everyday reality of our involve-ment with OSNs, and it would blind us to ourselves as human beings. Not every aspect of life is political or ideological (which, of course, does not mean no aspect is).

Part of our intellectual responsibility involves determining the real-ity of our concepts, what we might call their ontological status. This can be a problem in the physical sciences as well as the social sciences. Our ideas about light and waves encouraged 19th-century physicists to imag-ine something called the ether through which light waves could propagate beyond earth's atmosphere. The ether, however, did not exist; our assumptions about light were wrong. For social concepts like power and class, asking if they exist is less useful than asking how they are manifest to us: how they are manifest, for example, through our actions, within our experience, relative to other people. Always our concepts must be manifest as something, even if they should not be reduced to that manifestation. Power may be something other than any particular manifestation of what we call power. Or it may not be. To understand what power is relative to what we take as its manifestation is exactly the kind of work that must be done in the social sciences. And what is true of power is true of every other social concept, including information and misinformation, and even the metaphor of the so-called information ecosystem.

We will argue, therefore, that many of the fundamental problems and questions about our engagement with OSNs are *not* simply questions of fact and are not open to statistical research or the raw collection of data. These problems and questions are often (although not always) conceptual. One common problem, for example, is to understand how online behavior differs from (exaggerates or diminishes) modes of behavior that are common in life separate from online modes. Our initial interface with computers is isolated, individual, and private—but then we can enter into virtual public spaces, where various rules for public behavior are weak, encouraging, for example, trolling behavior. But this same process of public criticism can create group conformity relative to the group identification of the particular people involved. Information diffusion supports such group conformity and can look similar to crowd behavior, and like what Freud called a group-mind. Crowd formation and action, however, depends on physical proximity, as Elias Canetti and others convincingly argue. Online crowds lack this kind of proximity. Are they, therefore, really crowds or some new kind of group-mind? How will artificial intelligence (AI) effect and affect such group-minds, if they exist? Answers to these questions can only be determined after the fact. Whatever the answer, the key factor in shaping, creating, and maintaining communities online is gossip.

The primary conceptual terms in CSS and other data-focused sciences fit inseparably with other concepts. The concepts of information and misinformation, for example, are entangled with ideas (and prejudices) about knowledge—about how and what we know and the status of this knowledge. Epistemological questions naturally lead to questions about truth, falsity, consistency, and coherence. Various theorists have also attempted to derive theories of information that go beyond Shannon's minimal, statistical definition of information to semantical theories, in which, as John Mingers and Craig Standing argue, information is necessarily objective and veridical (2018). We will argue that such a definition and similar such theories that support or depend on such definitions are false, incoherent, and by and large unnecessary. But to do so, we will again demonstrate how our concepts are entangled with other concepts and how even some computational concepts are entangled with sociological and psychological concepts (this is especially the case when informational notions are used to replicate human cognitive behavior). This entanglement of concepts means that confusions about information are often confusions about epistemology or warrant or semantics. If we are to describe well, we must untangle the knot of interrelated concepts that produce misleading descriptions of the social phenomena we are attempting to study. One cannot stipulate definitions, one must discover them. To do that requires one to go back and forth between the phenomena examined and our various theoretically-infused descriptions of them. This is partly what it means to take part in a scientific practice of organized skepticism.

One of our central claims is that information spread should be modeled on and understood as a form of gossip. This can seem like a simple and unsurprising claim. As we have mentioned above, it goes against the prevalent ideas informing current models for information diffusion. Understanding information diffusion as gossip significantly alters how we understand information and the possibilities of the internet and social media. In support of this central claim, we provide a description of the essential elements or aspects of gossip as a discursive practice. The practice of gossip does not have a logical form. If it were to have a logical form, there would be some set of necessary aspects or factors without which it would not be gossip. The assertion of necessity is too strong. We argue that gossip has a kind of grammar, as Wittgenstein might have called it. But really it is a practice—with essential aspects that characterize that practice.[2] One might describe these factors differently, highlighting psychological motivations, for example. Our goal is to describe the form of the practice, identifying the factors that we understand as contingently necessary. This conditional aspect of common human practices fits with what we are attempting to understand more generally—the contingent patterns of human life.

One contingency that will gain the force of a seeming necessity is the growing power and presence of generative AIs. The rise of generative artificial intelligence models has increased the power and effectiveness of deepfake imitations of people, producing misleading portrayals of individuals and actions. Generative AI software is now being blended with presentation software. School children, for example, can ask the software to generate a picture representing a "dusty battleground sky in the French-Indian war" for their school presentation in history class. In other uses of AI, grammar gets effortlessly corrected and normalized, words are suggested, and sentences are completed. Software code is being written on command. Entire essays, books, songs, marketing copy, case law briefs, and speeches are generated through these machine learning tools. These generative AIs will not only become quasi-agents in the web gossip economy but will create a new kind of virtual environment, a quasi-society within which many people will engage with each other as they already do on Instagram and TikTok. We will conclude this book by **touching on** how these generative AIs alter and augment the gossip economy of the web, further accelerating the narcissistic forms of engagement encouraged by the ways we interface with OSNs.

The mimicry of generative AIs fits the pattern of mediation that defines the web and our interface with it. This should be called the culture of the interface. As is the case in every culture, this culture of the interface is a culture of conflict and accommodation. The internet externalizes aspects of our own minds into view and into conflict with an earlier vocabulary describing what we know and how we know it. The internet is both a conceptual accelerator of cultural change and a dynamic evolving mirror of ourselves and our offline culture. Consequently, it not just offers something to study in itself but also offers a way of studying ourselves, by offering large datasets of human behavior. It offers not just data but also new conceptual opportunities for our human self-understanding. We meet ourselves as we attempt to conceptualize the mediated and mediating forces of OSNs through disciplines like CSS and sociology, cultural studies, and philosophy of technology. The web and OSNs provide dynamic and evolving fields and forms of culture. They offer the tools, contexts, and even new agents for the creation of culture, social experience, economic opportunities, and personal expression and display. But what is often made with such tools are further precincts and forms of a virtual, networked, and highly mediated reality. This is a new kind of city, gathering and directing people and opportunities into patterns of shared behavior, although maybe not quite into communities. But OSN and other kinds of online platforms are themselves cultural creations, expressive of various socioeconomic factors and cultural values. A city is both context and work of art; so is the web.

Gossip is the monarch of the internet. We live in its kingdom. This book is meant to motivate, although not to accomplish, a dispossession of the monarchy. Revolt is impossible. Gossip is pervasively human. Nonetheless, we aspire to replace the kingdom of gossip with a republic of gossip. Gossip, itself, cannot be displaced. It will remain the master form of information. But if we become citizens of information, responsible for our informing and being informed, then we will more readily live flourishing lives amidst the powerful effects and contexts of OSNs.

The monarchy of gossip has several areas of vulnerability. The area of vulnerability that we want to leverage involves the crisis of knowledge amidst which we live. This will be the lever we use to clarify, describe, and diagnose the economy of information that supports the kingdom of gossip. In response to this crisis, we will pursue a practice of everyday epistemology and the study and evaluation of everyday practices of knowing (which will overlap and impinge on scientific ways of knowing). This everyday epistemology will provide the tools for our analysis of information and misinformation on the web.

In what follows, we develop a general and robust conceptualization of the problem of misinformation in conjunction with an analysis and derivation of the concepts of knowledge, information, data, gossip, and a few others. Unfortunately, the dangers of the internet cannot be cured, but only managed. The powers of technology encourage the notions that we, as human beings, are also a kind of technology, that information is a self-sufficient denizen of the universe, that knowledge can be absolute or non-contingent, and that misinformation is pollution, such that we can recycle it into truth or discard it as waste. We will argue against all of these notions. It is important to remember that before we can develop responses to the vectors of behavior and power evolving through the web, we must first understand what these vectors really are. Before we can be corrective, we must be descriptive. In describing the web and OSNs, we are describing ourselves through the distortions and augmentations that we ourselves have created and continue to create through and among our online interactions.

NOTES

1 For a recent account of the centrality of evidence in the scientific enterprise, see Strevens, M. (2020). *The knowledge machine: How irrationality created modern science*. Liveright Publishing.

2 Wittgenstein talks about grammar relative to what he calls language games and form of life. These descriptions are widely misunderstood. We avoid using them, and offer a more neutral characterization of grammar that does not rely on the specific modes of philosophical argument pursued by Wittgenstein in *Philosophical Investigations*.

PART I

**A Crisis of Knowledge and
Everyday Epistemology**

DOI: 10.1201/9781003401674-2

CHAPTER 1

Problems with the Concept of Knowledge

INTRODUCTION

Science spawns technology. Technology provides new means of exploration for science. A new and better telescope can provide evidence that can pressure our current theoretical understanding of the universe. The James Webb Space Telescope is currently doing just this, producing data that undermines the standard picture of the origins of the universe. More significantly in our everyday lives, science and technology together provide us with powerful ways of altering our physical and social environments. Paul Valery (1989) in a famous essay argues that the advance of science and technology creates a crisis of the mind:

> But once born, once tested and proved by its practical application, our science became a means of power, a means of physical domination, a creator of material wealth, an apparatus for exploiting resources of the whole planet—ceasing to be an "end in itself" and an artistic activity. Knowledge, was a consumer value, became an exchange value. The utility of knowledge made knowledge a commodity, no longer desired by a few distinguished amateurs but by Everybody.

> *"The Crisis of the Mind"*

The power of science and its knowledge created what has been called later a knowledge economy. Knowledge within the advanced societies of the West

DOI: 10.1201/9781003401674-3

became a high-value commodity. Along with this high-value knowledge, trivia, propaganda, bullshit, noise, opinions, rumors, and gossip proliferates. Kierkegaard in the 1840s already saw this proliferation, but the primary instrument and perpetrator of this noise at that time was the free press and its audience. He called this kind of 'knowledge' "windbaggery." Public talk and opinion, masked often as knowledge, produce a public stage in which personal display becomes a kind of psychological impetus and a public transaction.

The crisis of the mind that Valery identified in 1919 has evolved and mutated into what David Weinberger (2012), in his book *Too Big to Know*, calls a crisis of knowledge. One aspect of this crisis is the sheer explosion of the amount of knowledge discovered, produced, and disseminated. The modern world is noisy with fact. A "[t]sunami of available fact," as David Foster Wallace (2012) calls it [G, 403]. This is one problem. But there is another. Some facts are facts, but not all of what we might take as fact is a fact. Some of what we call facts are maybe facts, half-facts, seeming facts, falsehoods, prejudices, assumptions, presumptions, ideas, ideologies, fantasies, speculations, hopes, fears, and theories of varying status.

One might describe the crisis about knowledge as an anxiety about the very status of facts. So, we tend to believe what fits our beliefs; we easily believe so-called experts. Much of the content offered online are superficial facts, facts without context, and outside the complex web of other facts and ideas that make actual knowledge. And this follows from the truncated form by which these facts are posted on online social platforms such as YouTube, Instagram, and so on. But even in longer online formats, the presentation of 'facts' remains highly decontextualized. Without that context we cannot decide what is a fact, how it is fact, and how we might be wrong about that. Much of what becomes controversial in public discourse, as we should all know, are simply snippets, memes, and other such decontextualized bits of entertainment offered as fact.

We can get at these problems in a slightly different way. Weinberger reduces this crisis of knowledge into a single question: "is the *networking of knowledge* making us smarter or stupider?" [italics added]. This is an important question—and the answer seems to be that it makes us stupider, but offers some compensating benefits. But what does it mean to network knowledge? Is knowledge the kind of thing that can be networked? The phrase "the networking of knowledge" is rather odd. Can knowledge disembodied from anyone's understanding actually be considered knowledge? Knowledge is not networked on the web. What is networked are representations of knowledge, which is to say web pages. This is not a trivial qualification. Knowledge is not a set of lakes or reservoirs that can be linked together. Rather what counts as knowledge or knowing something always depends on our human involvement and understanding. In some ways, the web is simply a massive collection of data that our understanding sometimes allows us to process into some kind of knowledge or knowing. So, the first problem is that knowledge on the web is not yet knowledge. This problem is exacerbated by a further cultural confusion about how to understand knowledge, a confusion that ranges from disbelief and relativism, at the one extreme, to excessive and misguided belief in the idea of science, at the other.

THE ORIGINS OF KNOWLEDGE

Knowledge is a product of knowing. We do not just know something as if by magic. We come to know something. And thus, knowing is a kind of activity even if we are unconscious of the processes by which we perceive the world. Our perceptions can be partial and deceptive, and we learn to accommodate this. My knowing is not simply a state I am in, but an activity. What kind of activity is it? Sometimes it would seem to be a very basic cognitive and sensory activity. I know the color of the walls through perception and my conceptual ability to grasp and name colors. In other cases, it might be better described as a social practice. My knowledge of the American constitution involves not only linguistic abilities, but an immense background of social and political knowledge. Learning how to interpret and understand the constitution, which is what my knowledge requires of the constitution, takes place within a complex social context. Our dependence on language for much of our knowledge grounds our knowledge in social practices.

From these and other practices of knowing, we learn and know various things that we call knowledge. Knowledge is the product of our practices of knowing. Faraday's discovery of electrical fields and Maxwell's mathematical formalization of this physics into three field equations produce a different kind of knowledge about the physical world than my reading about their discoveries or about the physical world. And if I work through Faraday's experiments and Maxwell's equations, I will understand fields and their significance in physics with a deeper knowledge than before I did that. There are many kinds of knowledge. Knowledge also differs depending on its target. Knowing about physics is not the same as knowing that people tend to park their cars as close as possible to where they are going. Our claims about the origins of World War I are not subject to experiments and will always be open to debate and argument. This is the beginning of an argument that we will continue in the next chapter. Here, our conclusion is that *knowledge* is a label for a hodgepodge of thoughts, memories, beliefs, commitments, and more: a term of convenience.

Knowledge is not anything separate from our judgments and evaluations about what will count as knowledge. Understanding a statement about physics is not the same as knowing that the statement is true or knowing what it means for it to be true. The knowledge of physics entails a certain level and sophistication in understanding the descriptions and explanations of phenomena that physics offers. Webpages do not allow for the networking of knowledge, but for the networking of representations of knowledge. Even if the description of some physical fact or theory on a webpage is something a well-trained and good physicist might count as knowledge, it is not knowledge for me simply because I read about it after a Google search. But if I understand the sentences of an article about Feynman diagrams and quantum electrodynamics (QED), do I now know something about the physics of the universe? The answer to that question will depend on how well I understand physics and how much previous knowledge of quantum physics I have. The descriptions I read about QED might be true, but obscure, such that I have trouble drawing conclusions about what is said. I might accurately confess that I read about someone else's knowledge of quantum physics, but I don't yet know it. So that knowledge, which is some specific person's knowledge (or account), is not yet my knowledge. The characterization of knowledge as networked content creates problems because it obscures this basic fact.

We also come to know things through inquiry, but time, energy, and ability are limited, and so much of what we come to know (or think we know) is learned through acculturation, memorization, and reinforcement (in schools, primarily), and through the testimony of others. Much of this gathering and acculturation, however, is not part of a conscious, rational inquiry, and thus our ability to justify our understanding is limited. We become acquainted with facts, theories, ideas, images. We often learn in off-hand ways, from people we take as authorities, from baseless rumors, through presumptions and prejudicial judgments.

Culture is a repository of knowledge, often very practical knowledge about life as well as ideas, mores, religious stories, hierarchies, values, attitudes, and symbols. Gilbert Ryle (1945) distinguishes between knowing how (practical kinds of know-how) and knowing that (propositional knowledge). Hayek (1960) articulates a similar distinction, but develops it more broadly:

> Not all knowledge in this sense is part of our intellect, nor is our intellect the whole of our knowledge. Our habits and skills, our emotional attitudes, our tools, and our institutions—all are in this sense adaptations to past experiences which have grown up by selective elimination of less suitable conduct. They are as much an indispensable foundation of successful action as is our conscious knowledge.
>
> *The Constitution of Liberty*

These two different kinds of knowledge (and ways of knowing), a more theoretical, conscious and propositional kind of knowledge and a dispersed, embodied kind of knowledge, both exist amidst other evolving and traditional beliefs, assumptions, and prejudices.

This mixture of ways of knowing can also result in our holding a complex set of incompatible beliefs. In South Korea, for example, you might find someone who has studied biology and mathematics, and done well in those subjects, but who also frequents a shaman in order to discover if she will get married, get a good job, and so on. In this case, her school education and her acculturation are in conflict, but in her mind they are not.[1] This maybe a weakness of her education, or simply a result of different commitments that can be kept in different contexts. This is not an unusual situation. Most of us suffer from many such internal contradictions that we overlook or fail to notice. This kind of personal confusion and belief in conflicting ideas and commitments has always been the case. People have been endlessly superstitious, afflicted by half-truths, believing in mistaken ideas about everything from disease and astronomy to economics and history.

With the advent and success of science, however, two seemingly opposed consequences have emerged. The sciences in many ways have balkanized our understanding; scientists specialize and the body of knowledge has become huge and thus impossible to master. But as our knowledge expands so does our ignorance. Warren Weaver wrote that "[a]s science learns one answer, it is characteristically true that it also learns several new questions." Weaver then uses a metaphor that the physicist John Wheeler also is reported to have used: as the circle of our knowledge grows, "the points of contact with ignorance also gets longer and longer." Hayek agrees and notes that while the best scientists understand how we are becoming more aware of our ignorance, the scientism of the popular imagination, as well as too many scientists, imagine otherwise:

> Unfortunately, the popular effect of this scientific advance has been a belief, seemingly shared by many scientists, that the range of our ignorance is steadily diminishing and that we can therefore aim at more comprehensive and deliberate control of human activities.

To "aim at more comprehensive and deliberate control of human activities" is a form of intellectual hubris that expresses a political desire for control, order, and authority. It is exactly this mix of intellectual hubris and fantasy that the web, despite its decentralized network substrate, dangles in front of people with its promises of knowledge and information.

KNOWLEDGE AND THE WEB

In entry level psychology courses, you often read the *Diagnostic and Statistical Manual of Mental Disorders*, currently in its fifth edition (*DSM-V*). As you read the symptomatology of the various disorders, you find yourself recognizing yourself under the various descriptions. Maybe you have a mood disorder; or no, not that, maybe a personality disorder? It is unlikely that you do. But you find you can easily describe yourself using the symptomatology of a number of disorders listed. Part of the difficulty is that symptoms underdetermine the disease, so that the same symptoms could be the result of a vast array of causes. In addition, we can describe ourselves and our behavior and states of mind in various ways, such that one possible description might match a description in the DSM. We often slip from recognizing something is possible to believing it is probable. One might conclude that the issue here is that you, as a student, lack the adequate and relevant knowledge to properly diagnose mental disorders. This is likely true. But there is a further issue. Knowing some symptoms does not mean you understand how those symptoms fit together with their cause or causes. Knowing something need not entail that you understand it. Our engagement, reading, and reaction to the information on the internet and through various online social media is too often like the young student reading the DSM and fearing the onset of some mental pathology. Even if we are generous and imagine that a fair amount of information on the internet is in some sense true, that does not mean we or anyone else can easily understand it. It is a challenge to separate the gold from the dross, the wheat from the chaff. The internet encourages browsing, linking, quick reactions, and superficial engagements (although not always); this only further undermines our ability to adequately examine and evaluate what is offered to us as information or knowledge. Understanding takes time, discipline, testing, practice, and much else.

Such half-knowledge can encourage a common effect. When people research a medical symptom online, they gain an unwarranted certainty about their own self-diagnosis. They have not learned the complexity of medicine or of the human body; certainly, they have no diagnostic experience, nor do they have a systemic understanding of the body and illness. But they know a few facts and have read what they take as authoritative comments about various diseases.

This common tendency provides a metaphor for the general disposition towards information and putative knowledge gained through web browsing and online engagement. This is not to say that one cannot gain insight, knowledge of facts, and even reach reasonable and correct conclusions through the careful gleaning and consideration of online information. It is not that such online research, even about medical conditions, is all bad or useless. But even here your conclusions will often just be lucky. If they are well considered, this will be because you are drawing upon an already established background of not only knowledge but good judgment. This last aspect is critical and it cannot be derived from evidence and facts. Also, if one approaches the use of the web as a resource at the service of a serious inquiry, where a central part of that inquiry is dealing with opposing views, or other possible ways of understanding, then the web can be useful. Everything about the online social network (OSN) and much of our engagement with webpages undermines the disciplines of inquiry, highlighting instead the effects of entertainment.

THE CRISIS OF KNOWLEDGE ON THE WEB

The crisis of knowledge does not simply create anxieties about knowledge and information. In some ways, it encourages too much confidence in our own knowledge. Numerous studies have shown that our dependence on the web for information and knowledge has diminished our own memories and knowledge of the world. This reliance also encourages us to believe that we know on our own what we have in fact discovered online (Ward, 2021; Fisher et al., 2015). Adrian Ward (2021) reports, for example, that using Google to answer general knowledge questions artificially inflates peoples' confidence in their own ability to remember and process information and leads to erroneously optimistic predictions regarding how much they will know without the internet. When information is at our fingertips, we may mistakenly believe that it originated from inside our heads.

Some argue that in order to accommodate this change, we should alter what we mean by knowledge, so that we could treat information stored on devices as knowledge for us. We might extend our idea of our mind and thinking to include the tools we use to facilitate and clarify our thinking. Language, itself, is such a tool. But even if we might claim that our language, as part of our culture, embodies the history of past generations, we do not know that history simply by learning how to speak our language. There remains a difference between tools and those who use them, although this is exactly the difference that online technology and social networks seem to blur. But even if our vision gets blurry the things we see are not blending and fusing just because we see them that way.

The cognitive diminishments and distortions encouraged by our experience with the Web exacerbate already active and recurrent confusions about knowledge and knowing in our culture. Susan Haack has convincingly shown how the Supreme Court, let alone others within our society, confuse scientifically derived conclusions with what she calls reliable conclusions (Haack, 2008). Scientific inquiry, like all other forms of inquiry, relies on assumptions, guesses, and interpretive judgments that means it is neither certain nor reliable simply because it is scientific. The very complexity of modern life and our technologically infused environment creates a fog of half-knowledge and half-truths. Opinion becomes knowledge by courtesy and default. This further weakens the standards used by people to determine what will count as knowledge, about how to evaluate and understand not only the claims of scientists and experts, but one's own anecdotally defined beliefs about the world. As Herbert Dreyfus (1999) recognized many years ago, the web has augmented and accelerated the advance of Kierkegaard's notion of "windbaggery," encouraging and facilitating anyone and everyone to spout their opinions in public, sometimes under the ironic guise of following their preferred 'experts.'

We can usefully modify one of Nietzsche's (2023) comments in *The Joyful Science*, in order to highlight the way our ideas about knowledge are intertwined with our understanding of our lives. He writes that "the strength of knowledge does not depend on its degree of truth but on its age, on the degree to which it has been incorporated, on its character as a condition of life" (3.110). The venerable age of knowledge has lost much of its shine, since our knowledge about the world and ourselves has advanced and changed so much over the years. Other forms of epistemological authority have gained prominence. Scientific experts, whether they are reliable or not, pontificate. It is true that new discoveries are made, and the various sciences continue to advance, and our technologies become more powerful and more integrated in our lives. So, we might revise Nietzsche's observation: "Thus the strength of knowledge does not depend on its degree of truth but on the degree to which it has been incorporated as a condition of life."

The condition of life has changed with the advent of the web and OSNs. The environment around us has become infused with technology. Nature and technology blend within our urban and suburban environments. This technology, including the embedded technology in our refrigerators and cars, let alone the technology controlling traffic lights, the water supply, and networked payment systems, monitors and facilitates various actions, behaviors, and interactions. In many cases, it also tracks and gathers data about us. This smart technology, as it is called, gathers data about us and through that data gleans patterns and generates predictions. Businesses, and God knows who else, pay money for such information. Our relationship with this technology, embedded as it is in our environments, is increasingly unconscious. It is just part of the world we live in, hidden within things as the gods once were. This condition is what George Dyson (2020) calls the fourth epoch: "Machines taking the side of nature, and nature began taking the sides of machines, humans are still in the loop but no longer in control." He explains:

> The fourth epoch is retuning us to the spirit-laden landscape of the first (epoch); a world where humans coexist with technologies they no longer control or fully understand. This is where the human mind took form. We grew up as a species, surrounded by mind and intelligence everywhere we looked, sincere dawn of technology, we were on speaking terms with our tools. Intelligence in the cloud is nothing new.

CONCLUSION

The gods of the internet are new gods, more servants than lords, but as our dependence on them increases who knows what they might become. With the increasing power and presence of generative AIs, the already responsive online interface will become hyper-responsive and accommodating, as long as the current online economic model remains in place. Are we to become suppliants or priests? Or servants to our servants?

Such AIs are mimics of our intelligence; they themselves lack any conscious intelligence. But as mimics they fool us and in fact can sometimes perform what are for us real tasks, producing intelligent results, even if not through intelligent judgment. The cost of this success, besides our replacement by these devices, is cognitive confusion. The distinction between appearance and reality gets lost. It is not a simple distinction. But to live without that distinction lets loose narcissism and delusion. We start beautifying photographs and video programs; then get our faces altered through plastic surgery so that we look like we do online. And then we imagine, as do some philosophers and fantasists, that "simulations are not illusions. Virtual worlds are real" (Chalmers, 2022). If this becomes our world, then we will have all become psychotics.

We will not explore the metaphysics of such ideas. Instead, we will show how our confusions about knowledge, confusions encouraged, augmented, and accelerated by the web and OSNs, undermine our ability to adjudicate between delusive fantasies and creative innovations. For the moment, we offer an image of the epistemological challenge and possibility offered by the web. The intellectual historian, M.H. Abrams famously organizes the emerging intellectual world of Western Europe in the late 18th and early 19th centuries around the shift from mechanical and passive metaphors for the mind (mirror) to reciprocal, interactive and/ or generative metaphors for the mind (lamp).[2] These metaphors have remained dominant within Western culture. We oscillate between imagining we know the world through reflection or through projection, as mirrors or lamps. What has changed since Coleridge and Wordsworth is that we have invented an environment that is itself mirror and lamp: mirroring us and projecting on to us, as if the world we now inhabit were itself a kind of mind, if not quite divine, at least promising transcendence of our local context, our restricted condition. We are spectators, performers, and creators in an environment of mirrors and lamps.

NOTES

1 Personal knowledge.
2 *The Mirror and the Lamp*, see especially chapter III, "Romantic Analogues of Art and Mind".

REFERENCES

Abrams, Meyer Howard. *The mirror and the lamp: Romantic theory and the critical tradition*. Vol. 360. Oxford University Press, 1971.

Chalmers, David J. *Reality+: Virtual worlds and the problems of philosophy*. Penguin UK, 2022.

Dreyfus, Hubert L. *Kierkegaard on the internet: Anonymity vs. commitment in the present age*. HL Dreyfus, 1999.

Dyson, George. *Analogia: The emergence of technology beyond programmable control*. Farrar, Straus and Giroux, 2020.

Fisher, Matthew, Mariel K. Goddu, and Frank C. Keil. "Searching for explanations: How the Internet inflates estimates of internal knowledge." *Journal of Experimental Psychology: General* 144.3 (2015): 674.

Haack, Susan. *Putting philosophy to work: Inquiry and its place in culture: Essays on science, religion, law, literature, and life*. Prometheus Books, 2008.

Hayek, Friedrich A. *The constitution of liberty*. University of Chicago Press, 1960.

Nietzsche, Friedrich. *The joyful science / Idylls from Messina / Unpublished fragments from the period of the joyful science* (Spring 1881–Summer 1882): Volume 6 (The Complete Works of Friedrich Nietzsche) 1st Edition, Editor, Alan Schrift; Translator Adrian Del Caro.Stanford University Press, 2023.

Ryle, Gilbert. "Knowing how and knowing that: The presidential address." *Proceedings of the Aristotelian Society*. Vol. 46 (pp. 1–16). Aristotelian Society, Wiley, 1945.

Science and Imagination: Basic Books; 1932–1979; Warren Weaver papers; General Files, Series 8; Rockefeller Archive Center. Available at: https://dimes.rockarch.org/objects/mN8tWEUL7WUdNhkJ5LdJkN

Valery, Paul. "Crisis of Mind" In *The outlook for intelligence*. Ed. Jackson Matthews translated by Denise Folliot and Jackson Mathews. Princeton: Princeton University Press, 1989.

Wallace, David Foster. *Both flesh and not: Essays*. Back Bay Books, 2012.

Ward, Adrian F. "People mistake the internet's knowledge for their own." *Proceedings of the National Academy of Sciences* 118.43 (2021): e2105061118.

Weinberger, David. *Too big to know*. Basic Books, 2012.

CHAPTER 2

Knowledge Is Necessarily Contingent and Normative

INTRODUCTION

In the previous chapter, we argued that knowledge lacks a singular and general definition. We know things in varying degrees and not absolutely. In addition, what will count as knowledge in one particular case will be very different than what will count as knowledge in another case. Consequently, not only is our knowing contingent and not absolute, what counts as knowledge depends on what we are trying to know, and thus there are no absolute and universal grounds for our knowledge. Rejecting the notion of absolute knowledge produces a persistent anxiety in some people. They imagine that if there is no absolute knowledge, then there can be no knowledge at all, as if everything becomes mere opinion if we cannot know like God. If, however, we know things with varying degrees of certainty, and relative to different criteria, then knowledge should be understood as normative and contingent. In this chapter, we will explain what it means for knowledge to be normative and contingent.

What is knowledge? In asking this, our concern will not be with the kind of practical knowledge described by Ryle's (1945) phrase "knowledge-how." Riding a bike, making a soufflé, and throwing a powerful punch can all be described as knowing how to do something. But if I can describe how to do any of these, it does not follow that I can actually do any of

DOI: 10.1201/9781003401674-4

them. There is a lot of mystery about our knowing how to do things. In this chapter, however, our concern will be with our knowing that something is the case, with our assertions about states of affairs and about generalizations about the world.

So, we begin again. What is knowledge? If we know anything, we know something. And so our knowing has a specific content which is often called a belief. This putative belief can be expressed through a sentence or proposition. What kind of belief? A true belief, of course. A false belief would not count as knowledge. But how do we judge if what we believe is true or false? If I blindly guess at the answer to a problem and give the right answer, I do not by virtue of giving this answer know the answer. My supposed knowledge must be confirmed and I must have some warrant or some justification for my belief. For these reasons, philosophers have imagined that knowledge could be defined as justified true belief (JTB). Such a definition has many everyday uses. In particular, many of our confusions, false beliefs, and misunderstandings rest on inadequate justification or warrant for what we believe. But there are problems with defining knowledge too strongly as JTB. As we will examine in a later chapter, the evidence or data we might use to justify a belief always underdetermines any explanatory conclusion we might draw from such evidence.[1] And thus our justification for our beliefs rest uneasily on the foundation of evidence. The problem of the underdetermination of explanation from evidence can take a number of forms. But, we will not explore these problems in this chapter. Instead, we will show the ways in which each of the terms in the JTB definition of knowledge—Justified True Belief—are less clear and stable than we might imagine. In so doing, we will highlight the necessary normative form of our knowledge. If knowledge is normative, then it is not absolute (that is, non-contingent). The same will also be true of the concept of information, which overlaps in various ways with the concept of knowledge

We will begin by examining the normative and contingent forms of epistemic justification.

PROBLEMS WITH JUSTIFICATION

Using two thought experiments, Edmund Gettier, in 1964, identified a weakness with defining knowledge in terms of justification. I can, for example, validly infer some proposition P from a set of propositions, at least one of which is false, but in which I was justified in believing. In effect, I can seem to know something for the wrong reasons. With this argument, Gettier famously undermined the characterization of knowledge as JTB, sending philosophers in search of new vocabularies with which to describe knowledge. Our goal is not to enter into the debates about how to respond to Gettier's challenge. Rather, Gettier's argument is symptomatic of our confusions about knowledge. It reveals the looseness and vagueness that infects JTB.

The following is a Gettier-like thought experiment that reveals that I might be justified in a belief, but that does not mean that the proposition in which I believe is true and should count as knowledge. I look up at a clock and see that it says 1:35 P.M. I glance at my open computer and see that its internal clock displays the same time. I later tell someone that the clock on the wall is accurate. I am justified in this belief by virtue of my earlier experience in which I confirmed that the clock on the wall matched my computer time display. But in fact, the clock on the wall is broken, and only by chance did its hands, which were stuck at 35 minutes after 1, match the actual time indicated by my computer. My conclusion was faulty, since I was inferring something about the world by induction using only one example. But of course, I had no reason to test the clock further. All things considered, I was justified in my conclusion. I assumed since the clock worked yesterday, it still works today. Another observation would have shown my failure. But we usually need a reason to doubt how things seem. Otherwise we might find ourselves paralyzed by indecision. My justification seemed good enough, and in many cases, it would be, but not in all cases.

Stephen Hetherington offers a useful description of a strange version of a Gettier example. You see a sheep in a field and so you think there are sheep in the field. There actually are sheep in the field. You are correct, except that what you see as a sheep is not a sheep. It is a dog dressed as a sheep by the sheep rancher, who has a perverse sense of humor. Knowledge founded on observation, as Hume demonstrated long ago, can be faulty. As in this case, the observation is faulty. It is exactly the purview of science to limit and correct such mistakes. There is a generalization problem in this example as well. I may correctly state for the wrong reasons that there are sheep in the field. But it is more correct to say there are sheep and there is a dog dressed as a sheep. But I do not know that fact, nor is it something I normally worry about in my sheep-watching activities. In any case, strictly speaking my generalization about the sheep in the field, which is meant to include the dog-sheep, is actually false. The foundation of my generalization was faulty, because I simply relied on appearances. Of course, it is an unlikely occurrence to have dogs disguised as sheep. And so, it was a rational generalization, since in all probability it would be correct.

At this point we meet again the problem of underdetermination. No matter how much evidence or data we have their will be a jump from the evidence to some generalization about that evidence. How we make this generalization will be determined by how we frame our data, and we can do that in a multiplicity of ways, all leading to different conclusions. Similarly, we can offer different generalized explanations of the data even if framed in the same way. Of course, like in this dog in sheep's clothing case, we will have incomplete evidence or information. And this opens up more variability in both the framing of the data and in the possible conclusions we could reach.

The original Gettier cases do not involve generalization in quite this same way. We will briefly describe the first thought experiment Gettier describes. Both Smith and Jones are applying for a job. Smith has good reasons to believe that Jones will get the job and also that Jones has ten coins in his pocket. Smith is justified in inferring from this that the man who will get the job has ten coins in his pocket. But in fact, Smith will get the job, and not Jones. In addition, unbeknownst to himself, he also has ten coins in his pocket. His inference still holds and he is justified in believing it is true. But it is not true. What has gone wrong?

Smith's knowledge is formulated relative to the contingent facts about the ten coins and it is a prediction about what will happen. That fact about the coins is simply another means of identifying Jones for Smith. But that fact can also identify Smith. And it can identify him after the job has been decided. Both before the job was decided and after, Jones was justified in believing that the man with ten coins would get the job. After the job was decided the claim was still true, but not in the way Smith understood. His justified belief in this case picks out the wrong person.

George Dreyfus offers another example that is useful because of its clarity:

> Imagine that we are seeking water on a hot day. We suddenly see water, or so we think. In fact, we are not seeing water but a mirage, but when we reach the spot, we are lucky and find water right there under a rock. Can we say that we had genuine knowledge of water? The answer seems to be negative, for we were just lucky.
>
> *(Dreyfus, 1997)*

Seeing the mirage of water is not a prediction about water. We do not see water, even though there is water where we think it is. Belief in the water is established by the mirage, so my belief that I was seeing water was not justified, even though it ended up being true. If experience confirms a belief we have, but if our belief was founded on the wrong reasons, making our knowledge was accidental, is it right to say that our belief counts as knowledge? The mistake of founding a belief on wrong reasons arises if we generalize our experience, and act relative to the principle 'If I see water, even in a hot desert, I can move to that place in which I see the water and I will find water.' This would be a faulty principle. And in this particular case, knowing water was present at the place of the mirage was only justified once I found it and realized that what I saw had been a mirage. This is a simpler case than those offered by Gettier, but it is clarifying. Any justification of our beliefs, if that justification and those beliefs are about states of affairs (and not about numbers, for example), will be itself in need of justification, confirmation, modification, and sometimes revision.

Gettier-type thought experiments are often understood as undermining the role justification can play in defining knowledge. This is a mistake. The role of justification in these cases is inadequate and misleading. This does not mean that it is wrong in all cases. But there is no reason to imagine that all kinds and cases of knowledge will be consistent with each other. Nor should we imagine that they will all depend on justification in the same way. We do not need, nor can we have a universal, unified definition or even description of knowledge. As we have argued, knowledge is not a unified category of beliefs, propositions, abilities, or commitments.

Nonetheless, Gettier-type thought experiments are useful and important. They reveal two important things about the fragility of justification. First, what counts as justification relative to some observations and beliefs has to be determined and also justified. In addition, 'true' as both word and concept often just means "it seems like" or "this is a reasonable claim" or "this is a good approximation (this is good enough)." I may not need an atomic clock to determine the time; sometimes, a sundial will be accurate enough. Are the times read from the atomic clock more accurate than those read from the sundial? If we say that they are, does that mean that before the atomic clock we lived with a false sense of time? Is the world more real if our measurements of it are more precise? (The answer to that question is not obvious.) Our statements about what is approximately the case can be as true as a similar statement given using some more precise measure, for example. The second thing that Gettier's argument shows is that our inductive conclusions are always open to disconfirmation. Who gets the job and what ends up being true about water in the desert are inferences from evidence about the world that can be wrong. There is no guarantee ahead of time. Any generalized conclusion based on specific instances will always be subject to various levels of uncertainty.

The weakness of epistemological justification is manifold. There exist further challenges beyond those revealed by Gettier. For example, what counts as justification for a particular belief varies according to the belief or issue involved. What justifies a common-sense judgment about whether I should put gas in my car is different from my putative knowledge of whether some action will lead to victory in a sports contest, or whether a murder was really facilitated by the perpetrator eating a Twinkie, as was famously and successfully argued in the Dan White murder case in 1979.[2]

Again, we are not focused here on what we might call practical knowledge, despite the role of action in the Dreyfus example. Justification is not always explicit in our practical knowledge. Justification still matters; we learn from masters or authorities, we learn from experience, we learn from observation, we learn through slow inculcation. In these cases, the justification is also practical or, we might even say, pragmatic. We evaluate the success of our understanding (our knowledge of what is the case) in terms of the consequences of our actions when we act on such putative knowledge. We ask, "does our knowledge lead to success or not"? Our knowledge plays a complicated and varied role in our choices and actions. We need not explore that further here. Instead, we will look at one more kind of justification that remains powerful in our epistemological negotiations with the world.

For most people, their justification for what they call knowledge will rest on some epistemic authority. For example, the reason I think I know that matcha is good for my health is because the trusted source X says so. If my belief in something derives from some authority, then my confidence will depend on my trust in that authority. My confidence will not ensure that my belief is true about the world, however. Of course, my trust in that authority may arise because I am already predisposed to believe in the positions exemplified by that authority. Sometimes I may be so committed to an authority (a religious authority, for example), that I will alter my beliefs to conform with that authority. In other cases, my trust and my attitude towards some particular belief will be shaped by my prejudices, my confirmation biases, anecdotal evidence, and various other assumptions.

In some cultures, for example, divination was understood as a form of knowing, leading to knowledge. Often the knowledge was negative; if the omens were negative, then a battle should not be fought on that day. We reject the legitimacy of such modes of magical knowing, since they are contrary to the world revealed by modern physics. They were, however, once a legitimate mode of knowing. What counts as knowing has a history and is contingent on various beliefs we have about the world. For many people their understanding of physics might as well be a belief in divination. We could argue that while this is true, what they believe in has a greater claim to truth than divination, and is thus justified. Given the difficulty in the replication of many experiments and the history of mistakes that characterize science, such faith is misguided. And while divination is open to interpretation by priests and others, it is not open to the kind of revision and testing that define modern science. This does not mean that science should be taken as an acceptable authority, while ancient Roman priests and religious culture should not be. People are being unscientific if they simply accept the authority of scientists, whose conclusions are often distorted, simplified, and even falsified by the media (Ritchie, 2020). If you look at Thomas Aquinas' great *Summa Theologiae*, you will see a continual appeal and consideration of previous authorities, as well as an appeal to the Bible relative to natural historical questions (especially relative to miracles). The appeal to those who speak with the authority of science, let alone the ad hoc collection of beliefs about the world that are accepted because those are dominant in some way in our society, has less justification than the appeal to the divine fathers and other theologians by Aquinas. He knows who he is citing and why; their arguments and authority are open to view and have the legitimacy offered by tradition. Even if we no longer accept Aquinas' criteria of justification, his use of those criteria justify his knowledge claims to a greater extent to many of our everyday appeals to experts and authorities.

A philosopher might step in at this point and assert that the authorities to which Aquinas appeals simply provide him with mistaken ideas about the world. Even if people once took such ideas as knowledge, they are not, and never were known. But such a reaction misses the point. The issue of justification does not depend on what is true given our current understanding, but instead on the idea that what we call knowledge is part of a particular culture and time. The questions of knowledge that we struggle with now are also bound up with our limitations and embeddedness in our own cultures and lives.

Gettier-type cases should not undermine the importance of justification. In fact, they highlight the importance of establishing adequate justification. Justification involves the same contingencies that afflict our beliefs. We can always make mistakes in our justifications. Certainty has no part in our epistemological lives (or in our lives in general). All of our justifications are normative and contingent, and will thus require further evaluation and justification. Science offers various practices and disciplines of justifications and warrant that have enabled a great increase in our knowledge of the physical world. But these practices are by no means simple, objective, or free from the same complexities and contingencies of our everyday knowledge.

We will not rehearse the various arguments about the complexity of the sciences and their various scientific practices. Our goal in this chapter is simply to highlight the necessarily normative and contingent aspects of our ways of knowing; and to argue that this normative quality in no way undermines our ability to know. Rather it defines it, and describes both our cognitive powers and their limits. Without these limits we could not think about ourselves or the world; we could only react by rote and instinct.

In any particular case, justification constitutes a judgment. A judgment can include determinations about salience, evaluations of the relationship of a proposition with other propositions, an evaluation of the facts that seemingly support a claim, and a recognition of our own limitations and perspectives. Any particular justification of some purported proposition about what is the case will be guided by the kind of issue at stake.

Knowledge is knowledge and not mere belief, opinion, prejudice, or speculation because of the role justification plays in one's commitment to some claim, understanding, or belief. The justification of our propositional knowledge should be explicit, open to further questioning, and is bound with the normative criteria that we find legitimate, salient, and convincing. But the need for justification will vary. I can reasonably claim that I know my friends, but at any time I might be called upon to show I do.

If knowledge is normative in the ways we have argued, then knowledge is not a kind of certainty, nor it is absolute or incontrovertible. Our arguments lead to an understanding of knowledge that is fallible and thus revisable or defeasible. A number of theories of knowledge highlight this de-feasibility; fallibilism being the most prominent. We are not providing another epistemological theory, but rather some epistemological reminders. The standards for justification, for example, will vary depending on what one is trying to know. All things being equal, we may be perfectly justified in taking our JTBs as just that. But not always.

PROBLEMS WITH BELIEF

Let us turn to belief as a way of characterizing the kind of thing we have when we have knowledge of something. A belief is a propositional attitude. As such, it has a specific content (the propositional part) and it is something we have (the attitude towards or about a state of affairs, that is, that proposition). Many philosophers imagine that such an attitude is instantiated as a mental state. All of these characterizations of belief we sketch here lead to contingencies that further reveal the normative dimensions of knowledge.

Let us begin with the notion that a belief is a mental state, since this notion is less important in our everyday epistemology. We cannot grasp, know, or individuate any state of belief except through some description of it. Even calling it a state or attitude is an abstraction that could be denied. An appeal to brain states measured through an MRI or other such device will not solve this problem. We will still have to correlate and label the brain states measured on such devices with whatever we take to be our 'beliefs,' and thus again, we must depend on our self-descriptions which are, of course, not reflected on such measuring devices. We individuate our beliefs relative to other ways we have of describing cognitive attitudes. We articulate the content of our knowledge by saying things like "I believe in x" or "I believe that x is the case" or whatever. We could replace 'believe' with 'think,' 'am committed to,' 'imagine,' or 'feel'; and we can even describe our knowing through saying: "I claim, assert, deem . . . x." One might argue that these are all synonyms for belief. But the implications of each of these descriptions are different. Some emphasize the internal states involved in knowing, others emphasize the linguistic practices; all of them point to the fact that I take as true whatever is believed as the case.

How do I determine if I believe, think or assert something is the case? Do I do all of these at once? Are they serial states of mind? Why would all these states be the same in form, when they are not the same in duration or function? These are all intentional verbs attempting to describe intentional states; so, they are about something. If I claim that a short story is about the moon (and under one description it is), then it is about the moon. In so saying I believe something about the story, which is my knowledge of the story. It is at least conceivable that the form of my belief (in this case involving my memory and my understanding of the story) is different in kind from my knowledge of calculus. Memory is involved in both cases, but the kind of understanding and even the form of that memory is likely to be quite different. While I believe the story is about the moon, this depends on and comes from my understanding of the story. Even if I believe that I should use the chain rule to solve a particular calculus problem, I know this from my practice or experience in using it, and so I know it in a different way than what I know about the story.

What are the criteria that determine a belief as a belief and not a speculation, or a thought, or a hope, or a commitment? How do we grasp and apply these criteria? If we just learn these distinctions as we learn our language, those distinctions need not be anything other than the contingent norms of our language. Why should we assume that there exists some common mental state for all cases covered by the notion of belief, let alone the word 'belief'? What evidence do we have that there is such a state that is common to all cases of knowledge (or knowing)?

To make sense of belief requires some appeal to what is the case: to what it is we believe. So, the similarity between my belief that water consists of two hydrogen atoms and one oxygen atom, ignoring impurities and so forth, and my belief that class prejudices are real is that I take both of these claims to be true. I might also believe in myself (as a form of confidence). Is that the same kind of belief as my belief in the composition of water? My belief in political ideologies and in certain psychological patterns have different criteria of justification. The criteria we use to establish the 'truth' of beliefs about physics will be different from those used for politics and psychology, let alone art and judgments about myself. So, if what we count as true depends on the criteria we use to establish what is the case, then beliefs are individuated by these criteria, not by my state of mind in any particular case. That I hold the beliefs I do is a fact about me; although how do I know what I believe? Do I know ahead of time what I believe in all cases? The answer is *no*, since my involvement with the criteria of evaluation and with the particularities of what I am judging are decisive in determining if I know something or not. My beliefs need not be a collection of states or ideas stored in a mental library, waiting for me to access. We use a range of criteria to articulate our beliefs.

We live and act in ways that suggest we have beliefs about many things about which we need not be conscious, unless something goes wrong. I believe that one should eat with one's mouth closed, but every time I eat I will not be thinking about this belief. But I will, if I am disturbed by the way an acquaintance eats. We believe in more fundamental things about gravity, about clothes, about walking versus crawling, and so on. Much of the knowledge that defines and enables our knowing how to do things, as well as the vast background of knowledge that each of us has (both conscious and half-conscious) are not propositional in form. In many cases, such knowledge could not be given such a form. What is the propositional form of my knowledge of what cinnamon smells like?[3] I can recognize the smell and if asked, I would say that I know it. That knowledge, however, is not propositional, but experiential. We believe so many kinds of things about how the world works and what and who we are that it is difficult to imagine that all of these beliefs exist as propositional attitudes.

What does the idea of belief add to our idea of knowing? Consider the example of an everyday occurrence. I know that there is Zhang mountain tea in my teapot. In knowing this, I know something about the state of my teapot, about the world: it is filled with Zhang Mountain tea. It is also something that I know, which is to say, something *I* believe. To know something is to believe that that thing is the case. That which I know is something that I believe. The content of my knowledge seems to be given as something I believe. What I believe is something that *I* take to be true. Our appeal to belief in describing our knowing is an attempt to make explicit the way we are involved in our knowing, that the force of the proposition or statement (sentence) is provided by us: that human beings are the ones who know. In many ways, belief does not add much to our understanding of knowing, since it either means the same as *knowing* or it is as mysterious as knowing is, and so not very helpful. And it *is* rather mysterious. But what we see in the preceding argument is that the idea of belief as a constituent of knowledge gives content to our knowledge and indicates that this content is ours.

Our beliefs are often a question of degree. I can legitimately claim that I only half-believe something. My beliefs involve many contingencies, one of which is me. Any one particular belief depends on my other beliefs, my sense of the situation and the people involved, and on my understanding. I might believe something for the wrong reasons or I may realize that I don't really believe that at all, even though until recently I had believed it, or so I thought. It would be strange to say 'It is raining, but I don't believe it.' But I can believe something in a contingent more or less way. So just as I can half-believe something, I can also say that I believe it to some degree. This is a metaphoric gesture, an attempt to capture the variability of belief and my relationship to what I believe. In saying this, I am not appealing to actual probabilities, as some philosophers and others do with their probabilistic models of degrees of belief, or credences.

Here are some other examples of epistemic beliefs that are limited or are questions of degree.

1. I know that my favorite pen is in the house, but not where in the house it is. Do I know where it is? Yes, and no.

2. I know exactly what she will say when I ask her about the election; am I certain? When she says what I thought she would, did I really know she would say that? Or is my knowledge just my expectation? Is an expectation the same as a prediction? In either case, my claim was based on the fact that I have some knowledge of her.

3. I know that a projectile fired at a 45-degree angle will follow an arc as it moves through space. Will it be a perfect arc? It will more or less follow an arc.

These questions highlight the contingency of our knowledge. They suggest that Quine (1987) is right when he says that knowing is like a judgment that something is big. The judgment that something is big is contingent on what the relevant criteria are for the particular case. The plate of stewed crabs in front of me is big if it is an appetizer, but not so big if it is a main course; the toddler is big for a toddler, but small for a human being as such. To claim something is big is to make a comparative and hence relative judgment. How certain we are in our knowledge will be similarly contingent, comparative, and relative. I know a fair amount of physics, but compared to a physicist my knowledge is limited, incomplete, and lacking in mathematical depth. I know many facts about the world, including the fact that Mount Everest is 30,000 feet above sea level. But measured how? National Geographic lists its height at 29,035 feet. I am sure there is some degree of error, but I don't know what it is. How precise do we need to be in order to say that we know the height of Everest? It depends on how we are using the facts. If asked—is Everest 33,000 feet high? The answer is no. My approximate height is good enough. But if I am planning my ascent of Everest, my approximate answer will not be good enough. Similarly, what does it mean to know calculus? I can solve certain kinds of calculus problems easily, I could once do calculus in my head, but no longer. So, I know it less well than I used to know it. But I still know some calculus. How much calculus do I need to know for it to count as knowing calculus? It depends. All our knowledge is like this.

We have seen that both belief and justification are contingent and case-specific. They do not need to be all or nothing affairs, but can be more or less: a question of degrees and not of absolutes. If knowing were not a question of degrees, then we could know nothing. The standards or criteria for knowing would require absolute certainty. How can we have that given our cognitive limits and the simple fact that our knowing is a judgment about something that we can get wrong (we will return to the way that knowing can never be certain and remain a knowing). If absolute certainty is the criterion for knowing, then only God can know anything. This is true because of God's absolute view and grasp of whatever is the case. If we appeal to certainty, we can only appeal to our feeling or thought or fantasy of certainty, as does Descartes, no matter how hard he tries to explain the subjective phenomenology away. If we fail to doubt something and imagine that something is certainly the case, we are using our own mental feeling of certainty as the criterion for truth. Such an appeal to ourselves would necessarily be contingent and suspect. Unless we were God, of course. My feelings are no justification for my certainty. Nor do my feelings of certainty confirm what is actually the case. No amount of fancy qualification will remove the necessarily subjective ground of appeals to certainty as a means of establishing the truth of something.

The appeal to epistemic certainty degrades into subjective feeling because there is no argument or proof that can establish absolute certainty. (We will set aside arguments about deductive proofs as not relevant in our everyday epistemological concerns. In such cases, 'absolute' is understood as necessary, and this will lead to metaphorical and logical arguments that would take us beyond the scope of this book). All knowledge claims are formulated through language or through some mode of human representation. *This fact alone shows that my justification for any claim cannot be absolute, but is contingent on my representation of that fact and on my interpretation or understanding of that representation.* 'A = A' even when what is equated are the symbols and nothing else, still ignores the fact that there are two symbols in different spatial relations to each other [e.g. one is to the left the other and one is to the right]. It is only when we add: "'A' as understood as a token of A" that we understand that the two symbols understood as marks [or sounds] are meant to be understood as the same kind of symbol and tokens of the same thing. Therefore, this is not absolutely true, but contingently true relative to our understanding of symbols in general and these symbols in particular (as well as much else). We cannot make sense of the notion of absolute in the phrase 'absolutely certain' except in such contingent ways. Philosophers attempt to escape this contingency. This is one motive for the recurrent idea that knowledge requires absolute identity between our knowing and that which we know. If knowledge requires this kind of certainty, then we would know nothing.

Thus, such an identity is impossible and unnecessary, since it would anni-hilate the possibility of representation, and thus the possibility of thinking about anything at all.

In our everyday epistemology, we want to understand how to adjudicate amongst different claims about the world. The appeal to certainty, let alone absolute certainty, distracts us from our everyday concern about the status of what we think we know with which we began this chapter.

PROBLEMS WITH TRUTH

We now turn to the remaining term in the standard equation JTB—'true.' *True* and *false* as concepts are not contingent in the same way as are *jus-tification* and *belief*. Something (some assertion, for example) would seem to be either true or false, and not by degrees. The contingency in this case does not rest with the concepts of true and false, but with what is judged to be true or false and according to what criteria by which that judgment given.

We should start with basic logic. The world is neither true nor false. Some state of affairs is neither true nor false. It just is the case, or it is not. True and false are judgments we make about sentences or propositions. I say about a sunny day: "Today is a sunny day." If you answer "True," you are not saying the sunny day is true, but that my sentence about today is true. What makes a sentence true or false is what is the case, which we can determine in various ways.

Further distinctions can be useful, although these distinctions also lead to complexities. We might say, as does Quine, that sentences are true and false, and that there is no such thing as propositions. Others argue that what is true is the proposition that a sentence expresses. There can be mul-tiple different ways of saying that the door is open, and what is true is not those various descriptions, according to this argument, but the proposi-tion that we express by means of those sentences. Therefore, the sentence 'The door is open' expresses the same proposition as 'Die Tür ist offen.' The various sentences I might use to say something might have different connotations, rhetorical effects, and might reveal something about me as a person. But, such things are logically irrelevant. What is relevant are the conditions under which my sentence (or statement) will be true or false, and whether what is asserted by a proposition is in fact true or false.

Something can be true only if it is possible for it to be false. It is true, for example, that the door is open, because it could have been closed. If doors could only be open, then there would be no way the sentence 'the door is open' could be false. The notion of being open would have no meaning relative to doors, since all doors would be open. In this case, to imagine a closed door would be to imagine something other than a door. This would be like saying—imagine a rock that could grow if you watered it; what would that rock be then? The answer might be—a plant.

We should note two things about our knowledge claims. First, we have to determine what is the situation, the state of affairs, about which we are making a claim. Such a determination is separate from our assertion about that state of affairs. We can make this determination in various ways depending on the kind of claim at issue. We make observations, do tests, ask other people, read many books, do experiments, ask people we trust, and so on. If the claim is that the light is on, we look to see if it is really the case that the light is on. We might see that it is on, but later realize we were hallucinating. Or we might realize that there is a hidden source of light that we mistook as coming from the main light fixture. About any situation judgment is required. And those judgments will involve sense perception and various thoughts about what I perceive, the look of things, and what is likely or not.

A proposition is not compared to the world in some kind of one-to-one correspondence, whatever that would mean. How do we compare 'The light is on' to a room in which the light is on or off? We cannot get them side by side so to speak, and so we cannot compare them as if we were comparing the color of two oranges. What a sentence means, let alone what a proposition means, is not commensurable with states of affairs or with things. In any particular case, we perceive something; we say and understand something. The sentence 'The light is on' does not agree with what is the case when the light is off. It does agree with what is the case when the light is on. We judge that it is the case that the light is on, which is what the sentence says. We do not match or compare like we do when comparing the color of a piece of fabric with a painted swatch.

Instead, we understand the claim about the light and then see or check if the light is in fact on. With more complicated propositions and claims (assertions) the process of determining the state of affairs, and thus the truth of the sentence of proposition, can be more difficult and theoretically inflected. But what is essential is to see that *asserting* that something is true or not is logically different from what makes a proposition true (which is that it is the case). A sentence or proposition can be true or false, states of affairs or that about which we make a claim can be neither.

The second thing to remember is that our statements and assertions about what is the case are all *ceteris paribus* clauses—that is, gestures that require a number of other conditions for whatever is said to be true, even if they are not specified in our assertion (the proposition we take as true). Any propositional assertion generalizes in some way. Any statement will be vague and underdetermined to some degree. In simple cases of sense experience, such as when we say the light is on, we really mean that a specific light is on, in a specific place, at a specific time. All of this ambiguity can be resolved through our involvement and understanding of the situation in which the statement is made. More complicated claims, again involve more generalization and ambiguity. If I say, 'This is excellent coffee,' I am generalizing from one sip (some small amount) to some greater amount. What is excellent to me may not be excellent to you—and in any case, some set of criteria must be invoked in order to make such a judgment. But how can such criteria be established? I am reporting my experience of the coffee, not measurements of acidity, and whatever else. We can often specify the relevant conditions, but there will always be more possible conditions that may or may not be relevant (my mood, the weather, the particular tilting of the earth, the color of the walls, and so on).

Our claims about what is the case and our determination of their truth (which we can call our coming to know something) should be understood as contingent knowledge (or contingent truths). Such contingent truths are always open to revision.

Let us return to Quine's suggestion that knowledge is a question of degrees, and thus of comparison. What this means is that many truths are approximate and relative and are not worse for that. For example, Dave is tall; that is true. Although next to an NBA player he might not be, although he has not changed in height. Although there might be exceptions with this comparison with NBA players. Some players may be shorter than Dave. So we can be more specific. Next to Kareem Abdul Jabbar, Dave is not tall, since Kareem is much taller. But if compared to 'Pistol' Pete Maverick, Dave remains tall. Instead of using NBA players as a way of measuring what counts or does not count as tall, I might discover the average height of the general population relative to which I am situating Dave. How much over average must someone be in order to be tall? Regardless, if you ask me, do I know if Dave is tall or short? I will say that I know he is tall. It is something I believe to be true and something I know about Dave. His height has caused him some social trouble, so it is a fact for him. Tall is a comparative judgment, but it cannot be separated out from knowledge and the notion of truth. It is not only not absolute, it is necessarily relative. This in no way supports relativism as an epistemological or metaphysical position. We are not arguing that all epistemological claims are equally valid, but that all such claims are determined by how we make them. The world can be accurately described in multiple ways. And thus, we are suggesting that our notion of truth misleads us when we talk about what we know.

With these basic descriptions of true and false before us, we can identify part of the difficulty with the concept of knowledge. If we understand that concept to require that what we take as knowledge must be true, otherwise it is not knowledge, then we will know very little. We do not know anything absolutely, but only by degrees and contingently. The absolute distinction between true or false, however, grates against the provisional and contingent nature of our knowing. Again, we often say (or should say) that something is true all things considered (*ceteris paribus*). What we know is often just probable or our best approximation.

It is Friday, so the store will be crowded.
Physics tells us the truth of the world.
Even though you disagree, I know that Primo Levi is a great writer.

These are all true statements, but only in limited ways. The store might not be crowded; it is just as likely that it will be crowded. I am making a prediction with such a statement, but it is one based on experience and I have good reason to believe it. Physics is not a single theory, and not all theories within physics are even consistent with each other. Famously, the theory of relativity does not fit with the mathematical theories of quantum mechanics. But whether the claim that physics tells us the truth of the world is even potentially true will depend on what we mean by 'the truth of the world.' Biologists might disagree; and so, would anyone who is in love. That last claim made above is the most contingent of these examples. Primo Levi is a great writer, but disagreement is possible. What constitutes a great writer is open to further elaboration and defense. Nevertheless, I think this statement is true, and I take it as something I know. All of these examples suggest that the judgment of truth or falsity is rather strong relative to the kinds of things we take ourselves to know.

In the popular imagination, science, understood as a kind of monolithic institution, is often treated as the authoritative adjudicator of what is true or false. There are many reasons to be skeptical about giving science such a role. All of the sciences have problems with replicating their results, and since such replication is one of the foundations of the success of science this failure represents a kind of crisis.[4] The issue here is simply to acknowledge that science is a human practice subject to the same foibles and possibilities for fraud and misunderstandings as any human activity. Despite this instability in results, especially in the human and medical sciences, many scientists continue to attempt to confirm and test the work of their colleagues. In fact, knowledge derived and developed within any particular science is always open to revision, correction, and rejection. Knowledge in the various sciences should be understood as best-case claims, that are likely to be criticized, corrected, and often replaced at some point. The criteria scientists use in evaluating data, claims, and theories are different in the different sciences, and are even contested within some of the sciences. The various sciences not only rely on different criteria, "[t]heory and experiment," as Ian Hacking observes, "have different relationships in different sciences at different stages of development. There is no right answer to the question: Which comes first, experiment, theory, invention, technology . . . ?" (1983, p. xi).

Even if we set aside the uncertain status of generalizations within the social sciences, we see variation in the criteria for what will count as knowledge within the natural sciences. The idea of physical laws plays a more extensive role in physics, for example, than in biology. And even within physics, we see different procedures of adjudication. A cosmologist collects data using advanced telescopes, but does not perform experiments in the way a particle physicist does. However, scientists are attempting to describe and explain a set of phenomena using mathematical means. Newtonian physics, for example, is true enough in its domain of calculation. We can still use Newton's equations for force and movement to describe projectiles and automobiles. But the underlying physics is not correct, and has been superseded in quite radical ways. Often in physics, what will matter most is the accuracy and precision of the equations used to describe some phenomenon.

What we have said here is a mere gesture to the highly contingent role truth and falsity play in the sciences. We are highlighting the normative qualities of our use of true and false as a corrective of the common tendency to talk and think carelessly about the ways in which scientific claims are true or false. We applaud, for example, the American Physical Society for amending their earlier and inappropriate use of 'incontrovertible':

> The world's largest organization of physicists clarified its position on climate change last week, and it no longer believes, as it did in 2007, that the evidence for global warming is "incontrovertible."

> *Gayathri Vaidyanathan,* Scientific American

Nothing in science is incontrovertible.[5] Science does not discover necessary truths, that is, truths that could not have been otherwise, or that are true in every possible world. It gives us accounts that can be tested by evidence, and can be revised and corrected: its claims and theories are only contingently true.

We are making a modest argument in praise of a modest use of the notions of truth and falsity when thinking and talking about knowledge and our ways of knowing. We will conclude this section with another everyday example, in order to bring out the essential point of this chapter. I may know that an elementary school is over to the east, which is true, but I may not know exactly where it is. So do I know where the school is? I do know something about the location of the school. I may not be able to give very precise directions to the school. And, as we argued above, knowing something does not require absolute certainty or correctness. What we know can be contingent in all of these ways, and many more. The notion of true or false, however, is not like this. A claim is true if the state of affairs it describes is as described; if not, then it is false. True and false are useful and even necessary in our practices of knowing. But they are concepts that push us away from the natural contingency of knowledge. We can say that what we know is contingently true, or true all things considered, or true given the best evidence to date, and so on. And when we offer these qualifications, we are saying that within some domain or relative to a particular description, the statement is true.

SOME CONCLUSIONS ABOUT KNOWLEDGE

As a conclusion we will examine two ways in which knowledge can be understood as normative. First, there is no single or unitary concept of knowledge, but rather various kinds of knowledge, a heterogeneous set of practices that help us grasp, represent, describe, manage, and alter how things are. Second, we will examine and show how even the most mundane and uncontroversial epistemic claims about states of affair are normative and subject to relentless contingencies.

We will recapitulate one of the conclusions from the last chapter—that knowledge is not a singular or even fully coherent concept—but we will argue for this conclusion in a different way. This new form of the argument will also provide an initial description of our practices of knowing as normative. If I ask you what you are doing, and you answer: "I am knowing," I will be puzzled. If you answered, "I am learning Korean," or "I am watching for gophers," I will understand. In learning Korean, I will at some point know the language. And in my gopher-watching I will need to know the difference between a gopher and a squirrel. The criteria for success in these cases is relatively clear. Knowledge comes from our knowing, learning or discovering, but what counts as knowledge can vary a lot. There are criteria for speaking Korean, and these will be manifest in how people do or do not understand me. The criteria for what will count as knowledge are not manifest in that way. The criteria for knowing Korean are different than those for knowing what causes the tides, which are also different from knowing why my colleague JF dislikes me and from knowing the history of sociology. Consequently, our examples of knowledge will be determined by the criteria we are committed to within a particular practice of knowing. The criteria will be very different within different practices of knowing focused on different kinds of epistemological targets—language, the tides, someone's particular animosities, a field of study, and so on. Consequently, knowledge is not one kind of thing, and is, therefore, not a coherent concept, but a hodgepodge of relative notions. There are different norms governing our various practices and ways of knowing. And as we have said, there are many different ways of knowing, including our knowing that, knowing how, knowing why, knowing where (including our own proprioception), and so on.

The normative form of knowledge defines not just different practices, but any particular practice as well. A straightforward everyday statement of fact remains subject to various normative qualifications that give us the particular form of what we claim to know. On a walk, I see a blue street sign on the corner of Washington St and Sorrel. The next day I mention to you that I know there is a blue street sign on the corner of Washington St and Sorrel. You question my knowledge, because you have seen that sign and think it is rather purplish. Maybe we could argue our way to agreement, or someone might help us adjudicate our competing color judgments. But already what I know is not certain; it is open to disagreements that rest on normatively defined color distinctions and identifications. We might agree that we mean the same sign, even if we disagree on its description. And in any case, I imagine your *purple* is just my *blue*.

Even if we provisionally set aside our color debate, we might disagree. We might disagree about what counts as the corner on which I situate the sign. What I know about the location of the sign, founded on observation in this case, is a particular proposition, the interpretation of which rests on normative distinctions. It counts as real knowledge, but it is neither certain nor indubitable, and to call it a fact is simply to restate the proposition that I take as true. The color may fade into something more greenish than blue; but we might still say that it is close enough to blue to make my initial claim true. I can notice subsequently that the sign is not quite on the corner. And again, we might reasonably claim that it is still close enough to the corner to count as a true statement.

What I know about the sign in this case is given a particular sentential form (a propositional form). My own knowledge, however, is not simply explicit in the form by which I express it. My knowledge depends on my particular understanding of that proposition. I mean something by means of the sentence I say. We must remember that sentences cannot mean in and of themselves. In fact, it is more accurate to say that we mean by means of sentences. As Wittgenstein comments: "Every sign by itself seems dead." We give them life. We have a life with words.

What I take to be true or false is what I mean to say when I make a claim about something; it is the proposition I mean to express by means of the sentence I say. You might accept the same sentence that I utter but interpret the sentence differently. This is what was made explicit in our initial argument. The point now, however, is not the *representation* of our belief, or thought, but is the thought itself. This returns us to Weinberger's claim about networking knowledge. What is networked on the web are representations of thoughts (and much else) not the thought itself. A thought is a thought for a person, just as knowing something requires that someone knows that which is known, that they understand what a sentence says such that they can know it as true (or false).The situation with the sign on the corner can get more complicated. In the year following my initial observation, city workers replace the sign with a new sign of a different color and lettering, and in the process, they change the position of the sign. It is now further away from the curb than when I saw it. Is my knowledge about the sign still accurate? Is my belief that there is a sign on the corner true?

All things being equal, we might say 'Yes.' But the state of affairs has changed, and it is not quite what I remember, not quite what I thought I knew. Changes continue. At some point a wall is built, and the street name is written on a stone plaque embedded in the wall. Is the name enough to count as a street sign? What I meant by 'street sign' is not the wall and plaque. So, it may still be true that there is a street sign indicating the name of the street it is not what I mean when I made my initial claim.

And, of course, one hundred years before my observation there was no city here at all, let alone a street and a sign. And in one thousand years from now not only may the street be gone, so might the city, and even the country. Consequently, my claim about the street sign is true as far as it goes, and how far that is involves various contingent factors. The point is not that our statements are somehow faulty in being specific to the time and situation in which the statement was made. Instead, the point is that our knowledge is always like this, and thus what we know when we know something is not true in any absolute sense. It is true as far as I know; and this is good enough.

In saying, I know that there is a blue street sign on the corner of Washington St and Sorrel I am claiming a kind of epistemological authority. I saw the sign. And if the sign has been replaced with a new sign, then I no longer saw the same sign, and my authority does not hold, even if it remains a fact that there is a sign more or less on the corner of Washington St and Sorrel.

I might respond that I know there is a sign there but now for different reasons. I still believe that there is a sign on the corner of Washington St and Sorrel because streets in cities in the United States have signs identifying the street by name. These signs are usually placed on the street corner. This claim about signs and street corners is normative, and thus I have confidence in saying that I know there is a street sign there. And how do I know about this norm? Simply from observation and extrapolation. These are reasons and justifications for my claim, as well; but they are different from my observation that there is a sign there.

Street signs are creations of particular human beings in a particular place and time, useful for contingent reasons. Some villages do not have signs. In Lisbon, the official street names often are not the names by which the inhabitants know those streets. My knowledge about villages involves actual observational experience in Greek and Portuguese villages, as well as knowledge gained from books and photographs. My knowledge about Lisbon is from both observation and testimony. My claim about signs in cities in the United States is founded on experiences of such cities and signs, but also on a general understanding of cities, streets, law, and much more. It is, however, only a probabilistic claim. Facts about street signs, like every other aspect of our earthly existent, are contingent. One contingency is that things change, and thus our knowledge is time-specific. In addition, it is not a truth of the universe that there is a blue street sign on the corner of Washington and Sorrel, but a contingent fact (truth) known under particular descriptions.

Given this normative quality of our knowledge, we should be modest in our certainties. At any particular moment, we might have to revise our knowledge. And so, a relevant question will always be: do I have reason to doubt this (whatever this might be)? In our everyday life, we cannot do this for everything, and so we have to have some reason to even ask the question about whether we have reason to doubt. But relative to those beliefs that are contested, that are bound up with ideology, we might find many reasons to doubt. Again, there are limits. We should recall Montaigne's modesty: since people have believed many different things, we should not assume that we are necessarily correct in believing what we believe; and certainly, we should not be so certain in our beliefs as to kill others who disagree. Of course, there are limits to what we can or should tolerate. The beliefs of a Nazi remain horrendous. But it is their actions for which they should be legally punished, not their beliefs.

This is to be modest about knowledge. There is no single kind of belief that will count as a knowledge belief. Our knowing something is always bound up with what we know and how we know it. Knowledge is by degrees. When we imagine knowledge is equivalent to what is the case, then we imagine our knowledge should not be in degrees. Instead, we imagine that what we call knowledge must be true without qualification, that is, non-contingently. What we know, however, is dependent on the descriptions we give of what we know and the context in which we purport to have such knowledge. We will examine this dependence in the next chapter.

NOTES

1 There is another form of underdetermination. Longino describes it this way: "it concerns the semantic gap between descriptions of single observations (or of sets of observations) that serve as data and the hypotheses the data are taken to support, when these are categorically articulated" (2016, p. 11).

2 Through this defense, White avoided a first-degree murder conviction, and was instead convicted of involuntary manslaughter; https://www.law.cornell.edu/wex/twinkie_defense.

3 We are not concerned in this case with the psychology of belief or knowing. Nor does it matter if we attempt to determine if a belief is logically prior to knowledge or if knowledge is logically prior.

4 See Stuart Ritchie's excellent critique and examination of the replication problem in *Science Fictions*.

5 Vaidyanathan, Gayathri. "How to determine the scientific consensus on global warming: An academic feud swirls around how best or even whether to express the scientific consensus around climate change." Scientific American (2014). https://www.scientificamerican.com/article/how-to-determine-the-scientific-consensus-on-global-warming/

REFERENCES

Dreyfus, George B.J. Recognizing reality: Dharmakirti's philosophy and its Tibetan interpretations. SUNY Press, 1997.

Hacking, Ian. "Nineteenth century cracks in the concept of determinism." *Journal of the History of Ideas* 44.3 (1983): 455–475.

Longino, Helen. *Underdetermination: A dirty little secret?* Department of Science and Technology Studies, UCL, 2016.

Quine, Willard V. "Knowledge." In *Quiddities: An intermittently philosophical dictionary.* Harvard University Press, 1987.

Ritchie, Stuart. *Science fictions: How fraud, bias, negligence, and hype undermine the search for truth.* Metropolitan Books, 2020.

Ryle, Gilbert. "Knowing how and knowing that: The presidential address." *Proceedings of the Aristotelian Society.* Vol. 46 (pp 1–16). Aristotelian Society, Wiley, 1945.

CHAPTER 3

The Practices of Redescription (Paradiastole)

INTRODUCTION

We live much of our lives amidst and engaged in social contests with others. The internet and OSNs have provided augmented networks that facilitate and shape these social contests (we will characterize the uniqueness of internet networks in later chapters). These contests often take the form of competitions over conflicting descriptions of people, situations, and things. Of course, sometimes these are competitions in good faith. But, too often they involve fraud: the deceptive and distorting elaboration of trivial phrases, bullying insults, illogical pseudo-inferences, lying, and most dangerous of all, the augmentation or diminishment of actions and statement using what the ancient Greek rhetorician Quintilian called *paradiastole*.

THE ORIGIN OF PARADIASTOLE

For Quintilian, paradiastole is characterized by a pattern of replacement of evaluative words in order to recast a description of someone or some situation in a way that is either better or worse than what one expects it to be. Thus, it is used as a means of accusation or mitigation. As such, in rhetorical handbooks it was classified as a form of amplification or diminishment. For example: if I assert that you are stubborn, when in fact you are anxious and reacting in panic to a perceived threat, the implications of my

DOI: 10.1201/9781003401674-5

stubborn-description deform my understanding and constitute a failing of moral apprehension on my part. Your self-understanding, however, may be no better than my understanding of you, and thus you overreact to my description, denying that you are stubborn and insisting instead in self-righteous anger that you are innocently reasonable, when in fact your behavior, however motivated, is narrow, distorted and ungenerous.[1]

The powers and dangers of paradiastole reveal an ever-present challenge to our ways of understanding and knowing: how can we determine which of a set of possible descriptions is legitimate in any particular case? Legitimacy is bound to constraint. Thus, how can we constrain the descriptive possibilities we might recognize such that we can produce or recognize legitimate descriptions? In order to answer these questions, we will first have to develop an account of the role of the descriptive instability exploited through paradiastole in our knowing and understanding of people, situations, and things. The answers to these questions will not be encouraging.

Any descriptive statement is better or worse in accuracy and usefulness relative to other possible descriptions. The point of the description may be relative to some state of affairs, and its accuracy will be partly a question of how well it represents that state of affairs, but only partially. For example, I can say the following true things about my ceiling fan. 'The ceiling fan is on.' 'The fan blades are turning.' 'The fan makes a breeze.' 'The fan cools me off.' 'The fan clatters as it turns.' Each of these sentences highlights something and ignores other things. I could also say 'The fan does not move the universe.' And also, that the fan does not move the house, or any object in the house, or any object in the world. Or that it does not cool people in Kenya, that it annoys me, but not you, and so on. All are possible, and the sense of what description I offer is relative to at least some of these possible descriptions (and possibly implicitly to a very large set of them). Descriptions imply comparisons, and are, therefore, analogical.

Paradiastole is a subspecies of this more general ability to redescribe actions, situations, and people in various ways. It involves the replacement of certain words or descriptive phrases in order to recast that which is described as either better or worse than another normative or possible description. As the intellectual historian Quentin Skinner notes, the earliest definition of paradiastole is offered by Publius Rutilius Lupus in *De Figuris Sententiarum et Elocutionis*. Rutilius also offers a set of influential examples: "that you should be recognized as wise rather than cunning, or courageous rather than overconfident, or careful rather than avaricious in your family affairs, or severe rather than malevolent" (I.4).[2] Paradisastole involves the augmentation or the diminishment of the moral valence of a particular description. More generally we can say that the evaluative implications of a description are manipulated using paradiastole.

DISTORTIONS AND CARICATURES

To say that a statement augments or diminishes some particular descriptive target implies some more neutral description. Paradiastole, therefore, as a distortion by augmentation or diminishment, constitutes a form of caricature, in which by description (or representation, as in a drawing) someone or something is exaggerated or simplified relative to some other normative description of that someone or something.[3] Your brave act is exaggerated into foolhardy recklessness; my timidity is reshaped into prudent discretion.

The role of exaggeration (or diminishment) shows that paradiastole can be construed as a form of caricature. We normally understand caricatures as cartoons that distort, exaggerate, and mock. One person's mock, however, is another's ideal. In politics such caricatures are often nasty and prejudicial, trading on falsehoods and innuendo. This is one use of and motive for caricature, but it is not essential. Caricatures simplify and abstract; they can do so in exaggerated ways or in ways that clarify. A map is a caricature of the landscape. It leaves things out in order to highlight others. This is true of any representation or description. Despite its unsavory, and even debilitating and irrational uses and forms, therefore, caricature describes how we describe anything. We think otherwise because we imagine the most complete representation of something would just be that something. If the best picture of the tree were a tree, then it would fail as a representation. And if you took a particular tree as representative of trees, then you were, in effect, logically treating the physical tree as a symbolic tree. You could use anything to do that; the physical tree could be replaced with a word without any change in its logical function. The critical thing to see is that caricatures are comparisons.

We often understand a caricature as an exaggerated, often distorted representation of something. We see a representation as an exaggeration relative to a less exaggerated representation. You see something as a caricature because you see it relative to something else, some other possible representation. You might want to resist this last claim and say: 'You mean exaggerates relative to what is the case. For example, his nose is not huge, but this picture of him caricatures it as a large pickle.' How do you compare a picture with the world, however? You say a picture does not look like that, explaining how it should look with further descriptions. You have to conceptualize her face, for example, if you want to compare it to a picture of her face. You can see her face, but to understand the difference is to compare two representations, even if one is derived from your memory or a vague sense you have. A caricature is like and unlike its target, and thus it works by analogy.

The role of norms here is fundamental. As we have shown, descriptions imply comparisons. What counts as a good description or a distorted description depends on accepted or discovered norms of description (or a normative form of description such as an idea of what a face should look like). Those norms can change.

Calling descriptions caricatures because they exclude and are limited and because they make sense relative to other descriptions seems extravagant; it seems paradiastolic! It is, of course, but so would seem any other description. A description can be true or false, but not simply true or false. It is true or false given a certain norm of truth or falsity, even if that is given by what the sentence says: snow is white if and only if snow is white; but that means snow is white understood in some normative way. (See our discussion about the problem of truth in the previous chapter.) 'White' can mean lots of things and snow can be various shades of white. So, it might be true that the snow is white according to some blunt (caricatured) notion of white. The point is not to undermine the truth condition of a sentence (a proposition) nor even to suggest that such truth conditions do not constitute its meaning (we can be agnostic about that in my argument). To call snow white means that it is white relative to the complexity of colors, even colors of white. Always to say 'something is the case' is to make an assertion relative to some normative understanding of what is asserted, and thus the assertion means relative to the other possible senses of the words that are ruled out under that normative interpretation.

Paradiastolic manipulations use the possibility of alternate descriptions to destabilize the normative standards that anyone might utilize, to in effect establish the paradiastolic description as the relevant norm and thus give the paradiastolic description authority as the salient description. To call something paradiastolic is just to acknowledge that such a description shifts away from the assumed normative description, or from the linguistic sense of the words used in what someone takes as the normative description. Paradiastolic descriptions, that is, normatively variant descriptions, prompt reflection and anxiety. The anxiety follows from the fantasy that a non-normative description is possible, which can then oscillate into the fear that the claim and authority of any description rests on questionable foundations.

The claim on us and the veracity of any description depends on the authority and grip of the normative means (and assumptions) used to evaluate and determine the sense of the description. But to determine the relevant norm of evaluation is as open to distortion or instability as any specific or particular description. The role of the norm is to delimit the possible ways a statement can be understood relative to the case at hand: norm governs interpretation relative to other possible interpretations. Such norms get their specific content and their claim on us, their force of authority through experiential learning, habit, association, prejudice, assumptions, and so forth.[4]

TYPES OF PARADIASTOLE

Descriptions are fundamentally implied comparisons with other possible descriptions; this returns us to the way in which all deceptions are caricatures relative to other possible descriptions. We compare our descriptions not with the world but with these other possible descriptions. Our comparisons are informed with our understanding and perceptions of the states of affairs, situations, the world, however, you want to phrase it.

Let's look at an example. You did not act in some situation. I insist that you were paralyzed by fear, but you were in fact acting from prudence. Because I fail to acknowledge or even understand your prudence, my understanding of you and your refusal to act constitutes a failure of moral apprehension. Let's say, however, that you were neither fearful nor prudent, but simply reacted from petty resentment. But you do not see it that way. Your self-understanding of yourself may be no better than my understanding of you. Thus, you overreact to my description, denying that you were fearful, insisting instead in self-righteous anger that you are innocently reasonable, when in fact your behavior was defensive, distorted and ungenerous.[5] These various redescriptions as we have described are examples of what one of us has called a Type 1 paradiastolic description.[6] It classifies the standard examples of paradiastole, which are characterized as the manipulative or tendentious shifting of a descriptive term with self-serving evaluative associations or implications.

For clarification, here is another example of Type 1 paradiastole. If we describe a spendthrift as generous, we are attempting to recast his behavior as a way of redescribing his character. The point is not just to get us to understand a certain kind of spending behavior as positive instead of wasteful, it is to get us to judge the character of the person in a certain way: to collect the action of spending within a particular beneficent set of motives, goals, and attitudes towards money and other people.[7] As a tactical move the goal is simply to replace a negative word with a positive word, and thus alter the judgments we might make about that person and his or her behavior. This is not to change the normative sense of any word, but rather to provide a different description of the basic action relative to a different account of the motives and goals of the action (at the very least). So, someone who seems wasteful in her spending might be redescribed instead as generous in order to suggest that her motives are noble and good. Or someone who seems magnanimous might be redescribed as a spendthrift in order to assert a lack of self-control, and thus to undermine the approbation attending her spending. In either case the spending is not at issue; its meaning is.

If there is a Type 1, there should be a Type 2 paradiastole. Type 2 involves a related but different kind of shift in description. In Type 1 the shift is tendentious and manipulative, exploiting the natural ambiguity in how we can understand our actions. Type 2 involves a change in the assumed or expected way of understanding a given action. The ambiguity remains, but there is now a substantive debate about how to understand that ambiguity. When 'ambition' or 'shrewdness,' for example, shifted in meaning from negative to neutral or positive in the 17th century, it indicated that a new framework, a new set of presuppositions about work and financial aspiration, was emerging. This new framework is not simply a shift in how to understand the motives and goals of some particular action. It is to suggest that what once was seen as a negative activity—shrewd ambition—has become a form of praise, indicating business acumen and responsibility. So, in 17th-century Europe, and in some places even earlier, loaning money had ceased to be a sign of moral depravity and greed, and instead as an intelligent and useful activity.

The description of the activity of loaning money remained the same, and its motives and goals remained the same per se, it was no longer seen as a moral failing, but either as a neutral activity or as a shrewd activity. What was labeled a vice had become a virtue. Such a change indicates a shift in sentiment, as opposed to a reinterpretation of an action relative to stable moral values. In the cases of usury and shrewdness, the moral criteria of judgment shifted within a particular community. This is a kind of cultural paradiastole—an evaluative shift, where the description gains new implicative connections relative to a specific set of values. In a verbal contest one might agree on a negative description—that someone is shrewd, for example, but shift the evaluative implications usually associated with that word from negative to positive. Such a change in moral valuation does and can happen in particular communities over time. The practices of loaning money, for example, did gain a different and more positive moral valuation in Europe during the early modern period. The meaning of words can change.

Skinner fails to acknowledge the difference between what I am calling Type 1 and Type 2 paradiastole, even suggesting that Quintilian is mistaken in his recognition that paradiastole does not always involve questions of application, but also of meaning.[8] (That difference tracks what I want to capture in my typology). Quintilian comments that he is not sure "that this device can really be classified as a figure of speech" (9.3.65). A figure of speech would be a particular configuration of words, a kind of usage. With paradiastole, however, "everything is made dependent on the definition of terms" ("*Quod totem pendet ex finitione*," 9.3.65). Usage and meaning are not so separate as Skinner imagines, but a distinction does still need to be made here. When a redescription is dependent on "the definition of terms" it would count as an example of Type 2 paradiastole. It involves a change in meaning for a particular community, as opposed to a redecription that retains a normative meaning, but is used in order to shift the implications and evaluative sense of a particular situation, person, or action.

Type 2 paradiastole is situational. A good example can be found in Thucydides. In his history, Thucydides describes the effects of civil strife (*stasis*) on Greek, especially when put at the service of self-justification. During the fifth year of the Peloponnesian War, the pro-Athenian democratic party at Corcyra revolted against the oligarchic party that controlled the polis. Such revolutions not only degenerated into explosive violence, but they also led to the deformation of language, as the meanings of words changed to fit the new contingencies of power and ideology:

> Revolution thus ran its course from city to city . . . Words had to change their ordinary meaning and to take that which was not given them. Reckless audacity came to be considered the course of a loyal supporter; prudent hesitation, specious cowardice; moderation was held to be a cloak for unmanliness; ability to see all sides of a question incapacity to act on any. Frantic violence became the

attribute of manliness; cautious plotting was a justifiable means of self-defense. The advocate of extreme measures was always trustworthy; his opponent a man to be suspected. To succeed in a plot was to have a shrewd head, to divine a plot a still shrewder; but to try to provide against having to do either was to break up our party and to be afraid of your adversaries.

(3.82, 199–200)

While behavior is praised or blamed through tendentious redescriptions, as in any paradiastolic game, the revolutionary conditions of the Greek world pressure the meaning of these words into new pathways. In this case, it is the meaning of 'prudence' that is changing. This means that what will count as prudent behavior is altering. Thus, not just the words, but human actions are shifting in their sense and import. This is a case where Type 1 becomes generalized into Type 2 paradiastole, where what is at stake is not just whether some particular behavior should be described as frantically violent, but rather what will *count* as such behavior has collected around a new norm. If one realizes that words do not mean in themselves, but gain sense through their uses, their uptake, and how they fit within a shifting and constantly revised network of implications, then shifting the normative application of a word can lead easily to establishing new criteria for its usage.

Our discussion of paradiastole helps reveal that anything we know we know under a description. We can even extend this to the claim that anything is something *for us* only under some description or other. The dependence on description is particularly striking with human actions. Actions, however, are not separable from our ways of understanding them. While the basic idea of understanding actions and people under a description can be found in Aristotle (e.g., Poetics cap 25), the modern account is offered by both Wittgenstein and then in a more influential form by his student Elizabeth Anscombe.[9] "[O]ne and the same action (or other event)," as Anscombe observes, "may have many descriptions" ("'Under a Description,'" 210). And again: "a single action can have many different descriptions, e.g. 'sawing a plank', 'sawing an oak', 'sawing one of Smith's planks', 'making a squeaky noise with the saw', 'making a great deal of sawdust', and so on" (*Intention*, 11).[10] Even if one rejects the idea, as one should, that there is a brute action which is the 'real action,' one might still wonder what is the best description. Often the best description will be a question of why one is offering a description and what distinctions one wants to make. Someone might describe your sawing the plank as "making a nuisance" or as "waking the baby." Your sawing intentions matter, of course, but you cannot simply say to yourself that you intend only to saw the plank and not to wake the baby, in order to avoid the blame when the baby wakes up screaming.

Any particular description is underdetermined by what it describes (i.e., we can always offer further and other kinds of descriptions). Similarly, any description underdetermines what we can conclude or infer from that description. Many of these implications are evaluative, hence prejudicial. Agreement about any description of human action or situation is a question of judgment, not of fact. There is no principled solution to the ambiguities attending descriptions of people and their behavior. Thus, relative to people, what we know, as that knowledge is given under a description, remains always provisional and dependent on norms.

The philosopher Frank Ramsey's characterization of truth inadvertently shows that if we are to believe anything we must believe it under some description:

> My definition that a belief is true if it is 'a belief that p' and p, but false if it is a 'a belief that p' and -p is . . . substantially that of Aristotle . . . a belief that Smith is either a liar or a fool is sure if Smith is either a liar or a fool, and not otherwise.

> *"On Truth," 1992*

The form of this characterization of truth is not surprising. His example, however, shows the role of description and judgment. What counts as being a liar, such that Smith is one? If he lies once, is he therefore a liar? Such a criterion is rather extreme. And does it matter if it is a white lie, a misleading statement, a self-serving distortion? And if we require that we lie on a more regular basis, how do we determine that 'regular' means here? Of course, one can say that as long as there are some accepted criteria for these descriptions, then the rest follows. But in many cases, arguments about whether it is true or false that Smith is a liar or not will rest on how we understand what it means to lie and be a liar. And such terms are exactly, the kind of descriptors utilized in paradiastole. I might counter and say Smith was being strategically careful with what he admitted was true, because he is a general, and that even when he took responsibility for the lost battle he was no fool, but rather brave, and so on. None of this undermines the notion of truth, but shows that our evaluation of what is true or false is bound to descriptions, and that the criteria for these descriptions can easily be contested, and have a complex evolution and etiology.

CONCLUSION

We understand people and situations also through descriptions, and these descriptions are also open to distortions and revisions. This dependence on description allows people to manipulate and distort how actions, events, people, and situations are described. We can generalize. Whatever we know, we know under a particular description. Sometimes if we alter the description, even if it is logically equivalent, we might thereby fail to recognize that the new statement is equivalent, and thus think we do not know it.

This leads to a simple conclusion, although one that is often forgotten in ordinary life: statements and descriptions about people and states of affairs *must* be open for revision, which is to say both to alteration and correction. And such descriptions must be understood relative to other possible descriptions, and we must beware of evaluating these descriptions relative to our own desires and goals.

What is less obvious is that any description implies a set of other possible descriptions that all can be construed, under some further description, as analogies of each other. Analogies are not true or false, but more or less plausible, salient, useful, and are determined by judgment and argument. Consequently, our understanding of a situation, action, or person is not a question of simply being right, whatever that might mean, but of understanding within a context of possible descriptions about which one must be responsible, what is likely the case, what is accurate, reasonable, just, likely, and so on. There is no formula for determining what a good reason is, just like there is no procedure to determine what a good judgment is. And this is what gives paradiastole part of its force for both revelation and distortion.

NOTES

1 Such contests emerge out of different values and ideas of social interaction, relative to differing ideas of ones' self, rights, and status, as well as of ways in which personality, character fit or unfit with roles and obligations.

2 Quentin Skinner has explored in great detail the intellectual history of paradiastole. His thoughts about the role and history of the term and concept of paradiastole have over the years. See *Reason and Rhetoric in the Philosophy*

of Hobbes, in particular, Chapter 4, "Techniques of redescription" (1996). Also, "Moral ambiguity and the renaissance art of eloquence" (2002); "Hobbes on rhetoric and the construction of morality" (2003); "Rhetorical redescription and its uses in Shakespeare" (2018). I am using Skinner's translation, which can be found in "Rhetorical redescription and its uses in Shakespeare," page 91.

3 It cannot be simply a comparison with how someone sees something (a perception), since that would involve recognition and some representation relative to which the caricature could be itself not only apprehended as a caricature, but apprehended as a caricature of something in particular.

4 Our understanding of people, situations, events, and things are stabilized through these normative patterns of interpretation. The world is complex, shifting, filled with unknowns. We need efficient and good enough strategies for understanding that complexity in a way that allows us to act and protect ourselves. Thus, we are highly invested in those norms through which we grow into maturity within our communities. At the same time, these interpretative norms understanding rests on a complex, hardly coherent background of assumptions. Norms are not rules or algorithms; they are general patterns of how to interpret and understand complex events that do not come with labels that are open to multiple descriptions. Consequently, paradiastolic descriptions can be very effective since what we describe is open to so many other descriptions that can seem reasonable and normatively plausible. The intersubjective form of our shared norms also means that we can ourselves become destabilized relative to these norms and our investment in and use of them.

5 Such contests emerge out of different values and ideas of social interaction, relative to differing ideas of ones' self, rights, and status, as well as of ways in which personality, character fit or unfit with roles and obligations.

   One exploits the possibility of describing something in a way that implicitly commends or criticizes, augments or diminishes; one can perform such redescriptions as tactical manipulations relative to one's ends or in pursuit of a greater justice to the complexity of person and character. Aristotle explains this kind of descriptive shifting as a consequence of the relative similarity between various virtues and vices—such that one can seem like the other, as in this case where liveliness can seem or be impertinence, depending on a number of factors. The replacement of terms is rhetorical if there is no attempt to determine these factors and adjudicate between the reasons one might call the behavior one or the other.

6 Elsewhere I have classified our everyday modes of redescription (Bourbon, 2022). I provide a summary of that classification.

7 Beliefs concerning both the motives and consequences of capitalist behavior change over time in Western Europe, in particular beliefs about the developing practices surrounding markets, capital exchange, and the flow of currency. The history of this is complicated and international. See Appleby (especially chapter 4), *The relentless revolution: A history of capitalism* (Norton & Co., 2010); Deidre N. McCloskey, *The Bourgeois virtues: Ethics*

for an age of commerce (University of Chicago Press, 2006); and Joel Mokyr, *A culture of growth: The origins of the modern economy* (Princeton University Press, 2017).

8 See 'Rhetoric and the construction of morality," in *Visions of politics*, vol. 3, 96–97.

9 See Anscombe, *Intention* and "Under a description." Ian Hacking (1998) develops this notion of description into an account of the self in *Rewriting the Soul*. See also Anscombe, "Modern moral philosophy."

10 G.E.M. Anscombe, *Intention*, 2nd ed. 1963 and "Under a description" in Mind and Collected Works.

REFERENCES

Anscombe, G.E.M. *Intention*. 2nd ed. Harvard University Press, 2000.

Anscombe, G.E.M. "Modern moral philosophy." In Mary Geach and Luke Gormally (Eds.), *Human life, action and ethics*. Imprint Academic, 2015.

Anscombe, G.E.M. "Under a description." In *Metaphysics and the philosophy of mind: Collected philosophical papers, v. II*. University of Minnesota Press, 1981.

Appleby, J. *The relentless revolution: A history of capitalism*. W.W. Norton & Co., 2010.

Bourbon, Brett. *Jane Austen and the ethics of life*. Routledge Press, 2022.

Hacking, Ian. *Rewriting the Soul*. Princeton UP, 1998.

McCloskey, Deidre N. *The Bourgeois virtues: Ethics for an age of commerce*. University Chicago Press, 2006.

Mokyr, Joel. *A culture of growth: The origins of the modern economy*. Princeton University Press, 2017.

Quintilian. *The Orator's education*. Books 9–10. Donald A. Russell (Ed. and trans.). Harvard University Press, 2001.

Ramsey, F.P. *On truth*. N. Rescher and U. Majer (Eds.). Kluwer, 1992.

Skinner, Quentin. "Moral ambiguity and the renaissance art of eloquence," In *Vision of politics*, Volume 2 (pp. 264–285). Cambridge University Press, 2002.

Skinner, Quentin. *Reason and rhetoric in the philosophy of Hobbes*. Cambridge University Press, 1996.

Skinner, Quentin. "Hobbes on rhetoric and the construction of morality." In *Visions of politics: Hobbes and civil science*, Volume 3 (pp. 87–141). Cambridge University Press, 2003.

Skinner, Quentin. "Rhetorical redescription and its uses in Shakespeare." In *From Humanism to Hobbes: Studies in Rhetoric and Politics* (pp. 89–117). Cambridge University Press, 2018.

Thucydides. *The landmark Thucydides* (Revised Trans. Richard Crawley. Ed. Robert B. Strassler). Free Press, Penguin, 1996.

PART II

Information and Misinformation

DOI: 10.1201/9781003401674-6

CHAPTER 4

What Is Information?

INTRODUCTION

In 2003, the editors of a special issue of the *Journal of Logic, Language, and Information*, entitled "On Connecting the Different Faces of Information," confessed that "there is no generally accepted definition or theory of information that covers all of its meaningful uses" (Van Benthem and Van Rooy, 2003). We still do not have an adequate definition or theory of information. The word and concept remain ambiguous. It is a term used by many, but understood by few. In fact, there cannot be a coherent concept that can include all relevant examples. The determination about what will count as a relevant example is a judgment and open to dispute.

In such a situation what is required is not further theories, but minimal descriptions of kinds of information. We need more examples and fewer theories. In the following chapters that make up Part 2 of this book, we will examine a vast number of examples as a way of clarifying the concepts of information and other related concepts like data, facts, writing, and counting. In addition, we will critique a number of important theories about information that create confusion about the kinds of information that dominate online social media.

AS WHAT DOES INFORMATION EXIST?

This chapter is ostensibly entitled 'What Is Information?' The title of this chapter should be: *As What Does Information Exist?* We know that this is a strangely formulated question, which can seem unnecessarily obscure. Isn't information just information? Doesn't it exist as what it is, that is, as information? Information, however, is a confused and incoherent concept.

DOI: 10.1201/9781003401674-7

And, therefore, our strange question is essential. If we are going to talk about information we must establish what it is, even that it is something at all. In other words, how do we see, understand, and grasp information as something? How is it manifest to us? As what does it exist?

We will look at specific cases and examples of what we call or should call information. But given the complexity of what we are trying to describe, we need to think about what it means for something to be manifest such that we can describe it, analyze it, respond to it. So, we ask again: How do we see, understand, and grasp information as something? How is it manifest to us? As what does it exist? Seemingly, in many ways. Here are four ways we might ask about how information is manifest or exists as something for us to describe. We choose these because each describes a radically different kind of thing that may or may not exist, depending on your ontological commitments.

Is It Like Love, Which Is Manifest by Many Different Gestures?

Love is expressed in various ways. The gestures could be anything, but they are understood to express or show the love of one person for someone else. In such a situation we would understand this love as something definite, although possibly hard to define. It is in any case a complex thing that does not exist as an object, since it is a feeling. But it is manifest, that is, expressed, in various physical ways. Is information, therefore, analogous to a feeling like love that is manifest by various physical means such as marks, words, or statements? Of course, information is not a feeling. The point is that, in this case, information would be one kind of thing and it would be made manifest by means of other kinds of things.

Or Is It Like the Way Tuesday Is Manifest on Calendars?

This mode of manifestation has some similarities with the previous example of measurement. Whether it is Tuesday or Wednesday is a question of fact. But it is contingent on our system of tracking time and days, our particular calendar and its general acceptance by us as legitimate. A day and the system of labels are in effect a measure of solar day relative to the lunar month (the solar year is only implied). Information would thus be one kind of conceptual measurement relative to other conceptual descriptions. Those who describe information as a midpoint between data and knowledge are offering an example of this way of manifesting the concept of information. One need not use the concept of data and knowledge, but some other set of related concepts.

Or the Way Temperature Is Made Manifest by Thermometers?

This mode of manifestation has some similarities with the previous example of measurement. The general heat of the atmosphere heats the mercury that is contained within a defined physical structure that is used as a measure. Information would be a conceptual measure of some aspect of the world or our behavior as effects of some more general cause. In the calendar case, the measurement is more like a ruler than a thermometer. The mercury inside a thermometer is causally responsive to the temperature. A calendar represents and organizes days into a structure that we can then use to organize our shared experience of these days. We organize the days into a series that then allows us to describe them using the terms and structure of our description. There is no causal interaction between days and calendar.

Or the Way Mother Nature Is Manifest in Nature?

There is no Mother Nature; it is just a phrase of convenience to capture nature's intelligibility and coherence - if this is the appropriate analogy, information would just be a metaphor to describe a range of human practices with facts, data, propositions, and so on.

We might characterize these for ways of existing using the following short-hand:

- Love: Actual, but an unstable and contested conceptualization of overlapping phenomena of human experience

- Tuesday: Conventional, but its form and particularity determined by intersubjective structure

- Temperature: Actual, given as a measure and conceptualization of a physical phenomenon

- Mother Nature: Non-actual, but useful as a personified characterization of actual phenomena

We will see that information is so varied as to include all four of these modes of manifestation. Our goal is not to offer some ontological taxonomy, but simply to encourage a cautionary modesty in assuming that information is one thing. Or, if it is many things, should we assume that there exists a primary paradigm for what it is, whether that paradigm is physical, abstract, formal, or epistemic?

'Information' and 'misinformation' are descriptive of phenomena. And their meaning as terms is determined not only by how we use them, but by how the phenomena we describe by means of them are manifest to us. Our exploration must be a posteriori. Everything we say about information must be determined by examples of what we take as information per se or of the actions or behavior of *informing* or *being informed*. If we do not derive our descriptions (let alone our definitions) of information from examples or from the action or behavior of informing or being informed, what we say about information will be vague and/or question-begging. Any arguments we might make about what it is would be viciously circular. Intuitions mean nothing without clear and relevant examples; and if you have the examples, you do not need the intuitions. Therefore, we ground our exploration in examples, or what we sometimes call and have been calling the phenomena. How to describe these examples and phenomena is always a significant conceptual or philosophical task. The form such descriptions take should not be assumed to be obvious.

We can inform someone about something by using different kinds of linguistic statements in particular situations. This is part of our social behavior. There are no specific linguistic acts of informing per se. We can also derive information from non-linguistic situations and behaviors, as well as from animal behavior, weather effects, stratifications of rock faces, and so on. Information seems like a species of knowledge, or what we might imagine is knowledge (about someone's beliefs, e.g.). Someone might, of course, imagine they believe something, but in fact not believe that. Things are seldom simple.

There are numerous problems with the various logical descriptions or definitions of information offered by various scholars, especially those who argue that information is necessarily veridical. Theorists can, of course, define something however they want, but that does not help us understand the actual examples of so-called information and misinformation, let alone the behavior in which the exchange, acceptance, denial, misunderstanding of information is a part.

EVERYDAY PRACTICES OF ONLINE INFORMATION AND MISINFORMATION

We can side-step some of these theoretical issues, since they do not impinge on our particular goal. Our goal is to understand and conceptualize our everyday practices of information and misinformation exchange on the internet. Thus, we do not need a logically universal description or definition of information, even if one were possible. We actually do not think such a universal definition is possible, since information is not a well-defined anything, but a vague term describing multiple things. Of course, some researchers will want to remove the equivocation by nominating some kind of things as paradigmatically or essentially 'information.' Not only will this be question-begging, if any one kind is taken as paradigmatic, it is irrelevant to our actual practices of information exchange, which involve many different kinds of information (including informing people of our emotional states and moods, and so forth). What we need is a description of the ordinary and pervasive practices of information exchange and uptake by various online means.

Before we look at a few examples, we need to make one further argument about our everyday knowledge that has a bearing on our uptake, that is, our reaction, either of acceptance or rejection, of information. In everyday life, most people can hardly justify or explain why they believe most of what they believe to be true. It is true that the traditional analytic definition of knowledge as justified true belief does not cover all cases, as Gettier (1963) was the first to demonstrate with his famous thought-experiment, as we have discussed in Chapter 2. It remains true, however, that if I cannot justify what I think I know, what I think I know, which may be true, is a form of prejudice (prejudgment) or accepted opinion (sometimes called common sense). This is often the case with so-called scientific information, which is widely misunderstood and has become separated from the processes by which such knowledge is generated and tested and revised. Most people have little to no understanding of why any scientific claims are thought to be true, or probably true, and understand neither the theories nor the arguments in their favor. It can all seem like magic. So-called experts also vary quite a bit in their judgments and understandings. Indeed, the advancement of knowledge is sometimes the result of the failure of these experts. The application of scientific judgment in particular cases is also not simply a question of knowledge or expertise. All of this is to repeat what should be obvious; science is powerful because it can be tested and revised, not because it is certain or absolute.

Few educated people can actually offer adequate justifications for their various beliefs about the world and how it works. Most people believe what they do about science for no better reason than what people believed in Europe about astrology in the year 1300. Even when they do know something about the scientific understanding of the world, their knowledge is often superficial and brittle. I have often asked my students if the planets of our solar system move around the sun at a constant or varying rate. On average, only 5% of the students can provide the correct answer. It is interesting to note that those who do know that the rate varies can provide the correct basic explanation why. If human beings are likely to share many true beliefs about the world in which they live, what the philosopher Donald Davidson (1984) calls the principle of charity, their beliefs about what they cannot test in their everyday experience are likely to fit a vast range of ideological commitments, superstitions, self-serving opinions, and so on. In addition, having true beliefs about biology, for example, need not entail being able to justify those beliefs. At best such beliefs would constitute a weak form of knowledge. This is to suggest that relative to people's belief and uptake, information rests on no more certain foundations than does misinformation.

CONCLUSION

Our reactions and responses to what is presented as information will be infected or even determined by our moods and dispositions, and by our various personally motivated and ideological commitments and preju-dices. Thus, we often believe or disbelieve in what we should not. What we know matters because of how it guides us in making our own decisions. The world is complex and our knowledge of ourselves and others is not only limited, it is not clear that there is always a fact of the matter to know in every situation. Someone may imagine that they are so important that they must do everything to improve their longevity, including following the latest fads. They might also neglect their children, their mate, and vari-ous activities that they deem dangerous. Maybe this will pay-off or maybe not. They may end up living in fear and in self-absorption, however, and so the natural risks of life that end in the valuable experiences of love, athletics, nature, and so on will be avoided in the pursuit of self-important longevity. We have met more than one person who thinks like this, as we are sure many of us have. The information used to pursue this goal may all be correct (or it may not be), but the way that information is used and how it fits with other assumed facts are not simply true or false. Even the idea that eating well will lead to a long life is not necessarily true: cancer can still claim you as can a car accident, and so forth. Our point is not that one should eat poorly, but that so-called information fits with a complex set of beliefs, aspirations, fears, anxieties and so on.

Information, like anything which is supposed to function like a fact, or as data, is entangled with what we sometimes call value. The goodness or badness, the relevance or irrelevance, the saliency or lack of saliency of some belief are not facts of the matter. But neither are they simply subjec-tive. What it means to be a good sea captain is not simply an opinion, even though judgments about the issue will vary.

Again, our goal here is not to offer theories about facts and values (a recurrent issue in philosophy at least since Hume). Our point is simply to resist the simplistic and reductionist attempts to define information as simply one kind of thing. In fact, we would suggest that information is not a thing at all, but simply a vague label to collect a vast range of kinds of statements and of ways of knowing, communicating, and understanding human behavior.

When we use the word 'information' to describe contingently true (or false) propositions, then we need not concern ourselves with more problematic notions of information and data that might be relevant in certain interpretations of quantum physics, for example. But this proviso is ignored by many, and this is another path that can lead to the claim that all information must be true and that thus misinformation is necessarily false and not information at all.[1] We take this to be misleading, and encourages a polarizing notion of misinformation and mischaracterizes what we take as information, circulating through not only the internet but in everyday social 'offline' life.[2]

NOTES

1 A number of theoretical attempts to argue that information must necessarily true, including Dretske (1981), Floridi (2004, 2009); Barwise and Perry (1981); Israel and Perry (1990); Mingers and Standing (2018); Swire-Thompson and Lazer (2020). We will look at elements of Dretske's theory and of Mingers and Standing, as the most representative for arguments about online information. Within media studies and computational social science, the idea that information must be true can take a less theoretical form. In these cases, the assumption is pervasive that the primary way to counter misinformation is through the truth. The literature about this is extensive. A recent sampling would include the following: Li and Chang (2023); Prike et al. (2024); Lewandowsky and Linden (2021); Chung and Kim (2021); Clayton et al. (2020); Babaei et al. (2021).

2 We want to be clear what we are trying to explain. Our concern for judgment as reflected in our questions about whether some statement or information is true or false is a judgment within and about some kind of discursive situation. This is true even if we are just reading something on the web that has been posted. These judgments are required regardless of how our language works. We do not think language can be explained using a causal theory of language. Such theories sometimes appeal to information as the conceptual magic to explain how to get meaning out of cause. Our argument, however, is not about the mechanisms or processes or practices that allow language to mean or to be meaningful. However, we mean and understand within the practices of our language use, we make judgments. And these judgments are what we must understand if we are to understand our lives with information online.

REFERENCES

Babaei, Mahmoudreza, et al. "Analyzing biases in perception of truth in news stories and their implications for fact checking." *IEEE Transactions on Computational Social Systems* 9.3 (2021): 839–850.

Barwise, Jon, and John Perry. "Situations and attitudes." *The Journal of Philosophy* 78.11 (1981): 668–691.

Chung, Myojung, and Nuri Kim. "When I learn the news is false: How fact-checking information stems the spread of fake news via third-person perception." *Human Communication Research* 47.1 (2021): 1–24.

Clayton, Katherine, et al. "Real solutions for fake news? Measuring the effectiveness of general warnings and fact-check tags in reducing belief in false stories on social media." *Political Behavior* 42 (2020): 1073–1095.

Davidson, Donald. "On the very idea of a conceptual scheme." *Inquiries into Truth and Interpretation* 183 (1984): 189.

Dretske, F. *Knowledge and the flow of information.* MIT Press, 1981.

Floridi, Luciano. "Information." In L. Floridi (Ed.), *The Blackwell guide to the philosophy of computing and information* (pp. 40–61). Blackwell, 2004.

Floridi, Luciano. "Semantic conceptions of information." In E. N. Zalta (Ed.), *Stanford encyclopedia of philosophy.* The Metaphysics Research Lab, 2009.

Gettier, Edmund L. "Is justified true belief knowledge?" *Analysis* 23.6 (1963): 121–123.

Israel, David J., and John Perry (1990). "What is information?" In Philip P. Hanson (Ed.), *Information, language and cognition.* University of British Columbia Press, 1991.

Lewandowsky, Stephan, and Sander Van Der Linden. "Countering misinformation and fake news through inoculation and prebunking." *European Review of Social Psychology* 32.2 (2021): 348–384.

Li, Jiexun, and Xiaohui Chang. "Combating misinformation by sharing the truth: a study on the spread of fact-checks on social media." *Information Systems Frontiers* 25.4 (2023): 1479–1493.

Mingers, John, and Craig Standing. "What is information? Toward a theory of information as objective and veridical." *Journal of Information Technology* 33.2 (2018): 85–104.

Prike, Toby, Lucy H. Butler, and Ullrich KH Ecker. "Source-credibility information and social norms improve truth discernment and reduce engagement with misinformation online." *Scientific Reports* 14.1 (2024): 6900.

Swire-Thompson, Briony, and David Lazer. "Public health and online misinformation: challenges and recommendations." *Annual Rev Public Health* 41.1 (2020): 433–451.

Van Benthem, Johan, and Robert Van Rooy. "Connecting the different faces of information." *Journal of Logic, Language, and Information* 12.4 (2003): 375–379.

CHAPTER 5

Shannon's Theory of Information

INTRODUCTION

Modern information theory derives in part from the seminal work of Claude Shannon, Warren Weaver, and Norbert Weiner. More broadly it is a subset of probability theory and mathematical statistics and derives from the work of R. A. Fisher and others. In order to understand the problems and powers of information and misinformation as these diffuse through the web, we do not need to enter into arguments about the mathematical and logical definitions of information. We will, however, look in a limited way at attempts to extend syntactical theories of information into epistemological contexts. Confusions about information are entangled in our confusions about knowledge.

How much information can we extract (or is embodied) in a Bach Cantata? The words have theological significance as well as poetic beauty. The music is sublime, consisting of patterns and inventions of various kinds. It is recorded on paper and then if performed recorded in other ways. We cannot determine how much information is involved in this cantata because we have not yet specified the terms and units of measurement. Information theory (it would be better if it were called Communication theory) provides a measure and a set of units to measure all kinds of information. It is not concerned with the meaning of the information transmitted, but rather with the quantity of tokens that can be transmitted through some channel. As Shannon says,

DOI: 10.1201/9781003401674-8

These semantic aspects of communication are irrelevant to the engineering problem. The significant aspect is that the actual message is one selected from a set of possible messages.

(180).[1]

Shannon conceptualizes information as "the resolution of uncertainty" (Shannon, 1948). Thus, the measure of information is the measure of the uncertainty that is resolved. The more uncertainty resolved, the more information conveyed. It is common to claim that the intuitive idea behind information is that if some message is more uncertain or less probable, then it provides more content relative to other possible messages. If we are more surprised by the message than we would be with other possible messages, then we get more information. The idea of surprise provides some psychological justification for the theory, but it is not necessary for the mathematics. The theory can be given a purely statistical form. But the importance of the theory lies more directly in its modeling of communication systems. We will provide a basic description of the theory in order to identify one of the key ambiguities in our use of the concept of information.

STRUCTURAL LIMITS ON INFORMATION: NOISE, ENTROPY, CAPACITY

The measure of the quantity of information is given by the probability of any particular message given a set of possible messages. The less probable, the more information, and hence, the inverse of the probability. This gives us the basic mathematical measure of information: $\log(1/p)$. The base of the logarithm provides the unit of measure. For the sake of efficiency and reliability, Shannon uses base two. This equation defines what has come to be called a bit of information (sometimes called a Shannon), which is the amount of information required in order to choose between one of two options. Characterizing the amount of information relative to two options conveniently allows us to represent that information in binary, using 0 and 1.

Here is an example. Imagine there are eight dishes on a restaurant menu. Of these eight, I have chosen one to order. All of the choices are equally probable. I have made my choice, and you will ask me questions in order to figure out which dish I have chosen. You could just begin guessing randomly. You might get lucky. But by this approach it could take you anywhere from one question to seven questions. If we approach the problem differently, we can measure the reduction of uncertainty by determining how many questions would be required to determine my choice. Your first move would be to divide up the options into two sets of four, and ask if it is the first set (we can label with a 0) or the second set (we can label with a 1). In answer to your question I reply, "1." This is what Shannon called one bit (an abbreviation of 'binary digit'). Then you divide the set indicated into two sets, again labeling one with 0 and one with 1. This time I chose 0: a second bit of information. Finally, you label the two remaining choices with a 0 and a 1, and ask which dish I want. I reply 0: a third bit. The reduction of eight choices to one embodies 3 bits of information. Shannon used this measure of information in order to describe how much information can be communicated between two devices in a communications system.

Shannon's theory of information (or communication) defines bounds on the capacity C of a channel, beyond which error-free transmission is impossible. He called it as "nature's payment": "Nature takes payment by requiring just that much uncertainty, so that we are not actually getting any more than C through correctly." Prior to Shannon, this payment in the form of errors was thought to be unavoidable. Noise is a component of every communication channel, and the only mechanisms developed for mitigating the impact of noise were either related to increasing the transmission power or decreasing the transmission speed. But Shannon's theory showed that the noise characteristics of a channel define its capacity, and as long as the transmission rate is below the capacity, error-free transmission could be achieved. All that was needed for efficiency was the right code for the symbols of the message. This characterization allows for a new label for the uncertainty or entropy. If information is a measure of the entropy of a random variable, entropy is nothing more than what is called the self-information of the random variable (Cover and Thomas, 2005). Self-information describes the probability of a set of events of some random variable, like the flipping of a single coin. We can also calculate what is called *mutual information*, which is the measure of the amount of information one random variable contains about another. Thus, mutual information is the reduction in uncertainty of one random variable due to knowledge gained about another random variable. In the presence of noise, mutual information denotes the maximum possible communication rate on a channel. These fundamental concepts in Shannon's information theory leave no room for a characterization of misinformation. Any such notion of misinformation is simply the presence of noise that limits the ability to transmit more than the capacity of a channel and ultimately manifests as *errors*.

The reason for the absence of misinformation in Shannon's theory is straightforward. Misinformation expresses a judgment about the content of the information. Information theory describes the amount of information, understood as differences between two defined states. We can speak of errors in transmission, but such errors can be mathematically corrected. Far from being evidence that information must be true and misinformation must not be a kind of information, this suggests that Shannon's use of information is misleading (as he confessed). His use of information marks a distinction with noise, not with misinformation.

As powerful as Shannon's theory and the theories and algorithms it has spawned, it has left us with a core problem, that percolates throughout information theory, including in our constructions and interpretations of Large Language Model (LLM) Artificial Intelligences (AIs). J. Michael Dunn (2008) offers an evocative characterization of this core problem: "I believe that the fundamental philosophical question regarding the representation of information is: how much "lies in the eye of the beholder?" This is meant metaphorically of course. We can replace the word "eye" with "interpretation" or even "mind" to make the question clearer. Dunn is right: this is the essential question. Is information informative in itself, without our interpretation? The idea that information can exist simply in the distinctions produced in the natural world hides a set of personifying moves. Anything we perceive is potentially informative, but that fact does not mean that what we perceive is in itself information. A bobcat running across a fence does not embody the information that it is running *in* its running. It is simply running for whatever reason. And whatever information we might derive from that action does not exist in the bobcat or that action.

CONCLUSION

We might redescribe Dunn's question in a simpler communication engineering form: What does it mean for a signal to carry or convey information? Or, what is actually conveyed versus what is inferred from what is conveyed? Theories that insist that information must be true and that misinformation is not a form of information often collapse this difference: equating what is conveyed or carried by a signal or medium with what is inferred from what is conveyed.

Terrence Deacon offers another way of characterizing this issue (Deacon, 2007). Shannon's theory provides us with a means of measuring "the information-conveying capacity of any given communications medium, and yet we cannot give an account of how this relates to the content that this signal may or may not represent" (189). Information theory describes the medium and the tools (possible symbols or possible messages) that enable the transmission of meaningful information, but those meanings are not created by the medium or tools. Similarly, we can move our hand in a gesture of frustration, but neither the hand nor the movement contains the meaning of the gesture. There are many ways of describing this differ-ence between how something meaningful is manifest and the meaningful-ness expressed (our grasping of it).[2] The concept of information embodies an ambiguity that encourages people to imagine that this difference can be absorbed in that concept. But this is simply to imagine an ambiguity can resolve a difference, when in fact it reveals that difference. Philosopher David Chalmers describes this ambiguity well:

> When we talk about information, we encounter a central ambigu-ity. In one sense, information is the realm of facts. In another sense, information is the realm of bits. These are two very different things.

Facts are propositional. We grasp them as meaningful such that we can evaluate them as true or false. They constitute kinds of knowledge. Bits are syntactic and not semantic. Chalmers calls this kind of information structural, in order to suggest that its significance is a function of the role it plays in structures, like codes. Chalmers does speculate that information can offer a link between matter and mind. We do not think that this is the case, but such speculation would lead us beyond the scope of our focus on everyday information.[3]

In order to understand our current entanglements and confusion about information, we need to shift our ground from the mathematics of infor-mation theory to the relationship between counting, data, and informa-tion as an everyday concept. This is what we will do in the next chapter.

NOTES

1 Claude Shannon, "A mathematical theory of communication", *The Bell System Technical Journal* 27.3 (1948): 379–423 (1948, 1950 [1993: 180]).
2 There have been attempts to build a semantics of information from the syn-tax of information. Floridi (2009), for example, offers a theory of semantic information, but it is guided by technical concerns that come out of Carnap and Bar-Hillel's (1952) earlier attempt to describe the semantics of informa-tion (see Dunn's comments about this). We will return to the question of the truth status of information in Chapter 8.

3 Chalmers (1997) makes the following claim in *The conscious mind*: "We might put this suggestion as a basic principle that information (in the actual world) has two aspects, a physical and a phenomenal aspect. Whenever there is a phenomenal state, it realizes an information state, an information state that is also realized in the cognitive system of the brain. Conversely, for at lease some physically realized information spaces, whenever an information state in that space is realized physically, it is also realized phenomenally" (286).

REFERENCES

Carnap, Rudolf, and Yehoshua Bar-Hillel. "An outline of a theory of semantic information." Technical Report, Massachusetts Institute of Technology, Research Laboratory of Electronics (1952): 247.

Chalmers, David J. *The conscious mind: In search of a fundamental theory.* Oxford Paperbacks, 1997.

Cover, Thomas, and Joy Thomas. *The elements of information theory.* Wiley, 2005.

Deacon, T. W. Shannon–Boltzmann–Darwin: Redefining information (Part I). *Cognitive Semiotics* 1.s1 (2007): 123–148.

Dunn, J. Michael. "Information in computer science." *Philosophy of Information* 8 (2008): 581–608.

Floridi, Luciano. "Philosophical conceptions of information." In: Sommaruga, G. (Ed.), *Formal theories of information: From Shannon to semantic information theory and general concepts of information.* Lecture Notes in Computer Science vol. 5363 (pp. 13–53). Springer, 2009.

Shannon, C. "A Mathematical Theory of Communication." *The Bell System Technical Journal* 27.3 (1948): 379–423.

CHAPTER 6

Data, Counting, and Writing

INTRODUCTION

The prevailing assumption for many theorists of information is that information should be construed as something like a fact. If we formalize in a naive fashion the idea that information are facts derived from data, then we might conclude that information must be veridical, since facts are understood as true. Information would seem to be conveyed by true statements, while misinformation would be conveyed by false statements. There is no logical difference, however, in the information conveyed. That in one case the information is true and in the other false is itself a contingent fact, determined by the situation. Therefore, the distinction between information and misinformation when about facts or about what is the case is not a logical distinction, but an epistemological distinction. (The distinction we are making here is not absolute. An epistemological distinction, for example, can be used to make a logical distinction). In which case, the logical form of information and misinformation (so-called) need not be different. Even when I am misinformed, I am still informed of something. In some situations, however, what I am informed of will happen not to be the case. Therefore, what we call information and misinformation need not indicate a logical difference, a difference in the kind of thing so described. A false statement is still a statement. A false theory is still a theory. False information is still information. This argument will not be convincing for some.

DOI: 10.1201/9781003401674-9

In what follows we will make it more convincing. In this chapter we will analyze and clarify how to understand the relationship among the concepts of data, facts, and information.

INFORMATION FROM COUNTING AND COMPARISON

Writing is not simply a skill, it is a kind of technology, a systematic way of encoding language and speech. Language is not a technology in this sense. Language is a natural capacity of human beings. It has a logical form that allows human beings to express thoughts and communicate. It is learned and is governed by norms, but it is not a code.

A code is parasitic on the mode of cognitive understanding that we bring to it. A code specifies rules for transforming some input or target into some output; it is reversible, which means we can go from inputs to outputs and vice versa (if we could not do this we could not decipher the code), but also deterministic and complete. A language is not a set of rules; a language is not simply syntactical. As such a language is not the sounds and marks we make, not what we say, but our ability to say and understand each other. It is an activity.

Writing, of course, is distinct from language. Language can and has existed without writing, but writing requires some original language, even if that language has become extinct. Writing developed very late in our cognitive evolution. Writing as a technology encodes our speaking into a more permanent form. It was, as Denise Schmandt-Besserat calls it, "a revolution in communication when a script, providing a way to encode data, allows individuals to share information without meeting face to face" (Schmandt-Besserat, 2014). The data encoded in phonetic alphabets is phonemes, while a writing system like Chinese encodes morphemes. In both cases, meaning is not encoded—the meaningfulness remains a quality of the language that is represented through writing. Writing does not just allow the sharing of information, but all aspects of what languages communicate, from thoughts to expletives. As Solzhenitsyn observes in his Nobel prize acceptance speech: "Making up for man's scant time on earth, art transmits from one person to another the entire accumulated burden of another's life experience . . . and allows us to assimilate it as our own."

Script allows for our sharing of information without our being face to face—but there is an ambiguity in characterizing script in this way—as a technology for sharing information. This ambiguity is also part of the debate about the origins of script. Schmandt-Besserat and others imagine that script emerged from the use of tokens in counting—and that written script emerged from numeracy; while others argue that the development of numerical symbols was in parallel with the development of symbols for language.

As interesting as this debate is, our concern in this chapter is not with the origins of script. We are concerned with the ambiguities that attend symbolic representation and language (and thought), because these ambiguities are embodied in the concept of information.

The emergence of written language within oral cultures began a new cultural and cognitive process. An oral culture requires teaching, training, inculcation, and so on in order to pass on and stabilize its shared cultural system. In oral cultures, images and representative objects offer one way of stabilizing and sharing aspects of culture beyond shared memory. These pictures and objects are meaningful within the shared language and inter-personal culture of a community. A critical step in the development of the idea of information occurs with the emergence of numeration, which is a form of symbolic representation. A Tobias Dantzig and Mazur comments in *Number:* written "numeration is probably as old as private property" (21).[1]

An early form of counting is what we call tallying, which refers to the counting of some set of things, like sheep, and then representing that counting with tokens or marks. Tallies form an open-ended sequence. Such a marking requires that some particular things are understood as a collection and that this collection is understood as a quantity. Each tally is equivalent: it marks one kind of thing, and is, therefore, iconic.[2] Tallying is like saying 'one and one and one and one . . .,' or maybe 'a one and another one and another one . . .' If one wants to compare tallies, an idea of measure emerges: and idea, at least, of more or less. Tallying produces data, although it is only understandable within the relevant cognitive and social practices in which it is meaningful.

Tallying can also involve simple comparisons, such as a one-to-one correspondence between two sets of things (pebbles and pinecones, for example). By such methods the size of two groups of things can be compared. Such a mode of comparison is strictly speaking not a form of counting. Such a comparison of sets is precursor to what we call cardinality.

As Stephen Chrisomalis (2009) notes, tallying is different from counting using numbers. Such counting transposes the open-ended marking into an ordered serial system, a "*structured symbolic systems* of permanent, trans-linguistic graphic marks for recording numbers" (61). Numerical notation can be identified and used regardless of the language one speaks. Lexical numeration, like 36 and sechsunddreißig, are language-specific.

Counting and numerical representation, however, are culturally bound. Various peoples and languages have numbers up to three, which allows them to count to six. After this they simply say 'many.' (Hammarström, 2010). Tallying up some quantity of things and communicating that tally, as well as representing it by means of some token, constitute a primary form of information. We call such a tally and the information conveyed a fact. There are other kinds of facts, but again this would be a basic fact.

Counting with numbers can convey more information than can tallying alone. I can inform you that I have five oranges even if we do not speak the same language. A developed numeracy means that we understand that five can represent whatever we can quantify as a set of five. Such an understanding manifests an abstract sense of numbers that should be distinguished from a concrete idea of numbers that is more attached to the kinds of things counted.

Counting with numbers encodes objects (or that which is counted) as a quantity using the objective syntax of a numerical series. The recording of these numbers produces data that has a greater trustworthiness than if we merely rely on our memories, which can be both faulty and self-serving. Writing is like counting with numbers, as well, an encoding of a language into a mode of shared representation. We should, therefore, understand counting, beginning with keeping a tally as a primary information system. If you cannot count and do not have a stable and shared system of counting and doing arithmetic, you cannot keep or use records.

WHAT IS DATA?

We can tally and count as a means of producing data about our world. This is a datum or fact about data. And thus, we can see that data is not found, it is collected. A method of collection is required in order for the data to be structured and meaningful relative to some defined parameters. For example, the data derived from measurement must be based on a common mode of measurement.

Since I must extract data, the quality of data depends on my methods of extraction (and my use of these methods). If I can represent information in different forms (as a graph, as an equation, as binary code), then that representation (information) is not equivalent to what is represented, although both will be informative. Here we have a scale of abstraction and processing. The graph pictures a dataset in such a way as to reveal patterns that might be hard to recognize otherwise. But the graphic representation might not be equivalent to the data, which might be noisy and thus uninformative in its initial form. In this case, information is what we determine by means of the data, such that we are informed of something. It is for such reasons that information is often defined as meaningful data.

These observations prompt the following questions. Does data need a paradigmatically basic form from which we derive further less-basic representations? Can there be a form of information that is manifest in some ways (or else it would be nothing) and yet could not be represented? Or is all information a form of representing something that might not exist in that form, as information, separate from our representations? We might collect these questions into a single query: Is data information?

The notion of data, like that of information, is not a well-formed concept. It means multiple different things depending on how it is used, on the context in which it is used, and on whether the concern is with scientifically generated evidence or not. Data can be used either as evidence or examples, both of which also require careful conceptualization.

Data can be used to generate information. But it cannot generate information unless it is already informative. It must be framed and formulated, to even count as data, and that framing and formulation produces the data that at some basic level is then informative. If it is poorly framed and formulated, the data might be misinformative. It is still data, just bad data. Even if data is meaningful and thus informative, how informative and informative about what is a further question. Thus, data is contingently informative, and thus it can be reasonably understood as itself, a kind of information.

Data can be informative in different ways. It is often used to make more general claims or to develop explanations that are more general and extend beyond the cases from which the data was derived. But in other important cases, data is analyzed in order to discover patterns within it, prompting more abstract descriptions and theories. This is the case with numbers. Let us turn to the example of prime numbers. Prime numbers inform us of something by their very definition. Therefore, can we legitimately understand them as data? Any prime number is an example of the kind of thing we call prime numbers. An example can be construed as data, but it need not be. On the other hand, if we were going to use some subset of the prime numbers as the values to be input into some function, then they would certainly count as data, but relative to the function, not in themselves. Although why we were using just the prime numbers might also constitute a datum, and this might be informative.

ARE DATA FACTS?

Meaningful data are informative. Bad data we can dismiss as meaningless relative to the purposes that guided our derivation of the data. They are meaningful, however, as failed data, indicating some problem in its extraction or measurement. Given the role of data in our reasoning about situations or experiments or people, data can seem like a collection of facts. Are data facts? Not all data are propositional, although, to understand data requires propositions. If a list of measurements is given as a list of numbers, then in order to understand that data we would have to understand what was measured and why (and often how it was measured). Such framing knowledge and understanding would be propositional.

We want data to be factual, but that just means the data has been accurately derived from some source or by some legitimate means. Everyday data about someone (for example, let's say the data provided on a dating site) is different than the data generated from the James Webb telescope. The telescope data is highly processed, which does not mean it is inaccurate, just that it includes elaborate theoretical elements and depends on a complex technology. Data derived from medical studies will likely be processed in different ways than dating site data and astronomical data, even if it involves statistical analyses.

Data must be interpreted and further analyzed in order to become part of a claim or in order to support a theory or some explanation. Data, like all evidence, underdetermines the explanations and descriptions about it. (See Bruno Latour and Steve Woolgar, *Laboratory Life: The Construction of Scientific Facts*.)

Given all of this, it would be better not to describe data as facts. Instead, data should be understood as factual or not, accurate or not, or accurate to some degree. Data is either derived or recognized as data, and thus interpreted or defined as data relative to some question or problem or issue. Facts are better given in propositional form, and thus a fact includes a sense of aboutness; it is about something. A fact that is not about anything would not be a fact. The data generated by a photon detector in a physics experiment is not yet about anything, although we hope it is accurate relative to what it is measuring.

DATA FROM MEASUREMENTS

One important subset of what we call data are measurements of various kinds. Let's look at a simple example. If we understand ° as the symbol for degree, then without too much trouble we can read '42°' as a record of a measured temperature, although we might also read it as a measure of an angle. This number is not yet a datum about anything. We need to understand what was measured, using what scale, where and why (and maybe even how). When we learn that it is the ocean temperature at Dutch Harbor Alaska, on May 2, 2023 at 8:00 A.M. it becomes a datum—with a range of errors defined by where and how this temperature was taken. It is informative. We understand it as a bit of information relative to how it is framed, generalized, and fitted with other data, theoretical assumptions, and so on. The initial datum is used to produce a picture or claim from which further inferences might be drawn or conclusions made. I might conclude, given my tolerance for cold and despite my desire to swim, that I do not want to swim this morning in the Dutch Harbor ocean. We might read about other temperature measurements taken on other days of May, and take these data as informative about Dutch Harbor, if we believe the measurements are accurate. We might generalize this data into a belief about the Dutch Harbor water temperature in May, and call it knowledge. We can formalize our knowledge by taking the average of these measurements. The scope of our knowledge would be limited without further study of the ocean in the area, its currents, the possibility of hydrothermal vents in the area, and so on. If data is evidence, then knowledge would be a kind of claim developed from such data. If so, then data is already a kind of knowledge—limited in scope and import.

We can be informed of the temperature by various means and methods. (1) I can be told: "It is 30 degrees outside." (2) I can read a thermometer placed in an appropriate place and see that it indicates 30 degrees. (3) I can go outside. My skin feels cold, my breath freezes in the air, and I shiver. By means of these I may not be able to say that it is 30 degrees, but I can conclude that it is cold, because I am cold. Am I informed that it is cold by the cold?

Each of these cases allows me to gain information, but they are not all three communicating this information in the same way. In the first case, we have an act of communication. If we assume basic linguistic and epistemological competence to both parties, then the point of the statement was to convey something like '*it is cold.*' Of course, many other things might have been conveyed depending on the circumstances, motives, relationships, and so on. But in saying "*it is 30 degrees outside*" the speaker is intending me to understand something and I do understand this. So, the speaker has information that she then passes on to me.

In the other two cases, we do not have a speaker and the information is derived or determined by me in a way quite different from how propositions are understood (however they are understood). Someone might resist the idea that these scenarios are different. So you might suggest that since understanding thermometers also involves understanding human intentions and a human device, it can be modeled on our propositional understanding.

Why not imagine that a thermometer as a device is like a proposition? A thermometer seems to embody a syntax (rules of form) that allows the readers of the thermometer to understand the temperature. A thermometer is, of course, not a statement made by a conscious human being. Rather it expresses the information through the syntax of relationships that we simplify into the notion of measuring temperature. Why not imagine that the maker of the thermometer (its cause) gives the thermometer a propositional form? But that would be a stretch. He is not informing me of anything by making the thermometer. Nor should we say that the person who bought the thermometer and placed it outside was informing me. They are part of the causal chain that led to the thermometer's placement and functioning. But they are not speaking to me through their actions. It is the thermometer that is informing me, but it is not informing me in the same way as the person who says to me 'it is cold' or 'it is 30 degrees.' A thermometer has no intentions, no knowledge, no motives, and no ability to participate in either a concern about temperature or in the normative practices of speaking or informing.

Nevertheless, I am still informed by it that it is cold, just as I am by the person telling me by means of a statement that it is cold. Similarly, my shivering body, all things being equal, informs me that I am cold because the world around me is cold. I can tell the difference between shivering from cold versus from fear. I feel the cold, and that feeling is what informs me that it is cold. My shivering body is informing me, I am not informing myself. I might not have realized either that it was so cold outside and that I was cold. Similarly, my fingertips can feel much colder than my chest. I react to the cold, feel it, and so I know that it is cold. I can get so cold that I lose this awareness, and no longer feel cold. But in ordinary cases, I have learned what shivering means. (Of course, I can feel cold and not shiver.) The distinctions here, however, are less about the role of inference in these cases, than about what information is (or can be) relative to the means of our being informed.

The information conveyed or derived in these cases is more or less the same, although the means and mechanisms are quite different. As we can see from these examples, even if our grasping of it has a propositional form or is bound to our cognitive abilities of understanding or inference, the sources of information need not have propositional form. The general point we are making here is that information does not exist separate from our grasping of it as that. There is no information separate from our being informed. Information is nothing separate from us and our activities and capacities as human beings.

Information can be derived in various ways. An account of a situation, a crime report, for example, can count as subjective or qualitative data, as can an ornithologist's observations of the ritual behavior of Birds of Paradise in New Guinea. Quantitative data, while requiring a framing specificity, is both more limited in scope and can seem more precise, trustworthy, and generalizable than qualitative data. Whether it is any of these will depend on many factors—how it was generated, how legitimate the method of generation is, how well the statistical analysis was, if that is relevant, and so on. With most data there is no simple fact of the matter, like there might be in a list of telephone numbers in the cell phones of a group of friends.

The variability in what counts as data means that data should not be used as an atomic-like constituent notion from which knowledge can be built. Data, even so-called meaningful data, does not form a clearly defined something such that it can be used to characterize information without specifying what will count as data. Data is of too many kinds, and its status and even form depend on how it is generated and conceptualized.

Data can take many forms from a list of numbers, a collection of names, to some collection of facts. If a datum is taken as a fact, then it is understood as a claim about something. It is a fact that, when I write this, it is Tuesday, for example. The fact is an assertion you can take as true. A collection of numbers counts as data if we understand their source, provenance, method of generation or determination, and so on. We understand the numbers, have thoughts about them, scrutinize or explain them—and in so doing we situate these numbers within some set of propositions. We can use the data to explain something: the movement of a comet, for example. In these relatively simple examples, data is not simple, and to understand it as such is to abstract it from a proposition or embed it within a proposition. The reason for this is that some data are about something (about the planet Mercury, for example), while other data lacks a clear sense of aboutness (they lack intentionality, we say in philosophy). The results and the measurements taken throughout an experiment (data), organized as an array of numbers, are not about anything. We can instead use those measurements to talk about something.

Are such measurements true or false? A proposition can be true or false, and if some datum necessarily has that form, then we can say the datum is true, by which we often mean the assertion is true. But if the datum does not take propositional form, as experimental data often does not, then we might mean that the datum (from that data set) is accurate, that is, a good measurement, or that the method of generation is trustworthy all things being equal. We do not need to build up information or meaning from data; as we can see, data is already part of how we understand whatever the data measures, describes, reflects, and so on. It is an abstraction from a situation, and not a constitutive particle of that situation.

CONCLUSION

Abstracting phenomena into data is one of the purposes of scientific experiments and observation. Despite this process of abstraction, some people are tempted to understand the phenomena, itself, as containing or carrying information. Let us look at the example of a stellar explosion. If the information derived from some stellar event is understood as the radiant energy given up by that event, then we are tempted to think that information about the event is conveyed and is a part of that radiant energy. But in what way is the stellar event understood? Not from the energy alone—it has to be detected and understood as energy of a certain kind. We have to know about stars and about exploding stars, understanding not only that there was no such energy detectable and then there was and that it came from a certain location and so on. In fact there is an immense amount of knowledge, technology, and physical understanding required so that the reaction of our radio telescope to the radio waves it is picking up are seen as data let alone informative, and thus as information. Human beings with a certain kind of understanding can be informed of something. Information, therefore, is not the same as the event of the star exploding. The star exploding is not a datum separate from our taking it as that. In itself, it is not such a datum.[3]

We can collect our analyses of these examples into a provisional conclusion, which we can explain with an even simpler example. When you tell me that the light is on, you are informing me of that fact. The information conveyed seems to be the fact that the light is on. If the light is not on and you tell me it is, you would be misinforming me about what is the case. What is the case might be construed as a datum of some kind, although to call it that is misleading. In general, data are collected. Often in scientific analyses such data are numerical, which involves various forms of processing and experimentation (all of which can be good or bad, slanted or not). Thus, in many cases data do not play the same roles as the phrase 'what is the case.' We might use data to get a clearer picture about what is the case. Although that can often lead to false or unwarranted conclusions, as in the misuse and misunderstanding of statistical data. And we do not need to imagine some given objective condition that will count as a final arbiter of our claims. 'Data' and 'datum' are often used ambiguously in various arguments, as both something derived and as something given. Similarly, information is sometimes like a fact, but not always. And facts are open to dispute, clarification, and re-description. We can derive information from any sentence we might say, and we can be informed of something through a sentence. Nevertheless, information as a concept gets a special purchase in our cognitive understanding once we use writing or other ways of keeping a record of things over time (using tallies or numbers, for example). From record-keeping we get both a sense that information, including data and facts, can be objective and open to public view. And thus, information seems to be something separate from us. If this is misunderstood, then information can seem like it is some kind of thing or substance independent from our understanding. That is not the case.

NOTES

1 But language can also inform, as can numbers, which have a syntax (their order and the relationships), but no semantics (meaning). Numerical notation, as opposed to lexical numeration, may have developed independently from writing, although they both have many common features. Information as a concept, especially when understood relative to the notion of data, is usefully understood relative to numerical notation.
2 Stephen Chrisomalis, "The origins and co-evolution of literacy and numeracy." In David R. Olson & Nancy Torrance (Eds.), *The Cambridge Handbook of Literacy* (pp. 59–74). Cambridge University Press, 2009.
3 Theories like Buckland's theory of information, in which information is construed as a thing, confuse that which we are informed about (e.g., the exploding star) with the information gained about that thing. That we cannot have one without the other does not mean that they are the same thing. In physics and computational science a different concept of information is operative, a concept that is not equivalent to Buckland's (1991) usage.

REFERENCES

Buckland, Michael. *Information and information systems*. Praeger, 1991.
Chrisomalis, Stephen. "The origins and coevolution of literacy and numeracy." In David R. Olson & Nancy Torrance (Eds.), *The Cambridge Handbook of Literacy* (pp. 59–74). Cambridge University Press, 2009.

Dantzig, Tobias, and Joseph Mazur. *Number: The language of science*. Penguin, 2007.

Hammarström, Harald. "Rarities in numeral systems." In J. Wohlgemuth & M. Cysouw (Eds.), *Rethinking universals: How rarities affect linguistic theory* (pp. 11–60). De Gruyter Mouton, 2010.

Latour, Bruno, and Steve Woolgar. *Laboratory life: The construction of scientific facts*. Princeton University Press, 2013.

Schmandt-Besserat, Denise. "The evolution of writing." *International Encyclopedia of Social and Behavioral Sciences* (2014): 1–15.

CHAPTER 7

Is Information Subjective or Objective? Or Neither?

CONSTRAINTS OF COMMUNICATION

Our understanding of the concept of information seems to be recurrently found on an ambiguity that we can formulate as a question: Is information a kind of knowledge, open to all the uncertainties attending our knowing, or is it something like *what* we know, and therefore an objective constituent of what exists as the world? This question returns us to J. Michael Dunn's (2008) observation about information: "I believe that the fundamental philosophical question regarding the representation of information is: how much "lies in the eye of the beholder?" This is to restate the questions in the title to this chapter: *Is Information Subjective, Objective, or Neither?* We will provide an answer to this question at the end of this chapter. Our central purpose in this chapter, however, is not simply to sketch a philosophical answer to a philosophical question. As we have repeatedly argued, in order to conceptualize something like information, we cannot assume that we know what we are trying to understand separate from particular examples of we take as the phenomenon. Information is not a natural kind like water, the existence of which we can assume. In this chapter, we will investigate the possible objective and subjective qualities of information by analyzing an example of being informed offered by

DOI: 10.1201/9781003401674-10

the philosopher Fred Dretske in *Knowledge and the Flow of Information* (Dretske, 1981).

> Dretske's example involves bidding in a game of bridge:
>
> Recently, for example, I was asked by an opponent at a duplicate bridge tournament what my partner's bid meant. My partner bid "5 clubs" in response to my "4 no trump." (Blackwood convention). I replied that it meant that he had either 0 or 4 aces. This is the conventional meaning of that bid, and the meaning of all bids must be revealed to one's opponents. Puzzled, however, by our somewhat erratic bidding (and, doubtless, my incredulous stare at my partner), my opponent persisted: "I know what it means. What I want to know is what his bid told you, what information you got from it?" Now this, obviously, is a completely different question, one that (given the rules of duplicate bridge) I am not obliged to answer. For what information was conveyed (to me) by my partner's bid was that he had no aces. This information was communicated to me because I had three aces in my own hand; hence, he could not have all four aces.

Before we analyze this very interesting, but also rather specialized and constrained example, a few general observations will be useful. Like in bridge, when I address someone by making a statement, I may be informing that person of something. Sometimes that is what I mean to do when I make some statement, but, of course, not always. If you ask me the time, and I reply that it is 6:25, I am informing you of the time. That strictly speaking means that I think it is 6:25. It may also express something about my relationship with you, depending on the situation in which you made the request. I might have been cowed by your authority, and you may have asked the question in order to get me to reply immediately. We might add one more observation. If your question was in good faith, and my answer was also in good faith, then you were informed of something. But of what were you informed? It is possible that my watch might have just stopped five minutes before, so that my information is wrong and it is really 6:30. I still meant what I said and you were still informed about what I thought the time was, but not what the time in fact was. With these preliminary reminders in place, let us begin to analyze Dretske's bridge example.

The communicative situation when you are playing bridge is highly constrained, by the use of playing cards, by the form and valuation of these cards, by the rules of the game, by the way the cards are distributed, and by the particular distribution of cards in this particular game, and so on. The information is derived from the bidding relative to cards the player holds. Here the constraints include what can be said during bidding and the conventions recognized and governing what these bids mean to these particular players. Each bid communicates the bidder's understanding of her prospects relative to the cards she holds, and thus certain facts are communicated. The bid is informative and information is conveyed. In this case, as Dretske declares, his partner has "either 0 or 4 aces." The game situation and its constraints create an information system of a defined form, with very limited semantics. And thus, Dretske can also use his knowledge of his hand in combination with what his partner has communicated to realize that his partner had no aces, since he could not have four, given that Dretske has three.

Dretske rightly distinguishes between what someone might mean by means of some statement and the information that we might derive from that statement. He insists, however, that the information is carried by the statement. It is, as he claims, "embodied in a signal (linguistic or otherwise)," even if it is "only incidentally related to the meaning (if any) of that signal" (44). We might cry in pain, not intending to express our pain, but simply crying out: such a cry lacks either syntax and semantics. It is meaningful, but not intentional, and it lacks propositional meaning. But it is informative. Dretske is clearly right, therefore, that a signal can be informative in ways that may be independent from its meaning, if it even has meaning. But in what sense is my pain embodied in my cry? Let's alter the scenario. I might have a similarly acute pain, but not cry out. Does my silence embody my pain, as well? Remember I am not expressing my pain by crying out; my initial cry was involuntary. My silence may also be my habitual reaction to such an event. My reaction is meaningful and informative to some (even if I am silent); but the fact of my pain is not embodied in my reaction. We might say that it is revealed—but not to a frog; only to those who can and care to understand what I reveal in such a situation.

Given the particular distribution of cards and his partner's bid, Dretske was able to infer (rather straightforwardly, of course) where the aces were. In so doing, he learned more than his partner knew or meant to communicate to him. His example, however, does not support the idea that the information was embodied in the bid, even if separate from its meaning as a statement. Instead, the bridge scenario allows us to understand the role of constraints in such informative inferences.

Dretske, however, resists this conclusion. He characterizes information in the following way: "What information a signal carries is what it is capable of "telling" us, telling us truly, about another state of affairs" (44). We will set aside for now, his claim that information must be veridical. (We will examine this kind of claim in the next chapter.) Our concern for the moment is the question of what is conveyed by a signal (in the bridge game, the signal is the bid of his partner). In Dretske's characterization of information, we can recognize one of the confusions we identified in the previous chapter—the idea that if we can construe some datum as potentially informative, then it is in fact information. Dretske states that the information a signal carries tells us its potential information—that is, it tells us what it is capable of telling us. This is trivially true if we interpret this to mean that if some signal can be understood as informing us of something, then that signal was also capable of so informing us. But how does it carry this information, especially if the information exceeds the meaning of the message? That a signal or message is potentially informative, under some interpretation, does not mean that it already carries that information or that it carries a potential. It has potential. It might have more than one potential significance depending on the context and interpretation. Does it carry all of these?

Let us return to Dretske's claim that a signal carries the information that "it is capable of "telling" us, telling us truly, about another state of affairs" (44). Notice that he recognizes that he is personifying the signal but bracketing 'telling' with quotation marks. A signal cannot tell anything to anyone, since it is not a person who can tell things. (Can a pointer dog tell us where the prey is?) Dretske does not put similar quotation marks around 'carry,' when he asserts that the signal carries information. But this use of 'carry' is very like his use of 'telling'—both are metaphors that suggest the idea that the signal has information that is part of it, and so it can give (tell) it to the recipient of the signal. Both metaphors perform a conceptual sleight-of-hand, directing our attention towards the signal and diminishing the essential role of inference in order to derive information from any such signal.

Is the same true of a more mechanically defined code? A CD recording of a Chopin Nocturne would seem to be a recording of the information of a particular performance. Such a recording has the potential to be actualized not as the performance itself, but as a record, hence representation, of that performance, if played in a functioning CD player with speakers. Using a convenient shorthand, we might say that the CD is a recording of the information. This is fine if we do not take it too seriously. But it is misleading. To see why, let us alter the situation.

We can encode the Nocturne in a series of written notes organized according to the conventions governing such things. Where is the music in these marks? What carries the Nocturne? The individual notes or marks do not carry anything. They are informative through correlation with notes we can make or hear. And individually they do not constitute the Nocturne, but only as a series, all together. In other words, their configuration relative to the understandable conventions governing the writing of music notation allows them to inform us how to play the music. That configuration is informative as part of an intersubjective system of notation and correlation that we have to learn. Such a system is neither subjective (just in my mind) nor objective (embodied in the marks). If the notes carry the Nocturne, then so does the system of notation, as well as our understanding and ability to manifest those marks as the appropriate sound.

Does the Nocturne as music we hear embody the information of the Nocturne? Again, we can say trivially the Nocturne is the Nocturne, so in some sense, yes—the Nocturne manifests the information of itself (for some listener, we should add). We can write down the notes we hear, while we listen to it: we can encode it, and that would mean we were encoding information about how to play or sing it. The conversion of the nocturne into a code remains parasitic on our understanding of it as music and on our understanding of musical notation. It depends on us. We might in a fit of perversity, however, use the notes in a different way. We could develop a complex set of principled correlations such that we could encode anything using the Nocturne, as long as we know how it was encoded, including the system of decoding it. But that information—the system by which the Nocturne gains the information that we can read using that system—is not embodied in the Nocturne. It is as much, if not more, a function of the system as it is of the particular notes on the page.

A signal does not carry information like one might carry a suitcase, nor does it embody information. A signal, including the sheet music for one of Chopin's Nocturnes, is an organized structure of distinction, constrained in particular ways, such that with the right system of interpretation it can convey information to someone or some relevant interpretive device. Saying that a signal carries information is a useful metaphor, but misleading if the metaphor is turned into a theory.

Let us return to the example of the bridge game. Such a card game is a defined practice utilizing a constrained field of communication, a collection of rules, and a set of variables (the cards) about which statements are made and from which information can be inferred. It has important similarities to well-designed scientific experiments in the physical sciences. In these kinds of experiments, the relevant factors can be defined (quantified) and the hypotheses tested, which allows for scientists to make inferences of the sort Dretske makes in his bridge game.

The goal in a well-designed experiment is to limit to a very high degree the area of uncertainty, characterizing the possible solutions of a problem such that the experiment can provide relevant and trustworthy data, that can support and suggest to scientists a particular causal explanation. There are a wide variety of kinds of experiments, and varying degrees of constraint possible in any particular experiment. The more complex the system and the larger number of factors involved, the more difficult it is to draw reasonable inferences from experiments involving these systems. An experiment, of course, does not inform the researcher in the way a bridge partner does, but the point of the experiment is to gather information in such a way that further inferences about the experimental data and its underlying causes can be determined and supported, and from that, further inferences and conclusions can be reached about theories and other kinds of broader explanations.

In bridge and well-designed scientific experiments, we have feedback loops allowing us to correlate one kind of information (a measurement in an experiment) with a hypothesis or set of explanatory possibilities, such that we can infer something about the latter from the former. Another simple case will make this basic structure of inferentially useful information clearer. A speedometer indicates how fast your car travels by measuring the rate at which a wheel on your car rotates, multiplied by the circumference of the tire. Speedometers do not directly measure the speed your car is traveling. If your speedometer is working properly, then you have good reason to trust what it indicates, and you can draw a simple inference: that given what it says, your car is indeed traveling at the rate indicated by the speedometer. In the examples we have been examining in this chapter, some information is inferred about a specific situation, given the constraints by means of which the information is manifest or determined. In other words, no inference, no information.

Despite the differences between Shannon's notion of information and our ordinary uses of the term, Shannon's equations describing the information capacity of a channel (or medium) of communication also rely on constraint. The channel capacity is described probabilistically relative to uncertainty, or entropy. Information—or signal capacity—is a measure of uncertainty relative to an entropic limit. This is to describe the channel relative to its capacity—its syntactic organization and not its semantics; what the message might be has been bracketed or ignored.

In Dretske's bridge example, the possibilities are again contained relative to a limit—but that limit is defined not by noise or entropy, but by the possibilities defined by the cards and their organization and form as well as the relevant bidding conventions. Information, therefore, is defined relative to the kinds of constraints imposed or found within the system at issue. The bridge game is defined and constrained by what is possible to communicate given the cards and the bidding conventions. The information channel for Shannon is constrained not by the content of what is communicated, but by the limits of the channel as defined by a scale that goes from completely noisy or random at one extreme to completely ordered (with no change communicated) on the other.

Deriving or producing information requires constraints of some kind. Let us look again at counting. We can easily imagine a scenario in which I might wonder how many flints I have or how many tubers we have stored. I might count the tubers by saying, I have enough to last me for the cycle of a full moon. In this case, I am correlating our eating of tubers (an amount per day) with the cycle of the moon. We need the constraint of the moon to allow us to measure the tubers. If what I want to count gets large enough or if I want to communicate a more complex situation I might not only need something like numbers, but I would need a way of representing them or tallying that which I am counting. This is a basic scenario of extracting information and representing it. We constrain what we could say about tubers by some notion of quantity that we can measure, and then at some point represent. The argument that such counting (tallying) is the source of written language makes a lot of sense, since it refers to making a record and representing quantities.

In counting, we abstract and redescribe something, such as tubers, stages of the moon, sheep, or taxes, relative to quantity, which functions as a constraint, regardless of what we are counting. What we count are particulars, and thus have a syntax given by the series of numbers, but they have no meaning except as being a certain quantity. We might value tubers more than pebbles, but we can count them both using the same system.

Information, therefore, is often a derivation or redescription of something relative to some particular constraint. It could take the form of a sentence or a list of marks. The information is meaningful because it is framed relative to some further concern, such as by the game of bridge, by that which is counted and why, by the system of communication defined by input, channel, and output (and whatever else). The role of constraints in the derivation of information pushes against the idea that information is merely the creation of human beings, that is, it is radically subjective. The information we derive from and through these constraints, however, is still a part of our human practices of observation, inference, and judgment.[1]

SEMANTICS OF INFORMATION

As we have repeatedly observed, the concept of information is ambiguous. There actually exists a confusion built into the semantics of the term 'information,' which arises from its particular history in English, and indeed in French and Italian. Geoffrey Nunberg (2021) in his book "Information, Disinformation, Misinformation" writes:

> The association of information with the press and other printed documents shaped the way it was perceived, as a self-sufficient substance detached from its source and independent of any individual consciousness.

Information is meaningful for us, but it is also often understood as independent of our understanding, as if it existed in itself as information. We will trace and critique this confusion many times in our account of information as a concept (as we already have in previous chapters).

The idea that information is "a self-sufficient substance," as Nunberg describes it, is often understood to mean that information is objective. The argument for its objectivity, and therefore its factual and veridical status, often relies on a factitious dilemma, ignoring the fact that information in its content and uptake is normative. Mingers and Standing (2018), for example, claim that

> if information is to be a purely subjective phenomena, only occurring in the minds of observers, then it means that what we take to be repositories of information – books, newspapers, timetables, Web sites and above all information systems – cannot contain or process information but only data.

This claim partly rests on distinguishing between data and information and combines the notion of a book, for example, containing information, with processing information as a computer might. How a book would process information is unclear, but it is lumped together with information systems which supposedly do process information. A computer, however, is an input/output device which acts relative to our interests and our software instructions. It is a *syntactical* machine that can produce semantic results not for itself but for us. Information is about something, and that aboutness, what we call intentionality, is lacking in both inanimate things and syntactical structures. We extract information, for example, from rock strata about the causal events that led to the formation of those strata. Geological events in the past produced effects that we have learned to interpret. The rock strata do not cause our knowledge about their origin. Our knowledge is about that evidence and its causes. The interpretation generates both the data and the information. It is nonsensical (except as a metaphor) to claim that the rocks are informing us (as if they were human) about their past. The information is not in the rocks, but we derive that information from our understanding of geological processes. We can see in the rocks the effects of earlier events once we understand the geological and environmental processes that would in all probability had produced the configurations that we observe. When we say 'the rocks inform us . . .,' we just mean the rocks provide evidence for our analysis.

Information describes the interplay between objective elements and our intersubjective understanding and involvement with these elements. Here is an everyday example of how this works. A restaurant is arranged in a certain way with chairs, tables, pathways, and so on. The interior design of the restaurant informs me how to move from the front door to the table. If I can read this information off of the design, then does that information exist in physical space? That would be imputing something to space as if the idea of moving from door to table could be intelligible without human beings who have a desire to do such a thing. I am informed of what to do, but it would be better to say that the space and its design offer cues that I might be able to read given my specific cultural training. The information does not exist separate from that culture, from the ways of human beings (including our anatomical configurations), from my particular understandings, and so on. I could represent this information with a schematic of the space on which we include a dotted line with arrows. Of course, how to read the schematic also requires cultural training and habits of understanding (Wittgenstein's comments about reading signs remain a useful corrective to the idea that signs are self-explanatory or that they inform all by themselves).

CONCLUSION

To be informed about something is not simply to be affected by some cause. Information is a normative notion, that fits within our normative practices of understanding. We do not need an elaborate theory to support this claim. A normative practice (or the domain of normative practices) is not blindly causal, but involves judgments relative to norms that we learn, about which we can be corrected, and which we share with others. What we understand as normative is neither objective nor subjective, but rather intersubjective. Language and culture are both examples of normative practices.

The information conveyed or derived in these cases is more or less the same, but the means and mechanisms are quite different. Information can be derived in various ways. Even if our grasping of it has a propositional form or is bound to our cognitive abilities of understanding or inference, the sources of information need not have propositional form. And this means that information does not exist separate from our grasping of it as information. This does not mean that we make up what counts as information (as if it were purely subjective). Rather, there is no information separate from our being informed. Information per se does not exist separate from us and our activities and capacities as human beings.

NOTES

1 Our notion of information, let alone our use of the word, extends far beyond these kinds of constrained derivations of information from defined contexts, games, or situations. The constraints guiding our being informed can be practical and not epistemological, at least in a straightforward way. If I watch a YouTube video about how to install a dishwasher do I know by virtue of my watching how to install my dishwasher? I follow the instructions step by step and install the appliance. The next day, however, I may have forgotten the instructions. Should we say that if I have the information about installing a dishwasher available and in front me, then I know how to do it, but if I do not have that information, then I do not know how do it? Following instructions need not entail knowing how to do something.

REFERENCES

Dretske, Fred. *Knowledge & the Flow of Information*. Cambridge: MIT Press. 1981.

Dunn, J. Michael. "Information in computer science." *Philosophy of Information* 8 (2008): 581–608.

Mingers, John, and Craig Standing. "What is information? Toward a theory of information as objective and veridical." *Journal of Information Technology* 33.2 (2018): 85–104.

Nunberg, Geoffrey. "Information, disinformation, misinformation." In Ann Blair et al., (Eds.), *Information: A historical companion* (pp. 496–502). Princeton University Press, 2021.

CHAPTER 8

Is Misinformation a Kind of Information? (Or Must Information Be True?)

INTRODUCTION

Attempts to define information as necessarily true, and thus to define misinformation as not information all, begin with a formal understanding of information as defined by Shannon. Shannon explicitly stated that his theory described the syntax of information transmission and could not account for the meaning or semantics of that which was transmitted. Truth involves a judgment about the content, that is, the meaning of a statement or proposition. As such it constitutes a semantic judgment. If such judgments are normative, then, as we have argued earlier, no proposition can be necessarily true, since all propositions are bound to contingent normative forms. But even if one wants to allow for some analytical notion of truth ('$a = a$'), that would not describe the kind of truth that is at stake in and through information exchange or transmission. In this book, we are interested in information that is something to know or not know. We have argued that whatever we think we know, we know in contingent and normative ways. Similarly, what counts as information would also be contingent and normative. Only if one wants to argue, as some physicists do, that information is a natural aspect of that which exists and which we measure and describe in the science of physics can we mitigate the necessary normative aspects of our understanding of information.

DOI: 10.1201/9781003401674-11

Theories that define information as a kind of knowledge often attempt to reduce knowledge (and often language) to a causal system of interchange such that the meaning (or content) of some item of information is understood as an effect of some cause. We will not argue against such theories. Rather, we will further develop our critique of one aspect of such theories: the claim that information, to count as information, must necessarily be "objective and veridical." This is how Mingers and Standing (2018) in their influential and general theory characterize information, building from well-known arguments offered by Floridi (2009). Floridi's arguments, however, are motivated very differently, and are guided by an attempt to respond to the putative paradox generated by Carnap and Bar-Hillel's theory of semantic information (1953). In their theory, according to the standard definition of information, a contradiction would contain the greatest amount of information. A contradiction, however, would be meaningless, and so this conclusion seems counter-intuitive. This putative paradox depends on certain assumptions, in particular assumptions about the relationship between sentences and the world, as well as the belief that semantics can be derived from syntax. The details of this paradox and its putative solution by Floridi (2004), however, are not relevant in our account of information. Mingers and Standing, on the other hand, provide a representative and relatively comprehensive argument about information, claiming that it is necessarily true. One critical presumption of their theory is that information is a clear and coherent concept. We will examine their argument in order to further articulate our very different understanding of information.

Mingers and Standing (citing Rockness and Rockness, 2005) make the following claim:

> Information is the true or veridical propositional content of signs. It is that which could be inferred about states of affairs given that the sign has occurred, but could not be without the sign. (e.g., the true state of a company's finances rather than perhaps those presented for Enron).
>
> *(Rockness and Rockness, 2005)*

The idea here is that a sign is caused by a state of affairs. That is, the sign occurred, and from that sign, the true state of affairs can be inferred, but without that sign we would not be able to infer the true state of affairs. The sign is necessary for our understanding. They claim that information "at its most general, is the relationship between a token, sign or message and the event(s) that caused it." The causal structure is clear, because a sign is caused by that which it tokens, and thus we can read the cause from its symbolic effect. This model fits the idea that fire causes smoke and thus we can infer from smoke its cause (fire). They examine, however, a more complicated example: the financial state of a corporation. In this case, the companies' performance causes certain financial effects, that can be measured and recorded and from which we can infer their initial cause, which they call financial state of the company. The financial state of the company is not simply an effect of a set of actions, but is a judgment about the company relative to a number of factors that escape the underlying causal model. If the company is in debt, because they borrowed money to offset the failure of a buyer to fulfill their financial obligations, then we need more than a spreadsheet to understand the situation. The debt is a fact, but its significance as a measure of the state of the company will depend on the assumed risk, the likelihood of other buyers fulfilling their obligations, new sales, the general economy, the role of debt in particular industry, and so on. Determining how to assess these other factors will require judgments beyond the signs on the debt sheet. What debt means is not simply given by a record of that debt.

THE NORMATIVITY OF TRUTH AND FALSITY

It is critical to remember that true and false are normative judgments about a description or assertion or proposition about some state of affairs. The state of affairs is just what is the case. It is our talk about that state of affairs that can be true or false. And there is no necessary relationship between some state of affairs and our propositional statement about it. An example can help guide our critique at this point. Mingers and Standing state that a report of the "true state of the companies' finances" would constitute information. Such a report would be an accurate representation of some specific set of financial measures. Of course, any such measurements would involve all sorts of possible errors. In addition, any particular measure will be a very limited and constrained indication of the companies 'financial state.' Different financial modes of measurement, for example, produce different financial pictures. The financial state of a company is a conceptualized picture, not an object in the world; it is a partial and contingent characterization of something that is not a simply fact, but a complex, dynamic situation. There is no *simple* fact of that matter that counts as the state of a company's finances. A company might release its quarterly report. That would be a snapshot of its situation as given by the measures used. It might accurate as far as anyone knows, but accuracy is not truth per se. The example offered—"the true state of a company's finances rather than perhaps those presented for Enron" demonstrates that this is a comparative notion defined relative to other ways of computing and reporting these finances. One may produce a better picture, but that does not mean that such a picture is necessarily true. Maybe some more precise measures or different measures would present an even better picture. So, the true state of the company in this case just means that it is accurate and correct under some set of descriptive measures, as far as anyone knows, and not necessarily true.

The intuition underlying Mingers' and Standing's claim that information "is the true or veridical propositional content of signs" involves the fact that signals seem to carry information and that signals are caused. To more fully understand such theories and to further our critique we must ask: What does a signal convey or carry? This, of course, has been a recurring question for us.

Mingers and Standing (2018) do not explore in detail Fred Dretske's particular theory of what it means for a signal to carry information. They are concerned with theories of information that go beyond the more limited account offered by Dretske, in which he focuses on perceptual knowledge, specifically on the knowledge that allows one to identify a specific thing or state. They do cite, however, the central principle on which Dretske builds his theory of semantic information:

> A signal r carries the information that s is F if and only if the conditional probability of s's being F, given r (and k, the prior knowledge of the observer) is 1 (but given k alone is less than 1).

Mingers and Standing this principle by explicating Dretske's own explanatory example of a gas gauge as in information device:

> . . ., a petrol gauge carries the information that the car is half full for an observer with appropriate knowledge of cars and gauges (and also assuming that the gauge is working correctly) if the observer can be certain that it is half full with the gauge, but less than certain without it.

The observer of the gas gauge has prior knowledge about cars and gauges, and given the signal r, he or she can know that the car's gas tank is half full (with probability of 1), but "less than certain" without this information (probability less than 1). Mingers and Standing, as well as Dretske, take this example to support the idea that the signal, or rather the gauge, carries information about the amount of gas in the tank. Does the gauge carry this information, or does the gauge allow us to interpret what it shows as informative?

Let us look at the gas gauge example in more detail. Such a gauge is a causal mechanism correlated to a particular form and scale of measurement and embedded in our practices and understanding of gauges and cars. Our understanding of these things allows us to grasp what the gauge indicates as meaningful. The mechanism is built such that it is meaningful for us, but the causal functioning of the mechanism is not what has meaning. All the meaning is from us, and this allows us to read the signal from the tank as meaningful and as related to the amount of gas. Semantic information is not carried by the gauge or the signal per se. To think otherwise is to personify the signal, that is, to forget that the signal has the meaning we ascribe to it through correlation, and not as an effect of generated from the occurrence of a signal.[1] That effect matters and is interpreted and understood, but not because something is carried by the signal. The gauge correlates the signal with a system of measures that are meaningful because of how the designers have built the system. We can say the signals carry information, but we do that only given the design of the system and our understanding of it.

Similarly, a linguistic code or cipher does not have meaning in itself; it carries nothing. Rather the code symbols are correlated with a particular human language, like English. Our understanding and use of English gives sense to the code. A language is at a minimum a cognitive ability to formulate and understand thoughts by means of constituent words that function in various logical roles such that they can constitute a thought. Such a definition assumes a lot, but our goal is not to provide a complete account of language, but to distinguish it from a code.

Another example will clarify the role of correlation and interpretation. A traditional landline telephone involves a source, a channel, and a receiver. In such a device, the signal from the source (transmitter) does not carry the speech or language to the receiver. Instead, sounds are transformed into electromagnetic signals (these signals are continuous, not discrete) which encode those sounds. Those sounds can be reconstituted by the receiver, which mechanically decodes the electromagnetic signals into a facsimile of the original sounds. Those sounds can be understood, all things considered, as words, sentences, and thoughts by someone who hears them and understands the language expressed by those sounds. What we hear on the other end of the phone line (a person speaking) is not what is carried by the signal. We understand the decoded signal as a person speaking. The meaningfulness of the data sent depends on our ability to understand that data as speech. As long as signal error and channel noise are not prohibitive, the correlations of the signal frequencies can be reconstituted as the sounds we can recognize and understand as linguistic utterances. You can see in the details of this description that the correlations are governed by norms and those norms are those that allow the electromagnetic signal to encode meaningful sounds once those are reconstituted by the receiver. We are always tempted to personify this process so that we imagine that not only the voice but the meaning of what the person says is encoded in the signal. But it is not. Or rather, the meaning of the message is encoded in the signal in the way a word is encoded in written letters. If information is derived from a signal, then it is not something that flows or exists separate from us and our ways of measuring, knowing, and making sense. Similarly, the potential meaning of a word is nowhere in the written letters used to represent it; we use those letters and our knowledge of English to understand them as a particular word with its possible and likely meanings.

Let us return to Mingers' and Standing's attempt to extend Floridi's semantic theory. They say that their goal is the following:

> ...the information theory we propose will see information as objective and veridical, but it will recognize the subjective effects of information on receivers through the idea of import, which is essentially a form of meaning.

Floridi provides the following definition of what he calls semantic information:

> *r (σ) is an instance of information, understood as semantic content,*
>   *if and only if:*
> *r consists of data;*
> *the data are well-formed syntactically (well formed data: wfd)*
> *the wfd are meaningful*
> *the meaningful content is true.*

Mingers and Standing want to generalize this "definition to include both environmental information and pragmatic information within a social context." We will let Floridi's definition stand for now. Mingers and

Standing unsuccessfully attempt to generalize this semantic definition into non-propositional contexts (Floridi does not attempt such a generalization). There are numerous difficulties with such an extension. We will examine one critical difficulty with their theory. This difficulty undermines their attempt to combine the idea that information is necessarily true with the idea that it can be non-propositional fails.[2]

Mingers and Standing make two related claims:

1. "Signs carry information whether or not they are observed."

2. "A sign that is false, e.g., mistaken, does not carry the information it would appear to, but still does carry information concerning the actual reasons for its occurrence."

Claim (1) will be true or false depending on what counts as information. If we understand in a normative way, such that those signs are learned and can be used incorrectly, the knowledge of which is shared intersubjectively, then the situation is as we described with the telephone above. If you understand the language spoken on the telephone and if the correlation between sign and decoding device is within some intelligible range of error, then you can understand the sounds you hear as specific words. But that sound is not conveyed or transmitted. The code for those sounds is conveyed. Consequently, using the model offered by Mingers and Standing, neither the sound nor the words made up of those sounds would be the sign conveyed, it would be the electromagnetic signals that would be the signs transmitted. Those signals do not convey any information separate from the system of signal coding, which is parasitic on the correlations that enables someone to understand not what the system conveys but what another person (or a machine if it can speak) on the other end of the line conveys.

THE PROBLEM OF CAUSALITY

Given these difficulties with normative guided signs, one might be tempted to appeal to natural signs (again, like smoke from fire) that describe a causal link, which is what they do in their second claim above. This also returns us to the argument with which we began this chapter. If we imagine that all effects are caused (which is reasonable),[3] then should we say that all effects carry the information of their cause? Notoriously, many different diseases (causes) have similar symptoms (effects), such that one cannot infer the disease from the symptom. This is an example of underdetermination: more than one reasonable and logically equivalent explanation is possible. In addition, there is no necessary link between symptoms (data or effects) and explanation. By analogy, if all roads lead to Rome, you cannot infer which road someone took to get to Rome from the fact that they are now in Rome. The conclusion to draw from this is not that one should not infer a cause from what we perceive as an effect. We could be wrong and mistake a cloud for smoke, or mistake dust for smoke caused by fire. Nevertheless, we do make inductive inferences, and we are often correct. The underdetermination possibility is a way of highlighting that in making such inferences we are making a complicated judgment based on our understanding of how things are in the world.

Some animals respond with panic to the smell or sound of fire. The smell of fire produces an instinctive reaction in deer and elk; they flee. Smells, like sounds, can become strongly associated with fire. This correlation might be hard-wired sensitivity in the animal through evolutionary selection (Álvarez-Ruiz, 2021). Scent from a fire constitutes a signal caused by the fire. The signal does not carry information about the fire separate from an animal's ability to react to that smell in particular ways. Human beings can choose how they respond to smells and smoke, and that ability to choose is the result of their ability not to simply to react to smoke, for example, but to evaluate that smoke as possibly an effect of fire. We represent possible scenarios and make a judgment about what we are sensing relative to these other possible representations of the situation.

Someone might speculate that a signal carries information independent of our understanding, because animals do react to stimuli because of instinct. To explore this possibility more fully, we will look at an example of instinctive animal information processing. When a frog sees what it takes to be a fly, the frog will grab it with its tongue and eat it. The frog can be fooled, however, with a lead pellet or some other fly-like shape, and it will act just as it does when it sees an actual fly. What kind of information is transmitted by the visual signal that triggers the frog's grab-and-eat response?

Daniel Dennett analyzes frog fly-eating behavior as part of his attempt to account for the possibility of perceptual error. How can the frog make such an error? One explanation is that "the frog's eye tells the frog's brain to capture the object (Lettvin et al., 1959)." The information, however, carried in the visual signal underdetermines what the object is. It might be a fly or it might be a fly-shaped blur. Dennett explains:

If we interpret the signal coming from the eye as "telling" the frog that there is a fly flying towards it, then it is the eye that is passing mistaken information to the frog, whereas if we interpret that signal as merely signaling a dark moving patch on the retina, it is "telling the truth" and the error must be assigned to some later portion of the brain's processing.

(Dennett, 1989)

The signal carries the information it does; the frog's eye or brain processes it in such a way as to trigger a response. The frog is not making a judgment about whether the object is a fly or not. If its visual and cognitive systems process the input as that which causes a grab-and-eat response, this is what the frog does.

Whether it is the eye or the brain that processes the visual data, the visual signal produces an effect that is processed and decoded. The frog processes an input that produces an output. The frog is not capable of a judgment that distinguishes between fly and lead pellet. Dennett continues:

> If we are strenuously minimal in our interpretations, the frog never makes a mistake, for every event in the relevant pathway in its nervous system can always be de-interpreted by adding disjunctions (the signal means something less demanding: fly or pellet or dark moving spot or slug of kind K or . . .) until we arrive back at the brute meaning/n of the signal type, where misrepresentation is impossible.

At the level of "the brute meaning of the signal type" no misrepresentation is possible because the link is purely causal. The frog responds if it sees that kind of thing for which its system of eating has evolved. But if no misrepresentation is possible, then neither is representation. The frog's system is just built this way. It does not move from perception and understanding to a decision to act. Rather it simply acts. It does not make a judgment or decision.

A deflationary interpretation insists that the meaning of the signal lies in our judgments not in the signal. A frog, however, does not make any judgments. So, at the level of brute information, separate from any normative possibilities, no mistakes are possible because the signal is a stimulus that produces a response. This is what Dennett means by the signal being de-interpreted into a series of disjunctions that describe (for us, not the frog) the visual stimuli that produce its grab-and-eat response.

We will not enter into the argument about intrinsic or derivative intentionality, which is the main topic of Dennett's essay. We are using this example for a more limited purpose. Either we are deluded in our belief that we can make judgments and decisions, or we can judge and choose. Regardless, the input signals we receive would have the same content as they would if received by a frog. The visual signals are the result of the same physics regardless of whether we are a person or a frog. The difference in how we respond to that signal or in what that signal means is a result of our different forms of cognitive processing. Relative to the visual signal processed by a frog, Dennett citing Millikan (1987) describes two possibilities:

> No matter how many layers of transducers contribute to a signal's specificity, there will always be a deflationary interpretation of its meaning as meaning/n unless we relativize our account to some assumption of the normal (Normal, in Millikan's sense) function.

> *(Dennett, 1989)*

We can understand that the light signal is a mere cause that prompts an action by the frog, but that action is not a mistake even if the frog eats a lead pellet. Or we can argue, as Dennett does, that the frog's cognitive system of interpreting that cause has evolved such that it has a normative function. That is, it can function in such a way as to facilitate survival and thus reproduction. In either case, however, the visual signal only carries the potential to produce an effect in the frog. The meaningfulness of that effect is a function of the frog's brain processing capabilities.

So, again: a fly darting past our eyes and past a frog's eyes carries the same kind of visual information. The physics that describes reflection and absorption of light relative to the fly's body is the same for us and the frog. The difference in what we see lies in how we process and react to that light input. This is another counterexample to Mingers and Standing. A causal signal does not carry information separate from the cognitive abilities to respond to that signal by the animal perceiving it.

Consequently, the meaningfulness of the signal is always elsewhere than 'in' the signal. It would rest in how the signal is interpreted separate from the causal chain that proceeded the animal's reaction. Cause is one thing, aboutness is another. We are leaving room for a causal account of the mind, but we are denying that an information signal carries meaning in itself; it produces meaning within some further system of processing.

In an everyday sense, that processing is an interpretation or a judgment or a grasping of something normative within what Sellars (1997) calls the space of reasons, the normative space of possible understanding.

Let us now turn more explicitly to the second claim made by Mingers and Standing above:

> (2) "A sign that is false, e.g., mistaken, does not carry the information it would appear to, but still does carry information concerning the actual reasons for its occurrence."

Instead of talking about messages, which are propositional, Mingers and Standing, at this point, talk about signs, which is an ill-defined concept. Nevertheless, they claim that a false message does not carry false information, but rather no information. They immediately qualify this claim. They assert that even if a sign is false, it does still convey information about the reasons for its occurrence. Such a claim confuses what is false with what is nonsense. If a statement is false, it can be judged as false because we understand what it says or asserts. If we did not, we could not conclude that the statement is false. If something is nonsense, however, then we cannot determine what it says. Thus, it can be neither true nor false; we have no way of evaluating its content because it says nothing.

A message might be so garbled that we could not understand it, and thus it would be nonsense. If a message has content (that is, it is not noise), then for us to understand it as false is for us to make a judgment about the message, a judgment that it is false. If there is no content to the message, we cannot make such a judgment. But Mingers' and Standing's initial premise is that the message is false and that we recognize that it is false. Therefore, the message must have content, and not just information about the "reasons for its occurrence." As with any proposition, we can distinguish between what is said (the information, in this case) and the judgment about whether it is true or false. We should also add that the proposition must be asserted or understood as directed towards a particular state of affairs, but in this case the information asserted about some state of affairs is judged as false. This separation between what is said and the judgment of whether it is true or false is exactly what Mingers and Standing deny. For Mingers and Standing, information (what is said) must be true in order to be information.

The second part of their claim above also leads to other problems. They claim that despite the falsity of the message (the sign as they say) the reasons for its occurrence is still conveyed. If what is meant by 'reasons for' is the cause of the sign, then our argument above about inferring the cause from the effect shows that in most cases the information would be underdetermined (we know that it was caused, but not what caused it; there could be a vast number of causes, including enabling conditions). If we knew a lot about the source, we might develop a probabilistic model to describe some set of possible reasons for the message. But that would be to understand the source and not just the signal or sign, and that is not what Mingers and Standing are claiming.

Mingers and Standing admit that by talking about *reasons for the occurrence of some sign* they do mean the causes that produce that sign: "It is that signs carry information about their causal origin – what, given the occurrence of the sign, must be the case – whether or not it is observed or correctly interpreted" (97). In this case, all that they can legitimately say is what we have described above—given a certain system of correlations a sign might be construed as providing potential, not actual (or actualized) information. The actualization of this potential would require what they dismiss: someone's observation or interpretation of the sign as meaningful in a certain way. As we have been arguing, something is information for someone, even if not a particular someone. It is not yet information without our understanding that it is information, although it may be structured and have a form such that relative to our understanding it counts as mere potential information. It is important to note that qualification—"relative to our understanding." In making this argument, we are separating out from our discussion the very different usage and sense of 'information' developed and used in modern physics.

To construe something as information does not mean that information exists separately from our construal. And in many cases, we could construe things quite differently. Similarly, data is not something that exists separate from our understanding and construal. And it will not be of all the same kind. Data that is derived from my measurements, even if processed, are not the same kind of data as a propositional statement (let's say a description of something) which might also be called data (personal data, for example). We have discussed this in Chapter 6.

Mingers and Standing continually personify that which they are trying to explain, which is information, data, propositions. We have commented about this before. It is a continually repeated error. For example, they claim that data "if it makes some assertion as to how things are it may be true for false – it is a truth-bearer." Neither data nor sentences assert anything. We assert these (if the data is in a propositional form). Or we can understand the data or sentence as asserting something, which is to say we take it as asserted by someone. As Stampe (1968) argues, sentences do not say something; we say something by means of sentences.

There are many other problems with the Mingers and Standing's theory that information must necessarily be true. Some of these problems concern how they situate information within broader social contexts. In our critique, however, we will remain focused on their theory of information per se. They address an important argument made by Fetzer (2004) against Floridi. Again, we will not evaluate the effectiveness of this argument against Floridi. Sebastian Sequoiah-Grayson (2007) has offered one kind of defense of Floridi. Floridi's theory of *Strong Semantic Information*, as Sequoiah-Grayson describes it, is not an "Ur-concept with respect to theories of information." We are arguing that there is no such Ur-concept. Our goal at this point is to critique Mingers and Standing attempt to generalize Floridi's theory in a way that goes beyond the propositional focus of that theory.

Mingers and Standing ineffectively criticize Fetzer's argument in the following way. Fetzer argues that some kinds of meaningful data are neither true nor false, so that it is wrong to say that such data as information must necessarily true. He offers the samples of blood spots, photographs or tree rings. These can all be used as data, but they are not propositional in form, and thus cannot be true or false. Mingers and Standing claim that Fetzer is confusing data with propositional content. What does this mean? What kind of confusion is this?

Mingers and Standing claim that while it is true that only propositions can be true or false, data, like blood spots, provide true information. So blood spot would provide "(true) information about who shed it and when" (92). We see again the idea that signal (the blood spot) carries information. We derive information from the blood spot, which is just a something in the world for us to analyze. The blood spot, even at the molecular level, is not true; rather, it exists. But the blood spot as data is something that means within the context of our knowledge of human beings, biology, chemistry, and so on. Thus, it is meaningful for us as data, as information. But at this level of meaningfulness it is neither true nor false.

Mingers and Standing seem to be confusing data with judgments about propositions. Data can be meaningful like any aspect of the world can be meaningful. But that does not make it true or false. Similarly, the various elements that might constitute a rock are not true or false. A rock is potentially a datum in our attempts to understand the geology of some landscape. When we understand it as such a datum it becomes evidence. Our analysis might be faulty, and the data we extract from it might be correct or incorrect. Both the rock and our analysis count as information as part of our practice of geological analysis and questioning. That the rock is what it is does not make it necessarily true, it just makes it a rock which we take as evidence and as meaningful within our enquiry.

Fetzer is in fact distinguishing between data and propositional content. He is arguing that both can be informative. Here is what Fetzer (2004) claims against the idea that information must necessarily be true:

> Another perhaps equally serious reason to entertain a far broader account is that various kinds of meaningful data do not — even remotely — appear to be candidates for truth because they lack a propositional or a sentential structure. Consider, for example, blood spots, PET scans, photographs, geological strata, fossil records, tree rings, and the like. As a matter of common knowledge, blood spots can be among the most important kinds of information found at the scene of a crime, yet blood spots, as such, are not the right kinds of things to qualify as true.

His point is that such data is meaningful and informative and thus counts as an essential form of information. Such data, however, cannot be true or false, since it is not propositional. But this does not mean that it is not information. So, information need not be true or false, and is therefore not necessarily veridical. The argument also points out the sheer variety of what can count as information.

PROPOSITIONALITY AS A CONDITION OF TRUTH

J. Michael Dunn (2008) makes an excellent observation about ambitious relationship between truth and information. His observation does not solve the problem, but it does clarify it. Dunn (2008) notes that Fetzer (2004) in his critique of Floridi provides "several examples from ordinary life about false information, or 'misinformation,' e.g., giving wrong directions to Hyde Park." In addition, he acknowledges that Fetzer suggests a possible defense "Floridi might want to defend his position by claiming that false information is to information as artificial flowers are to flowers." The point is that false information would in fact be factitious information, artificial and fake. Dunn (2008) then offers his own example to undercut the identification of false with fake (factitious):

> I have heard a similar defense in a story of the "Information Booth" in a railway station and how it would be misnamed if it gave out

false information. But note that I said "false information" in a very natural way. I think it is part of the pragmatics of the word "information" that when one asks for information, one expects to get true information, but it is not part of the semantics, the literal meaning of the term. If there is a booth in the train station advertising "food," one expects to get edible, safe food, not rotten or poisoned food. But rotten food is still food.

Dunn (2008) distinguishes between the semantics and the pragmatics of 'information.' Dunn suggests that in our use of the word 'information' (pragmatics) we expect information to be true. But that is not a necessary element in what the word means (semantics). We do not think we can so neatly separate semantics and pragmatics. We would say instead that the use of the word (and the concept of) 'information' is fundamentally confused and equivocal. It is used in these theories in conflicting ways. It is used ambiguously, and the conflicting theories that arise from this usage, are exacerbated by the fact that information is not a natural kind like water or gold. If information does not exist in the world in the way water does, then it does not flow, except metaphorically, and maybe not even then. The concept of information has gathered a number of conflicting ideas under its name. In particular, information is something that is informative, because we understand it as meaningful in some way. It has also become associated with a notion that it is self-sufficient and separate from our understanding. These two senses are in conflict. We have discussed this in an earlier chapter. But, as Dunn (2008) states, in our actual use of the word, and thus relative to our everyday examples of information, we understand information as potentially false, and so we can say, as he does, that someone can give us false information.

Mingers and Standing refuse to accept this conclusion. We will look at another example to which they appeal that instead of supporting their argument, actually undermines it. They make the following claim:

> Indeed, DNA can now provide us with information about human population movements hundreds of thousands of years ago. The information has always been there, and it is only now becoming available.

The information provided by DNA in this case is about the movements of population over time. (See Jean Manco in *Ancestral Journeys for an excellent recent account of these movements.*) Mingers and Standing assert that DNA *contains* this information, as if it were gold ore in the earth that needs only to be extracted and smelted to reveal its gold content. But this is not how DNA markers work.

It is true that a certain percentage of DNA markers can be found in various populations. These markers can be used to trace the lineage of descent of individuals in this population to a common ancestor. Groups of people who share a set of DNA markers from some putative common ancestor are called haplogroups. Geneticists for various reasons have concluded that "where the greatest genetic variance of a haplogroup is to be found is likely to be its point of origin" (24). These genetic markers are found or are not found in different percentages among present populations. Given various assumptions about the rate of DNA mutation and variance, scientists can infer patterns of movement and migration of various populations over time. In addition, DNA markers have begun to be identified from human remains, and thus can provide direct evidence of the presence of certain DNA markers in a particular place at a particular time in the past. This information can be used in correlation with other archeological and linguistic evidence to suggest patterns and times of migration. The most common DNA evidence used to determine lineage are sex-specific DNA markers that can only be "passed down from parents to children without recombination" (Manco, 2013). Once we understand this mechanism of transmission, then in combination with knowing geography and the location of current individuals, we can infer that once an ancestor lived at a particular place and time, and now his or her descendant lives at this other particular place and time.

Establishing likely patterns of migration of people in the past is not information that can be found *in* the DNA. We could say that DNA contains information that we can decode about descent from some ancestor. But that, of course, is not its evolved purpose. That I have an eye shape like my great grandfather does not mean that my eye shape contains information about the fact that he lived in Chicago and that I live in Dallas. We can claim, therefore, that DNA contains the history of our lineage, but that is not the same as carrying information about migration patterns and events. We develop accounts of these patterns, relying on a vast number of historical clues, in order to establish a likely migration vectors and dates.

We can infer, therefore, that people from one place (the region around the Dneiper, for example) moved to another place (up the Danube into the Balkans), and certain DNA markers present in the current population is a consequence of that movement (Manco, 2013). The information about the movement of human individuals and groups from one place to another is not in the DNA. The movement is an inference made by using traces of certain DNA markers present in a percentage of individuals of a particular population.

We might claim that the evidence for this conclusion has always been present, but the evidence is not just the DNA markers, but involves our understanding, derived from a vast array of collected data, analysis, and inferences, grounded in geography, archeology, linguistics, human behavior and so on. And all of this allows us to conclude that one population descended from some individual or individuals that at one point we associate with some other location. In effect, our theories about population movement arise from our invention of a mechanism by which we can explain how the same DNA of some group found in one location (at some particular time) is also found in a certain percentage in another population. The fact of the existence of a particular kind of DNA present in a particular population underdetermines our explanation. That there is a fact of the matter does not make what we say about that fact necessarily true. If we misinterpreted the DNA or the mechanism of movement (imagining it was tribal migration when it might have been a consequence of slavery,) the DNA would still be informative. As our theories change, the information we infer from the DNA evidence also changes. The evidence exists and that can be informative, and we can understand it as information, even if we have less confidence in our actual interpretation of this evidence. The evidence is not true or false. DNA in this case would be like a bloodstain at a crime scene. Again, information does not exist in the world as something separate from our understanding of it as information; nor is it separate from the process of our interpreting it. It is neither objective nor necessarily veridical. And it is not one thing or a kind of thing that can flow like water, lava, or even air currents, since it exists always entangled with our attempt to understand it.

CONCLUSION

In conclusion, let us look at a more mundane example to clarify our argument. The slime of a snail can inform us that a snail has moved either into a part of our garden, because snails leave behind such slime as they move. The slime is not propositional nor is it about anything. It is just an effect of the snail's movement. It can be informative for us. It requires we know something about snails and movement. It is informative because of what we know about snails, not simply what we know about slime (we also have to recognize it as snail slime). So, this is a marker because it is an effect from which we infer a cause. It could be that our friend Chuck has collected snail slime in a squeeze container and was fooling us by leaving snail trails. This is again the problem of underdetermination. What makes something informative is our understanding or judgments and these cannot be necessarily true, but as we argued earlier only contingently true (they could be false). An effect is not information, but our understanding of an effect construes or grasps that effect as informative and thus as what we often call information.[4]

NOTES

1 Dretske deals with this problem by appealing to the necessities of the laws of nature, hence his focus on perceptual knowledge. Mingers and Standings more ambitious theory of semantic information cannot depend on the patterns of nature to prevent accidental correlations between two states.

2 Mingers and Standing also talk about signs conveying "pragmatic information within a social context." If this information is normative patterns of social discourse, then then the dependence of such normative content on interpretation remains in place. If this social information is understood as caused, then social context is construed as the same as "environmental information."

3 Quantum non-locality should not undermine the everyday sense in which we are appealing to causality here.

4 There are further argument in physics for information as a constituent part of the universe separate from our understanding. We think such arguments are flawed, but they are not relevant here since such arguments must construe information as non-propositional.

REFERENCES

Álvarez-Ruiz, Lola, Josabel Belliure, and Juli G. Pausas. "Fire-driven behavioral response to smoke in a Mediterranean lizard." *Behavioral Ecology* 32.4 (2021): 662–667.

Bar-Hillel, Yehoshua, and Rudolf Carnap. "Semantic information." *The British Journal for the Philosophy of Science* 4.14 (1953): 147–157.

Dennett, Daniel C. "Evolution, error and intentionality." In The Intentional Stance (pp. 13–53). MIT Press, 1989.

Dunn, J. M. Information in computer science. *Philosophy of Information* 8 (2008): 581–608.

Fetzer, James H. "Information: Does it have to be true?" *Minds and Machines* 14 (2004): 223–229.

Floridi, L. "Outline of a theory of strongly semantic information." *Minds and Machines* 14 (2004): 197–221.

Lettvin, Jerome Y., et al. "What the frog's eye tells the frog's brain." *Proceedings of the IRE* 47.11 (1959): 1940–1951.

Manco, Jean. *Ancestral journeys: The peopling of Europe from the first venturers to the Vikings*. Thames & Hudson, 2013.

Millikan, Ruth Garrett. *Language, thought, and other biological categories: New foundations for realism*. MIT press, 1987.

Mingers, John, and Craig Standing. "What is information? Toward a theory of information as objective and veridical." *Journal of Information Technology* 33.2 (2018): 85–104.

Rockness, Howard, and Joanne Rockness. "Legislated ethics: From Enron to Sarbanes-Oxley, the impact on corporate America." *Journal of Business Ethics* 57 (2005): 31–54.

Sellars, Wilfrid. *Empiricism and the philosophy of mind*. Harvard University Press, 1997.

Sequoiah-Grayson, Sebastian. "The metaphilosophy of information." *Minds and Machines* 17.3 (2007): 331–344.

Stampe, Dennis W. "Toward a grammar of meaning." *The Philosophical Review* 77.2 (1968): 137–174.

CHAPTER 9

Truth Is Seldom the Motive

The Complexity of Human Motives

INTRODUCTION

It is important to remember that people actually share and exchange information, images, messages, comments, and links for many reasons. In these exchanges, it sometimes matters if what is exchanged is true, but often it does not. If the perceived truth of information does not motivate people to share information, what does motivate them? We will offer here a survey of motives. The goal of this survey is to establish the secondary importance of truth or falsity in the exchange of online information, as well as to help us identify the actual gossip and rumor economy that best describes information diffusion online (and indeed, offline).

If we simply observe our own behavior honestly and over time, many of us (if not most of us) would come to the conclusion cited by Alice E. Marwick:

> But most importantly, within social environments, people are not necessarily looking to inform others: they share stories (and pictures, and videos) to express themselves and broadcast their identity, affiliations, values, and norms.

Her list of motives and desires is useful. People have a desire to express themselves or even display themselves in order to establish, confirm, or

 DOI: 10.1201/9781003401674-12

explore their personality, idea of themselves, and their group identity. Who we are is partly determined by what we care about (values, broadly understood), and our sense of what is normal, right, and comfortable. (It is also determined by our anxieties, by what we fear, and by our insecurities. We will discuss these below). Metzger et al. describe the motives for sharing content online using similar, overlapping categories as Marwick:

> Motives for sharing news include: acting as an opinion leader, advocating for one's own beliefs, socializing, gaining social status, sharing experiences with others, and informing others.

Metzger focuses on the social dynamics of self-expression and sharing. Claire Wardle also notes that if we are to understand online behavior we need to move away from our fixation on accuracy and zoom out to understand the characteristics of some of these online spaces that are powered by people's need for connection, community, and affirmation.[1]

Our online behavior has other more negative motives as well. These other motives include fears, anxieties, hurts, and confusions. Information is shared and criticized not only as part of political activism and social responsibility, but also as expressions of disdain and contempt, and sometimes out of a desire to hurt, prompted by anxieties about oneself and one's identity. Our sharing of information online can also lead to public confirmation, acknowledgement, and increased social status. And so, grandchildren attack their grandparents online for not conforming to their ideas of moral rectitude; colleagues attack each other with innuendo and mockery; peers find compromising posts of those they dislike and repost them; and so on (Cheng et al., 2017; March and Marrington, 2019).

Marwick's research also makes clear, as has the work of others (Jang and Kim, 2018; Dutton et al., 2017), that misinformation and disinformation can have a social and economic purpose:

> The second significant finding is that fake news and problematic content appeals to different people for different reasons. "Fake news" content is clickbait. The goal of the fake news producer is to have as many people spread their content as possible. The easiest way to do that is to find a news item that will be shared by people of different political proclivities. This can be a sensational claim about vaccinations or conspiracies or animals—topics that appeal across party lines—or it can be a story that includes both conservative and liberal points of view.

For many people, the truth or falsity of online statements or memes is irrelevant. What matters is that people click on the post or image and share it with as many people as possible. Sensational, extreme, and dubious claims will produce more emotional responses or will be more entertaining, and have a greater chance of being shared or liked.

Metzger et al. note the same kinds of motives, but also point out that sharing information or misinformation need not mean that someone believes it:

> For example, people might share misinformation for entertainment purposes, sarcastic reasons, or to illustrate a point counter to the message promoted in a false news story. Under such circumstances, the danger of fake news may be less than feared or, perhaps, even mitigated or reversed.

Life online is an extension of our ordinary social and personal lives. People do not simply mirror online content, they make that content and it reflects in various ways the confusions and mixed motives of all of us.

Both Marwick (2018) and Metzger et al. (2021) recognize that there is no simple and singular (magic bullet) way to resolve the complex conflicts and entanglements that characterize social life. Fact-checking sites and media literacy campaigns presume that people will not share news if they know it is inaccurate, imagining users as cultural dupes at the mercy of media elites. But this is simply a newer form of the "magic bullet" model of media effects that was popular in the first half of the 20th century.

In fact, fake-checking has proven ineffective in deflating or countering what the fake-checkers call false information. It has been observed many times that people will resist changing their understanding of facts. Given that we would find it difficult to justify much of what we think we know, it is not surprising that we tend to believe those we trust. Brandtzaeg and Folstad (2017) studied the use of three fact-checking websites (Snopes, StopFake, and FactCheck) and found that people's disbelief of some information was motivated by their lack of trust not only in the fact-checking website's recommendations, but also by a lack of trust more generally in the social and political environment. There is a good reason for this lack of trust.

The motive for belief matters more than the purported falsity or veracity of the information. Nevertheless, there exists a prevailing idea that if only people could see the other side, or if their misinformation could be corrected, then they would believe differently (invariantly like the enlightened researcher). There is good evidence, however, that exposure to competing, and especially conflicting prompts a renewed commitment to one's initial position. (Bail et al., 2018; Howell et al., 2009; Lord et al., 1979; Figà Talamanca and Arfini, 2022).

Lazer et al. (2018) note what we all should recognize, that we use OSNs in order to feel good, for psychological reasons, and not as part of some great and ideal pursuit of truth:

> Research shows that people more often use the media for personal gratification than for truth seeking. Additional research demonstrates that people prefer information that confirms their pre-existing attitudes (selective exposure) and view information consistent with their pre-existing beliefs as more persuasive than dissonant information (confirmation bias). That is, prior partisan and ideological beliefs might prevent acceptance of fact checking of a given fake news story. Our psychological and social desires, needs, anxieties, and pleasures will determine how most people interact with information.

Flaxman et al. (2016) studied the role of network structure, and investigated whether the Internet and social networks influence ideological isolation. They found evidence for both for and against. On the one hand, they found that online news consumption showed that information discovered via social networks exhibited higher ideological segregation and led to the formation of echo chambers and filter bubbles. At the same time, they also found that users of social networks were often exposed to information expressing opinions and offering perspectives with which they disagreed.

The increased activity of online bots did not seem to effect people's beliefs in any significant way. While bots are widely blamed for the spread of misinformation, Vosoughi and Aral (2018) found that bots spread both so-called true- and false- information in equal measure. Human attitude and beliefs were more decisive in the spread of misinformation that network structure or bot activity. In our analysis of the tweets from accounts related to Russia's Internet Research Agency during the run-up to the 2016 U.S. presidential election, we also found that claims about Trump and about Clinton were more less equal in number (Bourbon and Murimi, 2020). Garrett et al. (2009) found that readers were more interested in those stories that seemed to support their opinions, while also being willing to engage with other perspectives. On the other hand, Bail et al. (2018) in another study found that people who were exposed to political views they opposed were more likely to become more extreme in their beliefs: increasing the polarization of views, not ameliorating this polarization.

People are not simply shaped and determined by information and technology. Human beings are not simply passive. They react, resist, judge for themselves, assert themselves, search for what is intelligible and flea what is confusing and frightening. And thus, they can also be seduced by propaganda, they can conform to those around them, they can accept superstitions and stereotypes. We can all lose our way and fall into delusion and hysteria. And we can also resist this.

We do not mean to suggest, however, that we are all unfortunately prone to irrational behavior. People have diverse beliefs. We should not assume self-righteously that we are the anointed, while those we disagree with are the misguided. Our motives for sharing whatever we do online are part of our complex forms of self-expression and negotiation with others. Marwick cites a very telling example:

> At a recent workshop on partisan media, my friend "Carly" related her frustration. Her mother, a strong conservative, repeatedly shared "fake news" on Facebook. Each time, Carly would send her mother news stories and Snopes links refuting the story, but her mother persisted. Eventually, fed up with her daughter's efforts, her mother yelled, "I don't care if it's false, I care that I hate Hillary Clinton, and I want everyone to know that!"

"Carly's" mother wanted to express and affirm her dislike in a public fashion, both from her own personal commitments and feelings and as part of establishing her public political identity. What we share online, like our statements face to face, can have symbolic value, expressing feelings and asserting a public stance and identity.

This is a very brief and incomplete survey of the psycho-social motives behind the sharing of information and misinformation. We want to conclude this survey with a particular example offered by Wardle. Our political identities are often grounded in what we care about, what we value, and what we find essential to our sense of ourselves and our lives. Claire Wardle describes this well in her account of her team's investigation of online conversations about the COVID-19 vaccines:

> In November 2020, my team published a report on 20 million posts we had gathered from Instagram, Twitter, and Facebook that included conversations about COVID-19 vaccines. (Note that we didn't set out to collect posts containing misinformation;

we simply wanted to know how people were talking about the vaccines.) From this large data set, the team identified several key narratives, including the safety, efficacy, and necessity of getting vaccinated and the political and economic motives for producing the vaccine. But the most frequent conversation about vaccines on all three platforms was a narrative we labeled liberty and freedom. People were less likely to discuss the safety of the vaccines than whether they would be forced to get vaccinated or carry vaccine verification. Yet agencies like the Centers for Disease Control and Prevention are only equipped to engage the single narrative about safety, efficacy, and necessity.

I am not sure that everyone has as much confidence in the CDC's propagandistic storytelling as Wardle seems to. The role of the CDC is not simply a scientific one, however; it is political and social. Nevertheless, Wardle's team's analysis of these conversations reveals that information fits with patterns of sense-making, which she is calling narratives. She argues that our reactions to information are determined by how it fits or conflicts with the particular explanatory stories in which we are invested. The role of so-called narratives in forming our sense of self is a fraught topic that leads beyond our analysis of information and misinformation. Whatever role such stories might have in our lives, they express certain values and even ideas about ourselves and the world. That people talked about their ideas and anxieties about liberty and freedom, and therefore about the power and authority of government and politicians fits with our arguments that knowledge and information are part of a contingent web of concerns. We do not evaluate any particular claim in isolation, but as part of an imbricating web of beliefs, commitments, desires, fears, and much more.

We will bring this chapter and this second part of our book to a conclusion by recapitulating two fundamental arguments about knowledge and information that we have been developing. These two arguments are related but not identical.

THE FIRST ARGUMENT: THE PSYCHO-IDEOLOGICAL ARGUMENT

Let us first assume that information must be true. If, however, the motive for sharing information (understood to be true) is not because it is true but for a variety of other reasons, then we might conclude that the truth of information might be necessary, but it is not sufficient to prompt our sharing or taking up that information.

If our belief or attitude toward information is bound to how it fits with our ideologies, desires, experiences, and so on, then anyone's ability to evaluate information as true or false is compromised. And this will include those who research misinformation. If this is the case, then the putative truth cannot be separated from our ideological commitments. So, at least, from the outside, truth seems secondary to ideology.

If our motives for sharing are primarily psychological or ideological, and if we are either indifferent to the truth or falsity, or if we judge the value of information or misinformation relative to our social goals or our psychological needs or our social goals, then the truth of some bit of information is neither necessary nor sufficient to prompt our sharing.

And therefore, misinformation cannot be eliminated or even seriously diminished from our uses and involvement with information online or offline.

THE SECOND ARGUMENT: THE EPISTEMOLOGICAL ARGUMENT

What is the case and what will count as a fact are not simple to determine. In some cases, what will count as meaningful and true is itself an ideologically and psychologically motivated belief. Knowledge varies in kind. We rely on various and different criteria to establish the veracity and credibility of these various kinds of knowledge. There is no absolute knowledge or certainty. Instead, knowledge is normative and contingent on our descriptions. Our knowledge is a question of degree, and the denial of that creates a factitious simplicity that is itself a form of misguided belief. This does not mean that knowledge is subjective, but that it is contingent on our epistemological criteria and descriptions. And those criteria and descriptions can be better or worse.

Information is, in many cases, although not in all cases, a species of knowledge. And thus, it is also normative and contingent in the same way. It cannot be absolutely true. It has many different forms, all of which are case-specific. Since our knowledge is normative and not certain, our judgments about what will count as information being true and false cannot be generalized. It will require a case-by-case evaluation. Sometimes we will have to determine what will count as evidence and also what will count as *good* evidence. Any categorization of information as true or false (misinformation) will itself always be open to revision, criticism, and reevaluation. Such acts of categorization are not neutral, and given what we have argued about knowledge and information, they must be understood as contingent. This is true even if the claims are not about ideological issues, but it is even more the case if they are.

Identifying information and misinformation is not like identifying atomic elements or molecules or even like identifying animal species. Our involvement in determining what will count as knowledge and information means that our judgments about information and misinformation must be evaluated as judgments. In some of our judgments, we will have justified confidence, and in others, we will not (or should not). Studying the diffusion of information or misinformation through social networks is not like tracking a trace element as it moves through an organism.

Again, in making this argument, we are not arguing for some form of pernicious relativism. But we are suggesting that much of what is understood as information may not be information at all, and that all information is open to improvement and revision. Information and knowledge claims are necessarily given under some description or conceptualization (this is true even about numerical data, if it is meaningful). The truth or falsity of any claim is dependent on these descriptions or conceptualizations.

And thus, our knowledge and what we take as information will inevitably be dependent on descriptions that can and should be revised. As a result, information is necessarily entangled with misinformation, because statements of information or misinformation are not atomic statements that are true or false. Instead, they should be understood as contingent articulations of a process of knowing and understanding.

CONCLUSION

Information spread and our relationship with this information, and what many take as knowledge and authority, is guided by a varied set of emotional, cognitive, discursive, sociological motives, both rational and irrational. It is naive to imagine that this will ever change (or even that it should). Misinformation is a necessary and inevitable part of what we know and treat as information. The distinction between information and misinformation will be a part of how we know and understand ourselves and the world. It will also be a part of our psycho-social lives. It cannot and it should not be eliminated. The more we attempt to do that, the more we undermine our ability to know and be informed. The practices at the heart of the sciences (especially the physical sciences) constitute ways of taking responsibility for the normative and contingent form of our knowing, and thus to create processes that increase the reliability and explanatory power of our scientific descriptions, theories, and understanding. We cannot be right, if we cannot be wrong.

NOTE

1 https://issues.org/misunderstanding-misinformation-wardle/

REFERENCES

Bail, Christopher A., et al. "Exposure to opposing views on social media can increase political polarization." *Proceedings of the National Academy of Sciences* 115.37 (2018): 9216–9221.

Bourbon, Brett, and Renita Murimi. "The vagaries of online trolls." *Proceedings of the 6th International Conference on Computational Social Science (IC2S2)*. Cambridge, MA, USA, 2020.

Brandtzaeg, Petter Bae, and Asbjørn Følstad. "Trust and distrust in online fact-checking services." *Communications of the ACM* 60. 9 (2017): 65–71.

Cheng, Justin, et al. "Anyone can become a troll: Causes of trolling behavior in online discussions." *Proceedings of the 2017 ACM Conference on Computer Supported Cooperative Work and Social Computing*, Portland, Oregon, USA, 2017.

Dutton, W. H., et al. "Social shaping of the politics of internet search and networking: Moving beyond filter bubbles, echo chambers, and fake news (SSRN scholarly paper ID 2944191)." *Social Science Research Network*. https://papers.ssrn.com/sol3/papers.cfm?abstract_id=2944191 (2017).

Figà Talamanca, Giacomo, and Selene Arfini. "Through the newsfeed glass: Rethinking filter bubbles and echo chambers." *Philosophy and Technology* 35.1 (2022): 20.

Flaxman, Seth, Sharad Goel, and Justin M. Rao. "Filter bubbles, echo chambers, and online news consumption." *Public Opinion Quarterly* 80.S1 (2016): 298–320.

Garrett, R. K. "Echo chambers online?: Politically motivated selective exposure among Internet news users." *Journal of Computer-Mediated Communication* 14.2 (2009): 265–285.

Howell, William G., and Martin R. West. "Educating the public: How information affects Americans' support for school spending and charter schools." *Education Next* 9.3 (2009): 40–48.

Jang, S. Mo, and Joon K. Kim. "Third person effects of fake news: Fake news regulation and media literacy interventions." *Computers in Human Behavior* 80 (2018): 295–302.

Lazer, David MJ, Matthew A. Baum, Yochai Benkler, Adam J. Berinsky, Kelly M. Greenhill, Filippo Menczer, Miriam J. Metzger, et al. "The science of fake news." *Science* 359. 6380 (2018): 1094–1096.

Lord, Charles G., Lee Ross, and Mark R. Lepper. "Biased assimilation and attitude polarization: The effects of prior theories on subsequently considered evidence." *Journal of Personality and Social Psychology* 37.11 (1979): 2098.

March, Evita, and Jessica Marrington. "A qualitative analysis of internet trolling." *Cyberpsychology, Behavior, and Social Networking* 22.3 (2019): 192–197.

Marwick, Alice E. "Why do people share fake news? A sociotechnical model of media effects." *Georgetown Law Technology Review* 2.2 (2018): 474–512.

Metzger, Miriam J., et al. "From dark to light: The many shades of sharing misinformation online." *Media and Communication* 9.1 (2021): 134–143.

Vosoughi, Soroush, Deb Roy, and Sinan Aral. "The spread of true and false news online." *Science* 359.6380 (2018): 1146–1151.

PART III

Gossip and Rumor

DOI: 10.1201/9781003401674-13

CHAPTER 10

A Critique of Current Models of Information Diffusion

INTRODUCTION

Many theorists construe the problem of misinformation as a problem of knowledge, hence of ignorance. This assumption leads to solutions in which bad information (false belief) is resisted by good information (true belief). A vast number of studies pursue this idea that the truth, even if it will not make us free, it will free us from misinformation. See, for example, Li and Chang (2023), Prike et al. (2024), Lewandowsky and van der Linden (2021), Chung and Kim (2021), Babaei et al. (2021), Clayton et al. (2020), Swire-Thompson and Lazer (2020). The truth does matter. We should all attempt to debunk or counter opposing views, correct factual errors, and combat misleading claims and stories. We should not imagine, however, that we will all agree or, even more importantly, that our own grasp of the truth is apodictic. This book arose out of a resistance to the idea that misinformation should or could be effectively corrected by some method of truth-telling—fact-checking, source labeling, or censorship. In this chapter, we examine one of the dominant models used to describe information diffusion—the epidemiology model, in which information is characterized as something like a virus. The model fails to adequately describe, let alone explain information diffusion. It also perpetuates the idea that information exists independently of our human understanding

DOI: 10.1201/9781003401674-14

and involvement with it. This chapter is an examination of the conceptual failures that undermine the usefulness of describing information diffusion through causal metaphors.

THE ISSUE WITH EPIDEMIOLOGICAL MODELS

The dominant metaphor and hence model for the spread of information online has been epidemiological. Information infects us and can go viral, or that is at least the idea. In 2005, Eytan Adar and Lada Adamic wrote a paper entitled "Tracking Information Epidemics in Blogspace." It won the most influential paper of the decade award for their work modeling the spread of information in a network of blog websites as a viral infection. It prompted many other attempts to model information diffusion as infections, or as heat diffusion, which operates in a similar way. These are both attractive ideas, even though they are wrong.

If information can infect people, then people are cast as victims and viral hosts, and not as rational or independent agents. If information diffusion is modeled as a kind of epidemiological outbreak, then information becomes the de facto causal agent. If the infectious information is misinformation, or worse, then those infected (and those prone to infection) are the passive victims of the misinformation infection, although the assumption is that their information immune system is weak or diseased. With the viral metaphor in place, a simple solution to the spread of misinformation emerges. We need to identify and eradicate the misinformation virus; we need to cure those infected by the disease of their false views; and we need to identify those who are susceptible to this infection and inoculate them. Some might even dream of a misinformation vaccine for everyone. All attempts to diminish, let alone stem or eradicate misinformation, by using this protocol have failed, since it is built on an incoherent understanding of knowledge and information as we have argued in Parts 1 and 2. Curing people of their putatively false beliefs has also proved a failure, and in any case involves massive social engineering, manipulation, and political power.

That leaves the final option, which is identifying those who are susceptible and inoculating them. The first step requires that we identify those poor susceptible people. Given that requirement, the key question is again simple: Why are some people prone to this infection? The condescending and patronizing explanations are, of course, that such people are stupid, poorly educated, ideologically confused, lazy, evil, backward, ignorant, and so forth. Maybe some are. But the infection model is after all only a metaphor. And what the question should be, given the conceptual picture underlying this understanding of information diffusion, is: why are some people so passive, lacking in agency, choice, and judgment such that they get infected by misinformation?

The epidemiological model of information diffusion, however, fails to describe or capture how diffusion actually happens. The sharing and spread of information online (or offline) is seldom like the spread of a virus. As Zhou et al. (2020) observe, in "real-world diffusion, most receivers exposed to content chose not to repost it." A few important studies point to the inappropriateness of current models of information diffusion. An early study by Goel et al. (2012) shows clearly that information diffusion is seldom viral. While this does not directly support our contention that online information diffusion should be understood as a form of gossip, it does suggest that Internet behavior, while facilitated and constrained by network structures, is often more powerfully guided by the personal and social realities of which it is a part. As we have argued, this is not surprising given that information is not self-replicating. This does not offer direct support for our contention that online information diffusion should be understood as a form of gossip. It does suggest, however, that internet behavior, while facilitated and constrained by network structures, is also embedded and often determined by the personal and social realities of which it is a part.

Arvind Narayanan, using his own research as well as citing Goel et al., examines the rarity of viral events, while highlighting the manipulative and unpredictable effects of recommendation algorithms.[1] He cites in particular the failure of Travis Martin et al. (2016) to predict the likelihood that a particular tweet would be retweeted based on information about the content and the maker of the tweet. Narayanan's argument again suggests that the viral model for information spread gives too much power to the information, itself, and diminishes the role of human interests, judgment, and social dynamics.

Goel et al. (2016) returned to the question of how to determine if information cascades are viral a few years later. They discovered that fewer than 1 in 100,000 tweets are retweeted 1,000 times. Large online diffusion events did not conform to a decentralized viral model, but were rather better described as broadcast events, arising from spreaders who could broadcast the information or misinformation to their millions of followers:

> It could have been, for example, that the very largest events are characterized by multi-generational branching structures— indeed that is the clear implication of the phrase "going viral."

> So, it is surprising that even the very largest events are, on average, dominated by broadcasts. It is also surprising that the correlation between size and structural virality is so low.

Local networks of friends are unlikely to have the scope to spread information in a viral fashion. It can happen, but it would be rare. What is more likely is that the spread of information is similar to what Goel et al. observed due to top-down broadcast events where information diffused through users with many followers.

Zhou et al. (2020) have similarly argued that despite "the widespread use of such epidemic-like models, the mechanism of biological contagion and information diffusion are fundamentally different":

> In contrast to epidemic processes in which exposures to infection result in passive transmission, social contagion is a deliberate action taken by individuals who receive information. Empirical studies have demonstrated that simple generative models inspired by epidemic processes fail to reproduce some key features of the observed diffusion trees.

Not only is information not self-replicating, as we have observed, but human beings are not passive hosts for an information virus. Stano (2020) has also argued that infectious disease models are inappropriate tools for studying the spread of information, since infectious disease models assume that individuals are passive. In addition to these various studies, an array of studies have also argued that information diffusion does not match viral infection patterns: Liben-Nowell et al. (2008), Pei et al. (2015), Bourbon and Murimi (2021), Kauk et al. (2021), Narayanan (2023).

What should we conclude from these observations and studies? Given that information is not self-replicating like a virus, it should not be surprising that large diffusion events lack structural virality. Judgment and human decision is required in order to spread information. The factors, conditions, reasons, causes, and motives involved in deciding to share some information or content are various, labile, unsteady, and changeable. Patterns might emerge, but these are likely to be very specific to both the people involved and the content at issue.

The low virality of diffusion events of all kinds is what you would expect if the spreading of information was part of the practice of gossiping. We gossip relative to our local concerns among our friends and relevant acquaintances. Certainly, social media extends the geographical distribution and number of gossip-friends, but they still will be rather limited in number. Arnaboldi (2015) has demonstrated that the number of online friends that can legitimately be called as friends remains close to the Dunbar number of 150. In addition, our friends do not simply get infected by the information we send them. If they did, then a viral event could easily be precipitated by those with the largest number of susceptible friends. Social dynamics, however, as we know, are not simple.

We can also at this point identify two basic methods by which information is spread through OSNs. The first method is a bottom-up viral diffusion in which information spreads through local networks of friends. The second method is a top-down tree diffusion, in which information gets diffused through top-down broadcast events, which then might be taken up by local networks. (See illustrations below, which picture the different ways these two methods work within a network).

Figure 10.1 shows an illustration of bottom-up virality. Two nodes A and B in different, but overlapping communities, are sharing a rumor with their friends. Node A shares the rumor with a_1, a_2, and a_3. Node a_3 also receives the rumor from a friend in the other community, node b_1. Similarly, node B spreads the rumor with its friends: b_1 and b_2, who in turn share the rumor with their neighbors (b_1 shares the rumor with nodes b_{11}, b_{12}, and a_3, while b_2 shares the rumor with nodes b_{12}, b_{21}, and b_{22}). The two communities exhibit a few properties that are characteristics of rumor transmission: cross-community overlap and reinforcement. For example, reinforcement is observed in the rumor flow from node b_{12} to node B and from node a_{212} to node a_1 (represented by the dotted lines). Overlap is observed in information flow to and from nodes a_{22}, a_3, and b_1 who spread and receive information from nodes in the other community.

On the other hand, Figure 10.2 shows an illustration of top-down tree diffusion. Two broadcasters A and B transmit their information to nodes within their transmission radius. Two nodes ab_1 and ab_2 lie within the region of overlapping transmission zones of broadcasters A and B. Nodes a_1 through a_4 and b_1 through b_4 will continue the transmission in similar top-down tree-like manner to other nodes in their own transmission areas. We see that local networks function as gossip networks, whereas broadcast events function as distribution sources.

THE POWER OF FALSEHOODS

Another set of interesting studies suggest the centrality of human interest and engagement in information diffusion. These studies have revealed that

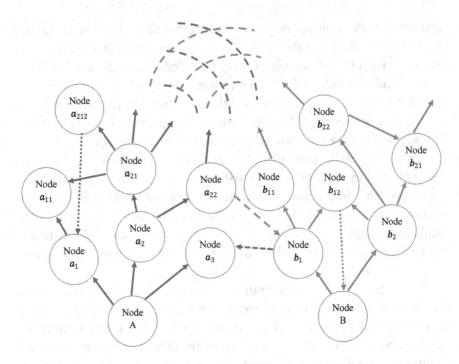

FIGURE 10.1 Bottom-up virality.

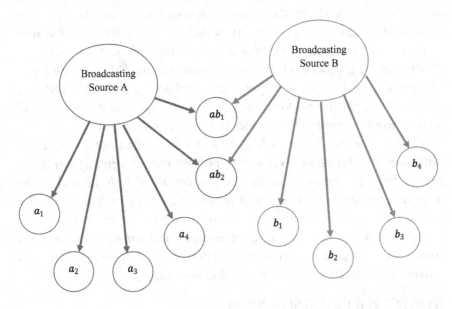

FIGURE 10.2 Top-down tree diffusion.

putatively false information spreads more deeply and quickly than puta-tively true information. There is some controversy here. But the effect has been found in a number of contexts (Hornik et al., 2015; Antypas et al., 2023). Similarly, Vosoughi et al. (2018) discovered that false information spreads more rapidly and more deeply through a network than does true infor-mation. This again points to the critical role of social dynamics in infor-mation spread, a social dynamics best modeled as gossip. The Vosoughi et al. (2018) study offers stronger corroboration that information diffusion is better modeled as gossip rather than knowledge. Vosoughi et al. (2018) discovered that false information spread more rapidly and more deeply through a network than did true information. It was not the truth or fal-sity of information that mattered, but how information fit with the per-sonal, social beliefs, and needs of the people spreading it. In other words, given the diversity of personal relationships and limitations in knowl-edge and understanding, information will spread like rumors do—that is, determined by the social interests of those involved. We suspect that people do not spread information because they believe it is true (certainly not because they have good warrant to believe it is true), but because it is socially and personally useful or meaningful.

The data from fact-focused information diffusion studies do not enable us to discover the actual reasons, judgments, or psychological processes behind the spreading of misinformation. We have no evidence from the data collected that people believed the information that they spread. We can, however, define certain range of possible belief attitudes towards the information and draw conclusions from these. Some spreaders may have known the information was false, and therefore spread it maliciously or as propaganda. Thus, they spread disinformation, and are a special case. Those that remain either thought the information was true or imagined that the truth did not matter. If we accept that they had no warrant to think the information true, then their belief in the veracity of the information and their spreading of it arose out of their motive for believing it to be true. For those who did not care about the truth, the same could be said. Those beliefs either motivated them to spread the information or not. If they did, then they were acting as a member of a belief community, sharing with believers or fighting against non-believers. Thus, in all cases, the informa-tion was spread as part of social purposes and dynamics.

Juul and Ugander (2021) reanalyze the data and conclusions of both Vosoughi et al. (2018) and Goel et al. (2012, 2016) compensating for the size of diffusion events, using a method of subsampling. Their conclusions were mixed. They found "that previously reported structural and temporal differences between true- and false-news cascades can be explained almost entirely by differences in cascade size, whereas the observed differences persist when comparing size-matched cascades of videos, images, news, and petitions." They note that the fact-checked true- and false-news cascades are naturally similar. They highlight the centrality of social dynamics and the particular interests of people who share information: "Our findings are consistent with the mechanisms underlying true- and false news diffusion being quite similar, differing primarily in the basic infectiousness of their spreading process." 'Infectiousness' means in this context a high rate of diffusion because of the content involved. Content is infectious because it is interesting to people in some way. Its truth or falsity might not matter at all. If someone spreads false news and they know it is false, then they are acting in bad faith or as propagandists. If they do not know it is false, then they are spreading the news in ways anyone who believes in something might. Those that spread this false news might, however, not care about its truth or falsity, in which case they are motivated by social and interpersonal concerns.

We should conclude from these various studies that those who spread misinformation do not necessarily believe in the news they share. We do not know. Whatever their motivations they are not centrally concerned with truth and falsity, but with personal and interpersonal factors.

CONCLUSION

A mistaken understanding of misinformation and information informs many of the attempts to model the spread of information. These models embody a set of assumptions that undermine their usefulness. These assumptions include the idea that information is like a virus, even though it is not self-replicating. In general, it is assumed that information flows or exists separate from our involvement and understanding. They also assume that people get passively infected with misinformation. Information, on the other hand, is not only active, it exists independently of human uses.

While the goal is to produce a model that will allow for the replication of information cascades, they are at best partially descriptive, and not explanatory. A model that produces the right kind of graph of a cascade has limited use, and tends to be very narrow in its accuracy and brittle in its application (if it ever gets that far). For example, the Ptolemaic model of the solar system, with its various epicycles and contingent add-on corrections, actually allowed a more accurate description of certain astronomic events than did the Copernican model. Of course, Copernicus incorrectly assumed that planetary orbits were circular. With correction, the Copernican model was descriptive in a way that opened up correct explanations of planetary movements. Similarly, if a model of diffusion is to be useful it should attempt to explain the mechanisms for information spread.

Infection models ignore the complex cognitive and emotional judgments that lead human beings to exchange messages. Although we are not examining them here, heat diffusion models fall into the same problems as do the other models. Such judgments and the conflicts out of which they emerge would be internal to each person. These internal aspects are flattened into distorting and simplistic external protocols. Even when these protocols are labeled 'believing' or 'hesitation' or some other psychological term, the protocols do not model our psychology, they simply correlate certain variable functions that activate or restrict the behavior of these nodes. (See the following for examples of this node personification: Tambuscio et al. 2015; Li et al. 2018; Xia et al. 2015; Zhao et al. 2013). The effect is to model nodes as passive and linear - when in fact our psychology constitutes complex non-linear system as do the various networks within which we participate. This last point is also of critical importance. Viral events, when they do occur, involve more elements than just the internet and OSNs. Beyond our many technologically constructed networks, we have our various offline social networks that remain powerful and often decisive in our everyday concerns.

When information, in the form of images, text, or links, does spread in something like an exponential way online, that spread is facilitated by broadcast diffusion and multiple reinforcement, both by people and algorithms creating feedback loops within the network. Marwick (2018) states the obvious, and yet it must be stated and restated:

> Information flows on and off platforms, between face-to-face interactions and broadcast media. Stories are discussed in person and on Facebook. In other words, online sharing does not exist in a vacuum. Isolating any single social technology ignores myriad others through which problematic information flows freely.

Marwick here is focused on what she calls "problematic information," but the point is more general. She uses the metaphor of "information flow," which we would resist, since it seems to exaggerate the independence of information from our human involvement. There is a certain degree of independence as we have argued in Part 2. Marwick's key claim, however, is correct and essential. Information on the Web does not spread in isolation from how it spreads and is meaningful offline. Zhou et al. (2020) conclude something similar, although using a different vocabulary:

> A growing number of studies have revealed that information diffusion is a complex process shaped by interacting factors such as network structure, information content, human activity, stochastic dynamics and even users' behavioral and sociodemographic characteristics. These entwined factors give rise to the diverse structure of diffusion paths observed in the real world, which obscures our understanding of the mechanisms driving spreading dynamics.

These conclusions are based on a variety of studies (Vosoughi et al., 2018; Iribarren et al., 2009; Salganik et al., 2006; Newman et al., 2011; Aral et al., 2013; Aral and Walker, 2012; Kwak et al., 2010; Goel et al., 2016). Information diffusion, shaped by network structures and focused by platform affordances, remains as diverse in its form as are our human social interactions. The failure of the epidemiological infection model rests on its failure to actually model human agency, action, and social behavior.

We also want to repeat an observation from earlier in the chapter. From these studies and attempts at modeling information diffusion we can extract two primary methods for information diffusion. (1) The first is a bottom-up, person to person (or node to node) sharing by both online and offline means of communication. (2) The second follows a top-down diffusion, utilizing broadcast methods, including legacy media, even if accessed through YouTube or another kind of online feed, aggregate services, or influencers (nodes with high degrees of centrality). The first method describes our everyday ways of gossiping both online and offline. The second method informs the first, as part of a communal involvement with sources of cultural influence. The interplay between these two is akin to the relationship between gossip and rumor, which we will examine in the next chapter.

NOTE

1 Arvind Narayanan (2023). Understanding Social Media Recommendation Algorithms: Towards a better informed debate on the effects of social media.

REFERENCES

Adar, Eytan, and Lada A. Adamic. "Tracking information epidemics in blogspace." *The 2005 IEEE/WIC/ACM International Conference on Web Intelligence (WI'05)*, Compiegne, France, 2005.

Antypas, Dimosthenis, Alun Preece, and Jose Camacho-Collados. "Negativity spreads faster: A large-scale multilingual twitter analysis on the role of sentiment in political communication." *Online Social Networks and Media* 33 (2023): 100242.

Aral, Sinan, and Dylan Walker. "Identifying influential and susceptible members of social networks." *Science* 337.6092 (2012): 337–341.

Aral, Sinan, Lev Muchnik, and Arun Sundararajan. "Engineering social contagions: Optimal network seeding in the presence of homophily." *Network Science* 1.2 (2013): 125–153.

Arnaboldi, V. *Online social networks: Human cognitive constraints in Facebook and Twitter personal graphs.* Elsevier, 2015.

Babaei, Mahmoudreza, et al. "Analyzing biases in perception of truth in news stories and their implications for fact checking." *IEEE Transactions on Computational Social Systems* 9.3 (2021): 839–850.

Bourbon, Brett, and Renita Murimi. "The Gossip Economy of Online Social Media." *ACM CHI Workshop on Opinions, Intentions, Freedom of Expression,..., and Other Human Aspects of Misinformation Online.* 2021.

Chung, Myojung, and Nuri Kim. "When I learn the news is false: How fact-checking information stems the spread of fake news via third-person perception." *Human Communication Research* 47.1 (2021): 1–24.

Clayton, Katherine, et al. "Real solutions for fake news? Measuring the effectiveness of general warnings and fact-check tags in reducing belief in false stories on social media." *Political Behavior* 42 (2020): 1073–1095.

Goel, Sharad, et al. "The structural virality of online diffusion." *Management Science* 62.1 (2016): 180–196.

Goel, Sharad, Duncan J. Watts, and Daniel G. Goldstein. "The structure of online diffusion networks." *Proceedings of the 13th ACM Conference on Electronic Commerce.* Valencia, Spain, 2012.

Hornik, Jacob, et al. "Information dissemination via electronic word-of-mouth: Good news travels fast, bad news travels faster!" *Computers in Human Behavior* 45 (2015): 273–280.

Iribarren, José Luis, and Esteban Moro. "Impact of human activity patterns on the dynamics of information diffusion." *Physical Review Letters* 103.3 (2009): 038702.

Juul, Jonas L., and Johan Ugander. "Comparing information diffusion mechanisms by matching on cascade size." *Proceedings of the National Academy of Sciences* 118.46 (2021): e2100786118.

Kauk, Julian, Helene Kreysa, and Stefan R. Schweinberger. "Understanding and countering the spread of conspiracy theories in social networks: Evidence from epidemiological models of Twitter data." *PLoS One* 16.8 (2021): e0256179.

Kwak, Haewoon, et al. "What is Twitter, a social network or a news media?." *Proceedings of the 19th International Conference on World Wide Web.* Raleigh, North Carolina, USA, 2010.

Lewandowsky, Stephan, and Sander Van Der Linden. "Countering misinformation and fake news through inoculation and prebunking." *European Review of Social Psychology* 32.2 (2021): 348–384.

Li, Chengcheng, Fengming Liu, and Pu Li. "Ising model of user behavior decision in network rumor propagation." *Discrete Dynamics in Nature and Society* 2018.1 (2018): 5207475.

Li, Jiexun, and Xiaohui Chang. "Combating misinformation by sharing the truth: a study on the spread of fact-checks on social media." *Information Systems Frontiers* 25.4 (2023): 1479–1493.

Liben-Nowell, David, and Jon Kleinberg. "Tracing information flow on a global scale using Internet chain-letter data." *Proceedings of the National Academy of Sciences* 105.12 (2008): 4633–4638.

Martin, Travis, et al. "Exploring limits to prediction in complex social systems." *Proceedings of the 25th International Conference on World Wide Web.* Montreal, Canada, 2016.

Marwick, Alice E. "Why do people share fake news? A sociotechnical model of media effects." *Georgetown Law Technology Review* 2.2 (2018): 474–512.

Narayanan, Arvind. "Understanding social media recommendation algorithms." (2023).https://knightcolumbia.org/content/understanding-social-media-recommendation-algorithms

Newman, Mark, Albert-László Barabási, and Duncan J. Watts. *The structure and dynamics of networks.* Princeton University Press, 2011.

Pei, Sen, et al. "Exploring the complex pattern of information spreading in online blog communities." *PloS One* 10.5 (2015): e0126894.

Prike, Toby, Lucy H. Butler, and Ullrich KH Ecker. "Source-credibility information and social norms improve truth discernment and reduce engagement with misinformation online." *Scientific Reports* 14.1 (2024): 6900.

Salganik, Matthew J., Peter Sheridan Dodds, and Duncan J. Watts. "Experimental study of inequality and unpredictability in an artificial cultural market." *Science* 311.5762 (2006): 854–856.

Stano, Simona. "The internet and the spread of conspiracy content." In M. Butter & P. Knight (Eds.), *Routledge Handbook of Conspiracy Theories* (pp. 483–496). Routledge, 2020.

Swire-Thompson, Briony, and David Lazer. "Public health and online misinformation: challenges and recommendations." *Annual Review Public Health* 41.1 (2020): 433–451.

Tambuscio, Marcella, et al. "Fact-checking effect on viral hoaxes: A model of misinformation spread in social networks." *Proceedings of the 24th International Conference on World Wide Web.* Florence, Italy, 2015.

Xia, Ling-Ling, et al. "Rumor spreading model considering hesitating mechanism in complex social networks." *Physica A: Statistical Mechanics and Its Applications* 437 (2015): 295–303.

Vosoughi, Soroush, Deb Roy, and Sinan Aral. "The spread of true and false news online." *Science* 359.6380 (2018): 1146–1151.

Zhao, Laijun, et al. "Rumor spreading model considering forgetting and remembering mechanisms in inhomogeneous networks." *Physica A: Statistical Mechanics and Its Applications* 392.4 (2013): 987–994.

Zhou, Bin, et al. "Realistic modelling of information spread using peer-to-peer diffusion patterns." *Nature Human Behaviour* 4.11 (2020): 1198–1207.

CHAPTER 11

Gossip and Rumor

INTRODUCTION

Information seldom spreads like a virus. Human judgment will always be a determining factor in how information diffuses through a network. The traditional name for such diffusion is rumor. We will examine some of the traditional descriptions and understandings of rumor in order to delineate how gossip and rumor fit with each other and how they both fit with our everyday forms of shared knowledge.

We can make some initial common-sense observations about gossip and rumor. They are, for example, not separable, but they are also not the same. All rumor depends on gossip, but not all gossip becomes rumor. Rumors must move beyond the local context of gossip exchanges. They must gain a life amidst the many local groups that make up a community. Gossip is the hearsay of everyday talk, sometimes founded on personal observation, sometimes not. It may be remembered, or it might be quickly forgotten. Rumor, on the other hand, is a pattern of gossip, reflective of and often reinforcing a community or group. All rumor spreads beyond its initial sources and resonates in some way with those who are at some distance from the source of the rumor. Rosnow and Fine (1976) make this point rather more strongly than we would: "the basis of gossip may or may not be known fact, but the basis of rumor is always unsubstantiated". The source of a rumor can sometimes be identified, but this will seldom diminish the rumor. In any case, gossip might be based on observation, or it might not; but a rumor necessarily has spread far beyond its initial source and thus for almost everyone who hears and retells a rumor, it is hearsay.

DOI: 10.1201/9781003401674-15

As a note, we should say that we will not be concerned with disinformation. The spread of disinformation would certainly follow the same patterns of diffusion of information and misinformation that we are discussing. Disinformation, however, has specific political or social purposes. In order to understand it, therefore, we would have to explore political and social issues beyond the scope of our particular concerns with knowledge and gossip.

RUMOR

All human communities are rife with rumor and gossip. Rumor, like gossip, exists intersubjectively—it exists within the interplay of social discourse and our mutually held beliefs. It is dispersed, and thus hard to kill and also hard to understand and grasp. This prompts the use of metaphors to describe it, like the current popular characterization of diffusion by infection, which we have argued is misleading and inadequate. In this chapter, we will explore some different kinds of metaphors in order to bring rumor and gossip more clearly into focus.

There are a number of metaphors for rumor that focus on its rate of diffusion. Rumors can be swift; they seem to fly from person to person. We often wonder how someone has so quickly heard a particular rumor. How did it travel? If asked how we heard some rumor, we can say 'A little bird told me.' Or we might say, 'I heard whispers.' The way rumors seem to move through a community also prompts personification; rumor becomes a kind of creature, sometimes a quite frightening creature. We find an example of this kind of personification in the poem 'Gossip' by Robert Graves:

> Gossip I heard in Mariposa town;
> The whispering ghosts of scandal walk the street,
> Eager to catch the innocent passer-by
> And drag him into an intimate talk.

Those who love tittle-tattle are transformed into 'whispering ghosts of scandal.' This even suggests that the gossipers, themselves, have become the gossip. And that is what rumor is: 'ghosts of scandal' that repeat their scandalous talk to those that they capture.

The Middle English poet, Geoffrey Chaucer, allegorically describes our social world as a house of rumors and tidings, ruled over by the goddess Fame. She hears everything, and in her allegorical form is a monster of many tongues, ears, and eyes. The story of the House of Fame is a kind of birdcage filled with tweeting, not unlike our online tweets. The story derives from the twelfth book of Ovid's *Metamorphosis*, in which the house of fame is a cacophony of "a thousand rumors" ("milia rumorum," 12.55).

These metaphors and personifications highlight the way in which rumor (and its attendant gossip) are both produced by us and yet exist somehow separate from us. The concept of information, as we argued in Part II, similarly involves us and yet seemingly exists separate from us. This pattern of involvement and separation is one of the primary sources of our confusion about gossip and rumor. It is also a source of the power of the idea of information, which seems to link the subjective and the objective. And it is what gives gossip and rumor its pernicious authority over us. It is as if the community is speaking about us with some special claim, and with at times great effect. Rumor can be difficult to resist and combat, regardless of its truth or falsity. We can feel powerless and it can seem unjust and destructive. Let us look at one more ancient figuration of rumor.

The great Roman poet Virgil can help us formulate a more comprehensive picture of rumor's oddness, and the inevitable entanglement of shared speech, gossip, rumor, and the social order. Aeneas, after fleeing from Troy, lands in North Africa and meets Dido, the queen of Carthage. He has been told that his fate lies in Italy, where he will found the city that will lead to the founding of Rome, but he feels the pull of the beautiful Dido. Dido calls her affair with Aeneas a marriage, "using the word to cloak her sense of guilt," as Robert Fagles translates the Latin. Her confession is both true and yet misleading. Since she was deceived by Juno to believe that Aeneas had consented to a marriage, it spawns a rumor that gathers form as it is spread throughout North Africa (*Aeneid* IV.219–248).

> Straightway Rumor flies through Libya's great cities,
> Rumor, swiftest of all the evils in the world.
> She thrives on speed, stronger for every stride,
> Slight with fear at first, soon soaring into the air
> She treads the ground and hides her head in the clouds.

Virgil turns rumor into a kind of god, a personification of human networks as an embodied divine force. The life of the rumor increases as it spreads, the exponential potential of a network transforming the slow beginning (slight with fear at first) into the speed of a bird. Rumor is a hybrid creature; walking on the ground amidst our lives but with her head in the clouds, she is not constrained by our pedestrian speeds (bold added for emphasis).

> Rumor is a goddess born of earth, a sister of giants, but herself a
>   monster:
> She is the last, they say, our Mother Earth produced.
> Bursting in rage against the gods, she bore a sister
> For Coeus and Enceladus: **Rumor, quicksilver afoot**
> **And swift on the wing, a monster, horrific, huge**
> **And under every feather on her body—what a marvel—**
> **And eye that never sleeps and as many tongues as eyes**
> **And as many raucous mouths and ears pricked up for news.**
> By night she flies aloft, between the earth and sky,
> Whirring across the dark, never closing her lids
> In soothing sleep. By day she keeps her watch,
> Crouched on a peaked roof or palace turret,
> Terrorizing the great cities, clinging as fast
> To her twisted lies as she clings to words of truth.
> (Bold added)

Rumor flies and terrorizes the great cities as if she were not made by and from their inhabitants. But who else sees and speaks with raucous mouths? Rumor is motivated by our anxieties, uncertainties, and desires. It is dispersed, and thus hard to counter. Rumor lives within a community and is expressive of it. In fact, rumor is a mocking version, a monstrous parody of all communities.

> And under every feather on her body - what a marvel -
> And eye that never sleeps and as many tongues as eyes
> And as many raucous mouths and ears pricked up for news.

The she-goddess Rumor emerges through our own talk and exists as the network of eyes, ears, and raucous mouths. She lives as a caricature of the community through which she is nurtured. The monster is a network given bodily form.

The rumor about the liaison between Arenas and Dido spreads and feeds the passions already alive in the heart of Numidian King Iarbas:

> Such talk the sordid goddess spreads on the lips of men,
> Then swerves in her course and heading straight for King Iarbas,
> Strokes his heart with hearsay, piling fuel on his fire.

Rumor sometimes offers confirmation of what we fear. In fact, we experience it as a kind of interface between the social order and our personal moral psychology. We too often react and believe rumors motivated by our own interests and passions. Part of rumor's power, her ways of reducing our belief, rests on the way she mixes truths and lies. We believe what we want to believe, prompted by a seeming confirmation coming from the world, from others, with an authority that is a mock version of the authority of the community. Rumor incites these however she can, often mixing both what is true with what is false.

> Terrorizing the great cities, clinging as fast
> To her twisted lies as she clings to words of truth.
> Now Rumor is in her glory, filling Africa's ears
> With tale on tale of intrigue, bruiting her song
> Of facts and falsehoods mingled.

Rumor's glory is her triumph over our reason and judgment. This is key. It strikes us as if it were an independent, external voice and force that prompts our reaction, sometimes against our better judgment. The diffusion of rumor within the community appears not as someone's opinion, but as the world speaking, and thus as something like a fact. We can see even from this description how rumor can seem like information that must be necessarily true. But, of course, this is not the case.

From Virgil's account, we can collect four critical aspects of rumor:

1. Rumor parodies the community. It presents to us a distorted picture of the social order.

2. People have many different motives and reasons for believing and responding, including passion and envy.

3. Rumor can be true, false, or even some mixture or amalgam of both. Since rumor need not be false, and our attitudes arise from our own prejudices and assumptions, our interests and fears, fact-checking, truth-labeling, and so on will seldom prevent its spread and influence.

4. Rumor seems to have a separate existence, a demonic power to which people react in various ways. It is less like a virus than it is like a kind of god that provokes, manipulates, and can be resisted, but often is not.

Virgil's monstrous goddess of rumor remains alive in modern times. She can spark and facilitate mass hysteria. Orson Welles' *War of the Worlds* 1938 radio play famously sparked a surprising panic that Martians were invading and conquering earth. Antisemitic enthusiasm, nurtured by rumors and prejudice, has continued to spark pogroms over the centuries (Wistrich, 2010). Witch trials still happen in popular culture. Property and investment bubbles expand and collapse because of many factors, one of which is rumors of various kinds (Aliber and Kindleberger, 2015; Reinhart and Rogoff, 2009). The recent COVID-19 reactions will at some point offer material for many investigations into mass hysteria (and political over-reach), although to say, that is also to risk a hysterical denial (Bagus et al., 2021, Frijters et al., 2021). Rumor is the imagination of a community. That imagination sometimes tracks what is happening in the world, and sometimes it distorts that into threat, fear, and self-delusion.

RUMORS AND INFORMATION DIFFUSION

Figuring rumor and information spread like a viral infection or as a monstrous god both characterize rumor as a power that is greater than any individual. It seems to have a life of its own. A virus, however, is a parasite, and infection can feed into an idea that rumor is what researchers have called "information pollution." The goddess of rumor is both a force external to us, but also a parody of us and our communities. We are fated to be afflicted by such monsters since we make them ourselves (or they are distorted versions of our communities). Of course, a viral metaphor can be mathematically modeled, while a multieyed and multimouthed god cannot. Nevertheless, Virgil's metaphor tells us more and shows us more carefully what rumor is. She cannot be killed without killing ourselves. The internet is itself a monstrous parody. In fact, this hybrid monster describes one aspect of the internet and web:

> And under every feather on her body—what a marvel—
> An eye that never sleeps and as many tongues as eyes
> And as many raucous mouths and ears pricked up for news.

The internet never sleeps. Its news moves from node to node, computer to computer, person to person. The web and OSNs merge into a body of images and eyes, tongues and voices; a raucous noise, endlessly available, never silent, a record of our own human noises, in which we mingle facts and falsehoods. This internet, web, and OSNs can be described as

Virgil's monstrous, demonic Rumor. The particularity of persons (eyes and mouths) fused into a collective whole.

As a rumor spreads, it ramifies into various strands. Tamotau Shibutani's excellent study of rumor remains an essential account of the non-linear patterns by which a rumor spreads. A rumor is "shaped, reshaped, and reinforced in a succession of communicative acts" (Shibutani, 1966). It is developed within a community, often in response to specific events. As such it can evolve into a kind of description and explanation of that situation. Consequently, Shibutani describes the spread of rumor as "the process of forming a definition of a situation" (Shibutani, 1966). We might replace 'definition' with 'description and understanding,' but otherwise this describes well how some rumors become part of a common understanding, part of public opinion. For Shibutani, rumor becomes a way of making sense of the world during times of stress and uncertainty, when the world does not seem to make sense. This is sometimes the case, although twisted and false explanations of what is happening can also occur. Conspiracies are invoked; dubious public statements about a virus and the proper response become sacrosanct, and remain so for some time even after they are debunked.[1]

Not all rumors need to be believed to be shared, just as we saw that misinformation is not posted or shared simply out of belief. Distortions and invented stories are common. In the 1960s, a rumor spread that Paul McCartney of the Beatles was dead, and that fact was hidden from the public. It was thought that you could find clues about his death in some songs and even on the album cover of Abbey Road. Maybe some people believed it. But even those who did not repeated the story. Such stories are sometimes called urban myths.

Cass Sunstein (2014), in his book *On Rumors*, highlights the role of belief in the diffusion of rumors. Sunstein, while acknowledging the many motives for gossip, defines rumor "to refer roughly to claims of fact about people, groups, events and institutions that has not been shown to be true." Rumors "move from one person to another, and hence have credibility not because direct evidence is available to support them, but because other people seem to believe them." These rumors are spread because they fit with the "prior convictions of those who accept them." There is no question that rumors sometimes spread in this way and for these reasons, but only sometimes. The motives for spreading rumors and gossip are as varied as the motives for any human action, as we discussed in Chapter 9. Recall the case, where a woman posted information online because of her dislike of Hilary Clinton and because of her desire to be seen as against her, regardless of the truth or falsity of the information (which she picked up from someone else).

Not only do the motives for gossiping and sharing rumors vary, our attitudes toward the rumors we hear vary. We might think: 'I don't believe this, but it is a good story.' Or 'I fear this is true, but I don't know.' Or 'sometimes this seems plausible and other times not.' Or 'This story makes me feel upset, but now I have no great confidence in it.' I may want to believe something is true. Or, on the other hand, I might just give lip service to some claim, fact, or idea.

If rumors are believed *in some sense*, what kind of sense is this? As Sunstein admits, we "lack direct or personal knowledge about the facts that underlie most of our judgments." He does not draw any conclusions from this admission. This simple fact suggests that much of what we believe is something like rumors; these beliefs are, at least, part of our acculturation and personal histories. It is rumored that the earth is hurtling through space, while the sun and solar system and galaxy are also hurtling through space. Some people know this from evidence and a solid understanding of physics. But for many it is mere rumor. And many others do not know it at all. There are also rumors that the moon landing was staged in Hollywood.

Philosopher David Coady (2006), on the other hand, argues that rumors have a reasonable epistemic claim on us:

> If you hear a rumor, it is not only prima facie evidence that it has been thought plausible by a large number of people, it is also prima facie evidence that it has been thought plausible by a large number of reliable people. And that really is prima facie evidence that it is true.

While Coady's description of a network as a filter through which true rumors are the most likely to be shared might sometimes be the case, it certainly is not always the case. Rumors are not just spread because they are believed, but for a vast range of motives and purposes, as we have discussed in Chapter 9. An information gatekeeper will naturally share the gossip and rumors that will satisfy the group of which he is a part, or, for more personal reason, in order to sustain his own self-understanding. Acting as a gatekeeper, for example, can provide someone with social status and authority. Building upon the work of Ma et al. (2014) and Lane et al. (2019), Metzger et al. (2021) comment:

> In this sense, the desire to act as a gatekeeper of information or an opinion leader may be a fundamental motivation for news

sharing. Indeed, research has found that self-perceptions of opinion leadership influence users' news sharing intention (Ma et al.
2014) and that political expression enhances people's motivations
to self-present as politically active on social media.

(Lane et al., 2019)

Information becomes a commodity, the value of which is to draw attention to oneself, to become a source of influence, and to gain prestige
by means of that influence. Metzger et al. (2021) quote Bernard Guerin
and Yoshihiko Miyazaki's (2006) study, in which they conclude that the
"primary function of telling rumors, gossip, and urban legends is not to
impart information to the listener or alleviate listener anxiety about the
topic, but to entertain or keep the listener's attention, thereby enhancing
social relationships." Gossip and the spreading of rumors allow someone
to perform as a kind of public poet, using information as a means of
entertaining others. Motives are mixed and varied. Truth may have little
to do with why rumors are spread. Metzger et al. (2021) go on to suggest
that people engage in rumor as a way to collectively reduce uncertainty,
enhance interpersonal relationships, and feel positive about themselves
(Bordia and DiFonzo, 2005), as may be the case with sharing news misinformation as well. What might matter more than adequate epistemic
justification is plausibility, "the perceived credibility of a claim itself" as
Axel Gelfert (2018) phrases it.

There is no particular reason to imagine that if a rumor is repeated
often within a community, this means that it have been established as true
by "a large number of reliable people," as Coady claims. More broadly, culture, itself, might be construed as the collection of accepted rumors by
some community or set of communities. In some cases, a rumor might
express the anxieties or hatreds of some group. Antisemitic rumors have
often been grounded in such feelings, as well as fitting within a cultural
history of scapegoating. Attacks against Jews in Europe and Russia have
recurrently been instigated by the hysterical spread of a rumor called
blood libel. Blood libel is the belief that Jews killed and used the blood of
Christian children to make matzahs for Passover (Teter, 2020). The most
widely distributed antisemitic tract in the 20th century is the infamous
Protocols of the Learned Elders of Zion, published first in Russia in 1903,
which purports to be a record of a series of secret meetings of Jewish lead-
ers who plan on taking over the world. Although they were publicly proved

in 1921 to be a forgery, the book and its paranoid antisemitic fantasy continue to circulate throughout the world.

The longer a rumor has been around, the more deeply it has penetrated a community. Such rumors gain a cultural force, expressing the very authority of the group. Consequently, a widely shared rumor creates a natural pressure within a community toward conformity, and thus acceptance. The truth of the rumor is not at issue; its social role in the community is paramount. The cost and energy to resist the rumor can increase such that it is easier to simply accept it. Such an act of acceptance "may be a passive and inevitable act, whereas rejection may be an active operation that undoes the initial passive acceptance" (Gilbert et al. 1993). Some rumors, especially if they are about something that might be determined as true or false, or at least more likely or less likely, might legitimately encourage our belief or trust; but others will not.

A rumor is often prompted by an event. Over time, if the rumor continues to circulate, becoming reinforced through retelling, it becomes part of the shared memory of a community. Such rumors become part of what we call *common knowledge*. The historian Chris Wickham (1998) examines a 12th-century property dispute in Tuscany that involved appeals to hearsay and gossip that were understood at the time as constituting common knowledge. He comments that medieval court cases, "like modern ones, generally used written proofs, if there were any relevant ones, and local knowledge if . . . there was not." This local knowledge is shared in various ways. It constitutes a subject of discussion and debate as and through gossip. Legally, local knowledge was categorized into three kinds:

> In Italy, as elsewhere, local knowledge was sharply distinguished between *per visum*, direct witnessing, *per auditum*, merely hearing about it from someone, and *publica fama*, what everybody knew, common knowledge. Direct witnessing was the only fully legally acceptable knowledge, but *publica fama* ran a close second; it was when everybody knew, so it was socially accepted.

Direct witnessing, while not always trustworthy, at least allows someone to be held responsible for the description of what is witnessed. What you hear from someone else is, of course, hearsay. Although, again in such a situation you can be held responsible for what you heard and you can identify from whom you heard it. *Publica fama*, however, is not like this. It has no clear source, and no one can be held responsible. I might treat my opinion as knowledge, but it is still my opinion. But it is not only that. I might confirm my opinion by asking my neighbor. The authority of such local knowledge, however, rests on it being generally shared by members of the community.

Common knowledge overlaps with two other kinds of shared beliefs. The first kind of shared belief is what we call public opinion or sentiment. Any community consists of shared and competing kinds of public understanding, moods, and attitudes. These understandings are based on various kinds of beliefs and propositional knowledge—about public events, history, technology, economic facts, and so on. None of what is believed needs to be true. Public opinion and the facts and ideas that provide its specific content are shaped and infused with competing fears, expectations, anxieties, desires, hopes, prejudices, commitments, and so on. This is often the realm of political contest.

In modern mass societies, especially democracies, public opinion is sovereign. Such opinion may involve kinds of public reasoning, but it involves much else. Like all rumor, public opinion is both public and personal in its content and diffusion. Lincoln understood this very well. Lincoln scholar David Zarefsky (1994) explains it this way:

> Lincoln's theory of public opinion reflected the paradoxical nature of persuasion in a democracy. The people rule not through their wants and desires of the moment, but through a durable public sentiment that transcends individuals and is the product of history and culture. Politicians and orators must respect this source of the people's power and yet not regard its hold over them as absolute. They cannot deny or discredit it, but they must seek to define, interpret, and stretch it. The people's will expressed through durable public sentiment checks against the people's will expressed through the momentary wish of a majority.

The political reality of any society consists of these vectors of public opinion, arising out of the past, reflecting current conditions, and oriented toward particular future possibilities. Lincoln understood democratic leadership as requiring a responsiveness to this opinion. No democratic leader, he thought, should dictate to people, but should consider a sensitive understanding of this opinion. Change evolved through public sentiment. Leadership attempted to persuade and inspire various elements of this sentiment. As he said during the Ottawa debate with Stephen Douglas:

> Public sentiment is everything,' he was expressing his own first principles of advocacy and of governance.

Common knowledge also includes a second kind of shared belief, what we can characterize as background on implicit knowledge. Let us quote Hayek (1960, 2011) again:

> Not all knowledge in this sense is part of our intellect, nor is our intellect the whole of our knowledge. Our habits and skills, our emotional attitudes, our tools, and our institutions—all are in this sense adaptations to past experiences which have grown up by selective elimination of less suitable conduct. They are as much an indispensable foundation of successful action as is our conscious knowledge.

Culture is a depository of shared knowledge. And our personal acculturation within our families, regions, communities, schools, and environment provide us with the equipment, senses of know-how, and a scope of possibilities and expectations that constitute our lives and world. Much of this is simply understood; it is implicit. The philosopher John McDowell (1998) describes a similar range of implicit knowledge, distinguishing it not from the intellect, like Hayek, but linking it with linguistic competence:

> [M]uch of the knowledge that enters into our possession of the world, even though we have it through language, is not something we have been told. It need never have enunciated in our hearing; rather, we find it implicit in the cognitive ways of proceeding into which we were initiated when we learned our language. This is knowledge that we grasp through language but which we did not acquire "by understanding a linguistic production".

McDowell is pointing out that as we learn our language we are learning about the world: that language and world come at us together, and we grasp one relative to the other in a kind of continual feedback loop of accommodation and adaptation. We live amidst public opinion and implicit background knowledge. This kind of knowledge is open to question, and can be modified, rejected, and validated. But this only happens under duress, in the face of challenges or because of some kind of failure. For many of us, our opinions and the cultural knowledge are inherited and, while not as labile, unstable, and of the moment, are taken up as the rumors of our cultures and communities.

CONCLUSION

Gossip and rumor operate within the substrate of knowing and understanding that constitutes the domain between public opinion and background knowledge. Gossip is a more localized and personal arena of exchange, while rumor involves both this local context and broader context. Gossip creates a feedback loop between the personal and the public domain, ranging from a community of two to communities of many. Rumor, and the gossip that nurtures it, exists as the way any community integrates public opinion with the common knowledge that forms a background for everyday action and judgment. That integration can be facilitated through epistemic criteria, but its dominant motives and facilitating forces are psychological and social. Thus, rumors can help make intelligible complex events, the form and effects of which can be hard to fathom from amidst uncertainty. But rumors can also be fueled by fear, shaped by prejudice, leading to hysteria and murderous rage.

Even though gossip and rumor are spread primarily for personal and social reasons, their truth value can be tested and evaluated. We might discover that we have good reason to believe something or reject it. Our background knowledge is like this too. But gossip is more conscious and lives in our awareness of ourselves and others. This allows it to function in the complex social ways it does. It is also what allows it to distort, hurt, and lead to misunderstandings or worse. Gossip, and much of what we call misinformation, is shared and matters in this in-between arena linking background knowledge and propositional claims. In the next chapter, we will examine gossip and rumor in more detail, providing an account of the discursive grammar of gossip as a social practice.

NOTE

1 See Frijters et al. (2021).

REFERENCES

Aliber, Robert Z., Charles P. Kindleberger, and Robert N. McCauley. *Manias, panics, and crashes: A history of financial crises.* Palgrave Macmillan, 2015.

Bagus, Philipp, José Antonio Peña-Ramos, and Antonio Sánchez-Bayón. "COVID-19 and the political economy of mass hysteria." *International Journal of Environmental Research and Public Health* 18.4 (2021): 1376.

Bordia, Prashant, and Nicholas DiFonzo. "Psychological motivations in rumor spread." In G. A. Fine, C. Heath and V. Campion-Vincent (Eds.), *Rumor mills: The social impact of rumor and legend* (pp. 87–101). Aldine Press, 2005.

Coady, David. "Rumour has it." *International Journal of Applied Philosophy* 20.1 (2006): 41–53.

Frijters, Paul, Gigi Foster, and Michael Baker. *The great Covid panic: what happened, why, and what to do next.* Brownstone Institute, 2021.

Gelfert, Axel. "Fake news: A definition." *Informal Logic* 38.1 (2018): 84–117.

Gilbert, Daniel T., Romin W. Tafarodi, and Patrick S. Malone. "You can't not believe everything you read." *Journal of Personality and Social Psychology* 65.2 (1993): 221.

Guerin, Bernard, and Yoshihiko Miyazaki. "Analyzing rumors, gossip, and urban legends through their conversational properties." *The Psychological Record* 56 (2006): 23–33.

Hayek, Friedrich A. *The constitution of liberty.* The collected works of F. A. Hayek Book 1 edited by Ronald Hamowy, University of Chicago Press, 1960, 2011.

Lane, Daniel S., et al. "Social media expression and the political self." *Journal of Communication* 69.1 (2019): 49–72.

Ma, Long, Chei Sian Lee, and Dion Hoe-Lian Goh. "Understanding news sharing in social media: An explanation from the diffusion of innovations theory." *Online Information Review* 38.5 (2014): 598–615.

McDowell, J. (1998). "Knowledge by hearsay." In *Meaning, knowledge, and reality,* Harvard University Press (pp. 414–444), Cambridge, 1998.

Metzger, Miriam J., et al. "From dark to light: The many shades of sharing misinformation online." *Media and Communication* 9.1 (2021): 134–143.

Reinhart, Carmen, and Kenneth S. Rogoff. *This time is different: Eight centuries of financial folly.* Princeton University Press, 2009.

Rosnow, Ralph L., and Gary A. Fine. *Rumor and gossip: The social psychology of hearsay.* Elsevier, 1976.

Shibutani, Tamotsu. *Improvised news.* Ardent Media, 1966.

Sunstein, Cass R. *On rumors: How falsehoods spread, why we believe them, and what can be done.* Princeton University Press, 2014.

Teter, Magda. *Blood Libel: On the trail of an antisemitic myth.* Harvard University Press, 2020.

Wickham, Chris. "Gossip and resistance among the medieval peasantry." *Past & Present* 160 (1998): 3–24.

Wistrich, Robert S. *A lethal obsession: Anti-semitism from antiquity to the global Jihad.* Random House, 2010.

Zarefsky, David. "Public sentiment is everything": Lincoln's view of political persuasion." *Journal of the Abraham Lincoln Association* 15.2 (1994): 23–40.

CHAPTER 12

A Discursive Grammar of Traditional Gossip

INTRODUCTION

When people talk, they mostly gossip. David Hume exclaims in a letter: "must our whole discourse be a continual series of gossiping stories and idle remarks?" Gossip is often petty, bitter, and trivial. Gossip is the hearsay of everyday conversation, from which rumor is born. On the other hand, gossip is also a primary mode of social negotiation. As Robin Dunbar (1996) argues, it is a sublated version of primate social grooming, but its value as a mode of discourse and a social practice remains labile. Gossip is bad, vicious, and distorting; or else it is bad, but fun, seductive, uncontrollable; or it is useful, a mode of practical reasoning about people and situations; or it is good, a form of public opinion, a way the powerless undermine the powerful, a facilitator of community and intimacy. Gossip can be any of these and often more than one at the same time: social life is endlessly ironic. Hence, it is a topic not only for sociology but also for novels, which rumor imaginary lives and gossip about gossip.

Gossip is the fundamental form of communal storytelling; all other forms of public storytelling are derived from it. Novels formalize gossip into art primarily by means of its particular narrative possibilities and the sympathy it engenders for its primary characters. Joyce's *Ulysses*, for example, is a compendium of kinds of gossip transformed into art, from the gossip of consciousness (the novel's occasional stream of

DOI: 10.1201/9781003401674-16

consciousness sounds an awful lot like a kind of self-gossiping) to the way rumors of the present and the past constitute the world that the protagonist Leopold Bloom travels through. Because of the importance of gossip in literature, we will use examples from novels and plays in our derivation of gossip's discursive grammar. It will provide us with clear and sophisticated examples. The use of literature in the examination of our social lives, and in scientifically infused sociology, is also championed by Jon Elster (1989, 1999), both in *Nuts and Bolts* and in *Alchemies of the Mind*. We feel we are in good company, therefore, in using the resources of literature to develop our understanding of gossip and the spread of information.

Any particular bit of gossip is not simply a kind of statement with a particular kind of content. It is part of a social practice. As a social practice, gossip and gossiping is bound to individual attitudes and interpersonal reactions. It is not simply a discursive linguistic practice. Gossip is dynamic and produces effects and events of social commitment and understanding, not relative to facts, but relative to shared beliefs about other people. Hence, in order to understand what gossip is, we need a description of that practice. As a social practice, gossip consists of an ill-defined range of discursive modes, from first-person observations and explanations to vague hearsay. Gossip, therefore, has both a social and a discursive grammar. It is something we say, but if we are to understand gossip we must understand the practice of gossiping. This is again why it lacks anything like a *necessary* logical form. It can take many forms, and certainly falls into patterns, but these patterns are not necessary.

The development of such a discursive grammar, however, is not a purely inductive research project. The goal is to derive a description of the essential normative characteristics of gossip as practiced within the communities of which we are a part. Those characteristics might be modified, by the further extension of the grammar to cover cases not at first envisioned. The evidence from which the grammar of gossip can be built is just what any competent speaker and social actor within a community would recognize as gossip. There will be liminal cases, of course. Relative to such cases, the ordinary discussions that language speakers might have about what counts as the normative sense of gossip would be what the theorist would also pursue. This makes the description of gossip contingent on the normative practices within any community. But those practices are in fact what we are trying to understand, not some theoretical, putatively necessary description, the relevance of which could only be determined by examining actual practices and modifying that definition relative to those practices. And that is tantamount to replacing a logical description with a discursive description of practice. Unlike the early work of Allport and Postman (1947), our goal once again is not to understand the psychology behind gossip, but to describe the discursive grammar of the practice (the patterns, norms, tendencies), so that we can compare that grammar to the practices of online information exchange.

Imagine that gossip is a practice not dissimilar from a game like American football. You could develop an interesting account of a particular game or series of games by investigating and describing the psychology of the players, the coaches, and the audience. You might also offer a sociological account of how football fits with post-World War II American culture. You could show how it has become embedded within the economics, history, and social practices and institutions of American society. These psychological and sociological analyses of the game would be interesting and revealing. They are also parasitic on the game itself, on what the game is, how it is played, its forms, grammar, and structure. Like any game, it is organized through a set of rules that are occasionally altered and adjusted. The game is played in particular ways. The current mode of play has evolved over time. The game has an internal logic, again shaped by rules, by the ability of the players, by practice regimes, by the structures by which various teams are organized, and by the creativity, intelligence, and leadership skills of coaches, and so on. There are offensive and defensive plays of great complexity, and ways of seeing and reacting to these plays. And these describe a kind of dynamic, responsive set of patterns; a grammar of play. The practice of football as it is played on the field remains the necessary and fundamental thing to be described. What is true of football is true of gossip. Our goal is to describe the essential elements of how gossip is played, separate from psychological and social concerns.

In what follows, we will provide an analytical characterization of the essential aspects of gossip as a discursive practice. We have identified four essential patterns. We will derive each pattern as briefly as possible, providing its grammatical form relative to a few examples. For each pattern, we will also include a subsection in which we will explore and elaborate more fully the grammatical form we have identified. There are two subsidiary patterns of gossip, and a number of variations which we will also describe after we have established the essential four patterns.

THE SOCIAL AND DISCURSIVE FORM OF GOSSIP

The practice of gossip can be characterized using four characteristics, which we will call grammatical/logical patterns:

    I. Irresponsible Speech

    II. Unwarranted Assertion

    III. Exclusion of Target of Gossip

    IV. Masked Implication and Import

These four patterns describe the differences between gossip and ordinary face-to-face discourse. We should all be able to recognize these patterns.

PATTERN I: IRRESPONSIBLE SPEECH

Basic Form

What kind of talk is gossip? Gossip exchanged lacks adequate warrant or justification; hence it is a form of hearsay. Despite its lack of warrant it is often presented and understood as if obviously true. We treat gossip as if we already had all the relevant knowledge to determine the truth of the gossip, of what we say and hear as we exchange observations and speculations.

In gossiping, we exchange impressions. We share things we see, or think we see. We do not determine what is actually happening, we simply say things like—'I saw him park his car near her apartment,' suggesting in saying that he is, therefore, visiting her. What we say may or may not be true. Similarly, we gossip by reporting what we have heard or what we have heard as hearsay. We say: 'Manager x said this to y.' Maybe manager x did say this or maybe she did not. Regardless, we pass it on.

While gossip can have specific origins, for example, in things seen by a particular person, no one is understood as responsible for what is said. Gossip is not speech for which anyone stands as a guarantor. One says, for example, "I am just telling you what I saw" or "this is what people are saying." Anyone can speak gossip because no one needs to be responsible for what is said or meant. In gossiping, it is as if we are exchanging quotations or our impressions of something, and thus we are simply saying 'This is what it seems.' When we gossip we act, or pretend to act, not as speakers or agents, but as vehicles, conduits, pathways. We have not confirmed what we are sharing when we gossip; or our confirmations are cursory, self-serving, and weak. We are not speaking as authorities separate from the quasi-authority founded in that we have seen or heard something (even if second, third, or fourth-hand).

Since we often act as if no one is responsible for what is said (and we are often vague about what might be meant by what is said), we do not often question the veracity of gossip. We do not determine its warrant (at least not rigorously or in good faith), especially if it fits what we want to believe or confirms our assumptions. All of this has the effect of lowering our resistance to sharing what we have heard, thus, facilitating its spread. Consequently, if no one is really responsible, then we can use what we hear for our own purposes; we react to it irresponsibly. Our self-interest and our self-doubts become sovereign in our interpretations and responses.

Further Exploration of Irresponsible Speech

The key observation here is that no one is responsible for gossip; it is as if it is always quoted, at second hand, thus hearsay. When I gossip, I do not stand behind my words (I am simply reporting). Because of this, gossiping talk can seem idle, pointless, and futile. Gossip is often exclusively defined as idle talk. This is a mistake. People gossip about political situations at work or in families, for example, that concern them. Gossip can be idle but it need not be. To make the point more carefully—the irresponsibility of gossip encourages the sense that one is just talking to talk. Heidegger (1962) in a comment in *Being and Time* makes clear how idle talk should be understood as irresponsible talk:

> Idle talk is the possibility of understanding everything without previously making the thing one's own . . . idle talk is something which anyone can take up; it not only releases one from the task of genuinely understanding, but develops an undifferentiated kind of intelligibility, for which nothings is closed off any longer.

Idle talk is one kind of irresponsible talk, but not the only kind. Similarly, idle talk is one kind of gossip, but not the only kind.

Another form of irresponsible speech (or we might also call it second-hand speech) goes all the way back to Homer. Homer and other Archaic Greek poets understood gossip of a certain sort as their own particular concern. Gregory Nagy, in *The Best of the Achaeans*, observes that "what the poets share is not knowledge but the stories of memory" (1997). He brings this out well in his translation of a passage from the *Iliad*:

> You are goddesses; you are always present, and you know
>   everything,
> But we [poets] only hear the kleos and know nothing.

(II 485–486)

What the poets share is not knowledge per se, but stories of memory. These poets are gossipers of what they hear from the gods (so they claim): they hear the glories (pl *kleos*) of men, which they memorialize. Even when translated as 'glory,' *kleos* describes not only the worthiness of the deed but the memory of it—so it also means 'fame.' The etymological sense of *kleos* is "that which is heard" (from kluo 'hear')—thus, to hear the muses, to hear the rumors of men, to hear the renown, the fame, and, thus, the glory of doing that which is worthy of remembrance.

> From the *Odyssey*:
> But when they had their fill of drinking and eating,
> the Muse impelled the singer to sing the glories [**kleos**, pl] of men
> from the story-thread which had at that time a glory [**kleos**]
>   reaching the vast heavens.

(NAGY, VIII 72–74)

The poet gives voice, infused by the Muse, to a story-thread, and in so doing memorializes the glories associated with particular names within the community of those who hear and value these glories. *Kleos* is gossip sifted and idealized; or, maybe, gossip parodies *kleos*, but in either case gossip is more fable than history.

PATTERN II: UNWARRANTED ASSERTION

Basic Form

We often gossip about things about which we know very little; or we gossip about things for which we have no adequate reasons for belief. Consequently, gossip is talk for which we lack adequate warrant or justification; hence it is a form of hearsay.

Gossip is not part of a practice of epistemological evaluation. Rather, it is part of a social economy in which beliefs and impressions are exchanged. It constitutes an economy because these exchanges are acts of social significance. Sharing gossip indicates or encourages an intimacy, a sense of trust, and thus can encourage a kind of alliance, even if momentary. Only when the gossiping becomes reciprocal and frequent is the social relationship (facilitating an alliance, for example) fully established. This is similar to grooming practices in chimpanzee groups, as we mentioned earlier (Dunbar has developed a theory about the evolutionary development of language from this observation). Consequently, people arbitrate and evaluate gossip relative to their beliefs and anxieties about things. As a consequence, it encourages facile belief, partly because of its lack of warrant. Gossip confirms prejudices more readily than it counters them.

Because gossip tends to be evaluated relative to beliefs and anxieties rather than to states of affairs, it is difficult to counter by evidence or counter-statement. (This does not mean that it is not about states of affairs, only that people's beliefs and anxieties about something matter more in how they respond, take up, and repeat gossip.) Because of this, one fights gossip with more gossip, not with facts or rational inquiry. By filling the channels of social gossip with new gossip and counter-gossip one creates noise and alternate descriptions. Gossip displaces gossip in the way that Hume argues affections displace affections (and for a similar reason). This is an important fact to remember when thinking about the role and forms of gossip online (Hume, 1993, 1999).

Further Exploration of Unwarranted Assertions

Let us summarize the logical grammar of gossip at this point. Because no one is responsible for what is said and meant, gossip exists in *the exchange and sharing*. Gossip can sometimes be true, but its truth is nothing to believe, since we have no warrant to believe it (yet). In the best case, gossip is unjustified true belief. Even when its source is known, gossip functions as gossip because no one is responsible for its particular claims. It circulates through a self-reinforcing mode of exchange. In gossiping, no one speaks in their own voice, they simply pass the information on. Gossip understood relative to these two patterns becomes more of an event that happens to people, than an action that people do; and so, people take it as something in the world, a kind of fact to which to react as much as it is also an opinion to dispute.

PATTERN III: EXCLUSION OF TARGET OF GOSSIP
Basic Form
Gossip is often defined as a conversation in which the target of that conversation is absent and cannot, therefore, take part in it. This definition is

misleading. I can tell a friend of mine what people are saying about her. In so doing, I share with her a bit of gossip about her. She is present. Her absence is not required for me to share this gossip. What is required, however, is her silence within the gossip conversation. She can protest, but that is outside the gossiping. She would be commenting about the gossip. She has, in effect, no voice in the conversation. She has become a spectator, even if a protesting one.

In gossiping, people often share secrets, and in so doing they share private concerns in a public forum. The sharing of privacy, usually of someone else's privacy, encourages a sense of intimacy with those with whom we share the gossip at the expense of the privacy of the target. The consequence of the exclusion and silencing of target removes one source of resistance to what is said about that person. The target of the gossip is often treated as if they were mere tokens in some larger game or as if they were simply objects of our voyeuristic fascination.

The exclusion (silence or silencing) of the target reinforces the community of gossipers at the expense of the silenced or silent target. This exclusion reinforces the inclusion of those who gossip into a kind of discursive community. This community may be very short-lived. Gossip, therefore, facilitates the formation of a community of intimacy, focused on a common friend or enemy.

Further Exploration of Exclusion of Target of Gossip

Community

Gossiping is a social activity, between friends, acquaintances, who live in some shared context, or in some kind of community. A community, no matter how superficial or attenuated, can arise around gossip itself, reflecting a certain set of shared interests, fears, anxieties, desires, aspirations, and so on. In addition, friendships and social groups are bound together through gossip. There is some evidence that negative, critical gossip is more commonly exchanged with close friends, than with co-workers and casual friends (Grosser et al., 2010; Farley, 2019). In some case, sharing of negative gossip would require a higher level of mutual trust between those sharing that gossip (Ellwardt, 2019). One is always vulnerable to exposure and exclusion. Sommerfeld et al. (2007) found that people are sensitive about their reputation in a group, and show more pro-sociality if interacting with someone known to gossip. People will privilege gossip even when they know from experience that the gossip is incorrect. The pervasive practices of gossip within any social group pressure individuals toward conformity with the understood beliefs and norms of the group. One risks the loss of reputation, status, and inclusion if one challenges the dominant sentiments of any particular small social group (Coleman, 1990; Merry, 1984).

Victims

The exclusion and silencing of the target of gossip removes one source of resistance to what is said about that target. The absent or silent target becomes an object, antagonist, or scapegoat. French theorist, Roland Barthes (1978) describes the target of gossip as reduced to a third-person position, becoming voiceless, denied the inter-locative powers of the first or second person. The target has no voice in the conversation, even theoretically. The target becomes depersonalized, more an *it* than a *person* (*Lover's Discourse*, 2010).

This discursive pattern is overtly manifest in the way gossip can be used to attack the socially vulnerable. All of us recognize the tendency, as Susan Farley (2019) describes it, "for low-status members of a group to be target of gossip" (Farley cites Eder and Enke, 1991; Ellwardt et al., 2012; McDonald et al., 2007). While those of low status can also gossip about those socially superior to them, they remain vulnerable and weak within the social order. Within any social group, scapegoating is always a threat that can be used against those who have insecure social power and status.

Self-Gossip

We gossip about those who are absent or silent. Gossip is a conversation about a person not involved in the conversation. If this is true, then we should be unable to gossip about ourselves, because we are neither absent nor silent; we are necessarily in and of the conversation. While the target of gossip must be somehow disjunct from the conversation, we should not conclude from this that we do not gossip about ourselves. This variation of gossip is critical to how we interact online, although it is an extension of a very common self-centered behavior. We will defer our discussion of offline and online self-gossip to Chapter 14.

PATTERN IV: MASKED IMPLICATION AND IMPORT

Basic Form

When we gossip, we are not taking responsibility for what we say. As seen in the pattern of irresponsible speech, we can mask our purposes when we share gossip. We seemingly highlight what we see or the literal sense of what we overhear, leaving the implications for others to draw. Consequently, we can use gossip to deceive by implication, protected behind a mask of innocence and obviousness. If I say, I saw Robert park his car near the house of ‹You-know-who›, I am not just reporting an observation. I am making a suggestion: implying a secret assignation. In this case, I am pretending simply to share a bit of information, telling you just what I saw. But what I mean is not quite what I say. Gossiping encourages us (and allows us) to understand statements relative to the inferences we draw from them. In other words, gossip as a social practice is often governed by a concern for secondary effects. Gossip prompts the imagination; it insinuates, implies, triggers associations, casts aspersions.

Further Exploration of Masked Implication and Import
Manipulation (Misinformation)
The implications and import of gossip target our fears, desires, anxieties, aspirations. In other words, gossip targets or affects the whole range of human psychology. Gossip suggests, implies, triggers associations, casts aspersions. We often gossip by presenting the appearances of something masked within an atmosphere of implications. A famous example is the way Iago gossips (although his gossip is mock gossip and purely manipulative) about Desdemona and Casio to Othello. Iago first starts Othello's interest with a negative comment about Cassio. He then suggests something by refusing to say what he is thinking. This is pure play-acting. Pretending reluctance, he describes a nefarious possibility by pretending to say that it cannot be the case.

Iago, on seeing Cassio leave Desdemona, says to the Moor, as if in exclamation: "Ha, I like that not."
Oth: what dost thou say?
Iago: nothing my lord, or if—I know not what.
Oth: Was not that Cassio parted from my wife?
Iago: Cassio, my lord? . . . no, sure, I cannot think it.

That he would sneak away so guilty-like,
Seeing you coming.

Oth: I do believe 'twas he.

. . . .

When Cassio left my wife: what didst not like?

(III.3.35–42; 114)

Othello takes what Iago says as innocent observation: gossip without ulterior motive. He is obviously wrong about this. Iago teases with implication, his innuendo prompts Othello's doubt and imagination; but Iago's gossip remains of impressions. It is imaginative in motive and implication, but not in what is stated—or not stated. The very obviousness of what he says gives his comments a seeming innocence that only furthers their power of suggestion. Iago's attitude is pretense, which is common in even ordinary gossip. Someone offers a pretend cautionary proviso—'I am just telling you what I saw, I don't mean anything by it.' Gossip is often manipulative in just this way. It is not simply an exchange of explicit information, but *the manipulation of possible interpretations.* Iago invokes a possible interpretation of Cassio's actions and behavior, only to pretend to deny it, and then asking what else can it mean. He relies on invoking an emotional response in Othello, triggering his fear and doubt that he is loved, allowing him to draw Iago's seemingly resisted conclusion.

Gossip as Low-Level Practical Reasoning

The destructive manipulation of gossip by Iago is possible because gossip is naturally a part of a low-level practice of social reasoning. We often share gossip as a way of understanding the behavior of those around us. While gossip can be true and used for rational ends, it is usually distorted, superficial, deforming, and defaming. It is founded in what is seen or heard; gossiping usually involves the sharing of what seems. That seeming is fitted with anxieties or resentments and comes to illustrate these. Arguments are formed out of these illustrations, confirming or undermining various beliefs. Because of this illustrative quality, gossip can at best have a kind of sifting categorizing quality. Gossip can prompt, as is with Othello's response to Iago, a recognition, even if prejudicial and false. When we gossip we share the appearance of things, cast and fitted with implications. Gossip prompts belief, despite its lack of warrant.

We do not arbitrate or evaluate the claims of gossip through an investigation of what is the case; that would undermine the conversational context and situation of gossip. We arbitrate and evaluate gossip relative to our beliefs, fears, desires, and so forth. Consequently, gossip confirms prejudices more readily than it counters them. For example:

I heard that she was leaving him.
Oh, I know, but it has always been bad.
Yes, I heard that too, such a shame, though since they seemed
   so right.

Well, I heard that he was a bit of a user.
She always does like that type.
She does, doesn't she?

Does she like that type of person? Such a conversation is a kind of sifting of judgments and observations that results in a consensus between the interlocutors. That consensus constitutes an agreement about their judgment of their friend. They are not changing their mind, but confirming publicly what both purport to already believe. The prompt is the action of their friend to leave her boyfriend. Their gossiping in effect situates that event within their previous understanding. This is a common mode of gossip-reasoning: a public reconfirmation of previous beliefs relative to a new event.

Gossip, therefore, would be better described as a parody of reasoning, since it often relies on and invokes prejudice, presents appearance with little concern for veracity, prompting the confirmation of dubious beliefs, and often producing scapegoats, in order to build or confirm intimacy and community. Gossip is a parody of practical reasoning in the way that obsession is a parody of love.[1]

A GENERAL PICTURE OF GOSSIP

We can collect these descriptions of gossip into two fundamental characterizations:

1. Gossip is more expressive of the community of gossipers than it is of the target of the gossip.

2. What is said in gossip, because of the irresponsibility in which it is exchanged and its lack of warrant, and because of the way gossip is dispersed and held within the community of gossip exchange, floats free from responsible counter-statement.

While gossip is often about states of affairs, it also invokes and provokes desires, vanity, distress, and anxieties. Gossip has no foundation or warrant that can be readily examined; it is by definition irresponsible speech, and thus bounded only by its transmission and the dispositions of a community to accept it. Small face-to-face communities, especially within cultures oriented toward honor and reputation, police themselves through gossip. Gossip is thus often a mode of social control and stabilization. The fear of being shamed or losing reputation induces conformity. Gossip is a kind of social mode of governance.

The volatility of gossip can be checked by the face-to-face nature of such communities, and limited by the stricter proprieties organizing life within clans and families. When breakdowns do happen in such communities they tend to be violent and extreme. See, for example, *Fanshen*, William Hinton's remarkable historical account of the breakdown of the traditional order in a Chinese village during the Chinese Revolution. Propriety, a normative pattern of behavioral constraint, infused with moral overtones, dampens the disruptive powers of gossip, which is often motivated by resentments and directed toward particular targets. When propriety breaks down through social change or ideological fervor, as in the Chinese Revolution, and even more so in Cultural Revolution, gossip becomes an unchecked form of social revenge and power. (See "Red Terror," Macfarquhar et al., 2006). Similar cultural conditions have been created by OSNs, leading to similar breakdowns in propriety facilitated by gossip.

One check on gossip in face-to-face communities, as we have mentioned, is social propriety, an accepted set of norms and standards of behavior governing everyday interactions among people within a community. They are forms of custom. Proprieties, even if misguided, express forms of respect. But they can be abused. Bad intentions and actions can be disguised behind proper manners, behind the proprieties of outward behavior. Corruption and manipulation can be hidden behind the decorous behavior. In such societies gossip can sometimes be used to puncture the masks of propriety. At other times, it can be used to undermine the status of those who would attempt to expose those who are corrupt and manipulate from positions of authority.

Gossip expresses forms of authority in the way that secret knowledge or propaganda can: a comment here and there, a casual observation by someone with authority, and someone can become ostracized and rejected. Proprieties can be abused and they tend to conserve inequalities. Gossip, as Tocqueville rightly understood, forms the context for egalitarian societies, which are stabilized socially and relative to individual anxiety by a tendency for individuals to fit themselves within mass beliefs, within forms of social gossip as opposed to structures of propriety. Proprieties and gossip can stand in opposition, as well as the former serving as a constraint on the latter.

Gossip and propriety constitute two complementary aspects of an interlocking social economy. However, gossip, as practiced in small face-to-face communities, differs from the type experienced in online settings. Modern media, egalitarian politics, consumer capitalism, and the internet all facilitate gossip and rumor in a public mode, but without the limits of a face-to-face society. In addition, one dangerous aspect of OSNs is that they further dissolve the proprieties that are already diminished in modern society. Trolling and other aggressive forms of behavior have become ubiquitous in the anonymous and mediated forms of expression allowed on the internet. This decay of propriety and unleashing of solipsistic aggression feed into the naturally irresponsible forces of gossip. The checks remain those Tocqueville recognized: the natural stabilization and inertia provided by public (majority) opinion and sentiment. The effect of these checks is balkanized on the internet, however, since people tend to interact within mutually self-confirming, often exclusive communities. This will be one of the topics we will discuss in the next chapter.

CONCLUSION

While we can gossip broadly about what we are largely ignorant (such as politics, celebrities, social opinions), our everyday gossip circulates through local topics and people, and it tends toward petty and trivial details of interaction and behavior. We often call this local gossip observation and opinion. Gossip's greatest weakness, however, is less its superficiality, than our lack of warrant in believing it. This lack of warrant and the consequent displacement of its sense into conflicts of belief among those who gossip constitute its primary discursive characteristic. Gossip seems non-fictionally true or false about the world; and yet when we gossip, we do not evaluate gossip relative to what is the case, but, rather, relative to what we, the gossipers, believe or want to believe or are afraid of believing.

The discursive grammar of gossip matches some of the logical characteristics of dreams. Dreams, whatever relationship they might have with the dreamer, and however expressive of the dreamer, are not dreamed on purpose, and it is strange to speak of a dreamer being responsible for the dream in the way he might be responsible for a statement. Within the dream one can recognize states of affairs about which judgments can be made, but once the dream has become mere memory, it is no longer possible to make such judgments or to recognize the relevant states of affairs without radical interpretation. The dream grips us not because it is true or false, but because it troubles our beliefs or confirms them. Gossip and rumor operate in much the same way. Gossip, while in some ways a parody of fiction, is more like a shared fantasy. By means of gossip we dream together, often in nightmare.

NOTE

1 We can shift gossip from parody into a part of our social reasoning, if we take it as self-descriptions of those who gossip, as opposed to descriptions of the targets of that gossip.

REFERENCES

Allport, Gordon W., and Leo J. Postman. *The psychology of rumor.* Henry Holt, 1947.

Barthes, Roland. *A lover's discourse: Fragments.* Macmillan, 1978.

Coleman, J. S. *Foundations of social theory.* The Belknap Press of Harvard University Press, 1990.

Dunbar, Robin Ian MacDonald. *Grooming, gossip, and the evolution of language.* Harvard University Press, 1996.

Eder, Donna, and Janet Lynne Enke. "The structure of gossip: Opportunities and constraints on collective expression among adolescents." *American Sociological Review* 56(4) (1991): 494–508.

Ellwardt., et al. "Who are the objects of positive and negative gossip at work? A social network perspective on workplace gossip." In *Social Networks* 34 (2012): 193–205.

Ellwardt, Lea. "Gossip and reputation in social networks." In Francesca Giardini, and Rafael Wittek (Eds.), *The Oxford handbook of gossip and reputation* (pp. 435–457). Oxford University Press, 2019.

Elster, Jon. *Nuts and bolts for the social sciences.* Cambridge University Press, 1989.

Elster, Jon. *Alchemies of the mind: Rationality and the emotions.* Cambridge University Press, 1999.

Farley, Sally D. "On the nature of gossip, reputation, and power inequality." In *The Oxford handbook of gossip and reputation* (pp. 342–358). Oxford Handbooks, 2019.

Grosser, Travis J., Virginie Lopez-Kidwell, and Giuseppe Labianca. "A social network analysis of positive and negative gossip in organizational life." *Group & Organization Management* 35.2 (2010): 177–212.

Heidegger, Martin. *Being and Time.* John Macquarrie and Edward Robinson (Translators). Harper and Row, 1962.

Hume, David. *David Hume: Selected essays.* Oxford University Press, 1993.

Hume, David. *An enquiry concerning human understanding,* Tom L. Beauchamp (Editor), Clarendon Press, 1999.

MacFarquhar, Roderick, and Michael Schoenhals. *Mao's last revolution.* Harvard University Press, 2006.

McDonald, Kristina L., et al. "Girl talk: Gossip, friendship, and sociometric status." *Merrill-Palmer Quarterly (1982-)* (2007): 381–411.

Merry, S. E. Rethinking gossip and scandal. In Daniel Klein (Ed.), *Toward a general theory of social control* (pp. 271–302). Academic Press, 1984.

Nagy, Gregory. *The best of the Achaeans.* Johns Hopkins University Press, 1997.

Sommerfeld, Ralf D., et al. "Gossip as an alternative for direct observation in games of indirect reciprocity." *Proceedings of the National Academy of Sciences* 104.44 (2007): 17435–17440.

PART IV

Online Interfaces

DOI: 10.1201/9781003401674-17

CHAPTER 13

Online Information Diffusion as Gossip and Dreamscape

INTRODUCTION

As one of the most important transactional spaces, social media has become a mode not simply of communication, but a means and a context for the formation of communities and the exchange of gossip. Since communication is highly mediated on online social platforms, information easily falls into the social discursive form of gossip, where no one is fully responsible for its content, and thus warrant is not relevant. Information becomes more rumor than fact. The easy proliferation of information and the speed and superficiality of our online interactions encourages often highly prejudicial and unthoughtful transfers of putative information, images, and videos. In this chapter, we identify specific similarities between the discursive grammar of gossip we have developed in the previous chapter and the patterns of behavior characteristic of information exchange within OSNs. We have organized our analysis into eight sections, within which we show how OSNs facilitate information diffusion as part of a gossip-economy. This gossip-economy, however, is part of a kind of public dreaming, or at least quasi-dreaming in which people enter into a mediated space in which their relationship with online content is akin to their relationship to their own dreams. How akin is something we will explore in this part of the book. In the rest of this chapter, we will examine

DOI: 10.1201/9781003401674-18

the eight characteristics of our OSN behavior that can be described as a form of gossiping.

1. FORMATION OF SOCIAL CONFIRMATION

The tendency of people to befriend others who seem to share similar beliefs and commitments and the design of social media algorithmic push-strategies creates a situation in which the targets of negative statements are absent and silent relative to those making or sharing these statements (regardless of whether these statements are true or false). This is a prime characteristic of gossip, which we identified as the third pattern in the grammar of gossip (see Section "Pattern III: Exclusion of the Target of Gossip" in Chapter 12). Such a situation is not only self-confirming, but it reinforces the group identity of those who gossip against those who are the absent targets of this gossip. Bessi et al. (2016) in their study of Italian Facebook, for example, found that communities supporting various conspiracy theories formed easily, leading to the formation of social "echo chambers." These echo chambers may not be as powerful as many have feared. Metzger et al. (2021) have found that people are not as isolated within information silos as had been reported earlier. What this shows is that some are consciously treating information online as gossip, and are thus reacting skeptically to the presentation of some evidence as prejudicial because the evidence is unwarranted (or propagandistic).

The sharing of gossip, even when this gossip is presented as video links, sustains online groups and friendships. Some of these online social groups and friendships overlap with offline friendships. When they do overlap, these friendships prove more stable. Nevertheless, modern experience, especially as facilitated by OSNs, is increasingly mediated. Mediated relationships lack the visceral power of face-to-face relationships. Without that face-to-face interaction, more abstract and ideological factors can become important in order to maintain some kind of group identity and continuity (Laslett, 1956).

2. LACK OF JUSTIFICATION

Many social media theorists construe knowledge as personal belief, and classify all information as data. This is misleading. Much that passes for informational data (hence as evidence) remains highly tendentious and untested. Similarly, personal belief hardly counts as knowledge, since knowledge must be not only believed, but also justified and true. (It is true, as we have discussed in Chapter 2, that the traditional analytic definition of knowledge as justified true belief does not cover all cases, as Gettier (1963) was the first to demonstrate with his famous thought-experiment. It remains true, however, that if I cannot justify what I think I know, what I think I know is prejudice or accepted opinion.)

Online interactions encourage factitious justification, too often tied to the perceived status and authority of the various people involved. The proliferation and display of putative credentials, certifications, and other gestures toward authority facilitate the acceptance of misinformation as true. Confirmation bias and a reticence to question one's own beliefs encourage an uncritical attitude toward acceptable information and an unbalanced critical attitude to unacceptable information. Consequently, our highly mediated interactions through OSNs often take the form of personal advertisements and displays of status. What is advertised and sold through OSNs are the means of confirming our beliefs. Information accepted without adequate justification manifests the second pattern characterizing gossip (see Section "Pattern II: Unwarranted Assertion" in Chapter 12).

3. BELIEF WITHOUT ADEQUATE WARRANT

Gossip encourages belief without adequate warrant. People with little understanding of science or statistics, for example, accept journalistic statements about scientific studies, without realizing how provisional such studies often are. Scientists are not immune from this. They, too, often draw erroneous conclusions and make numerous statistical errors, as well as being subject to confirmation bias and the negative effects of consensus (about statistics, see Reinhart, 2015; Spirer et al., 1998; about consensus errors in science, see O'Connor and Weatherall, 2019).

In non-scientific online communities, the exchange of information encourages superficial kinds of knowledge (often simply pseudo-knowledge). This information lacks context, and people often have little sense of the questions and controversies that inform any particular intellectual discipline. In addition, information is read (or 'consumed') amidst people's other activities. The prime activity on social media, besides passive consumption of various stimuli, is browsing, which is a kind of stimulus-response activity, the primary effect of which is entertainment, which tends again toward easy confirmation of previous beliefs or basic ideological commitments (Vitak et al., 2011). This matches the second pattern characterizing the grammar of gossip (see Section "Pattern II: Unwarranted Assertion" in Chapter 12).

4. SIMPLIFIED FORMATION OF SOCIAL CURRENCY

Online transactional spaces like Facebook and Yahoo! create the illusion of a **neutral** environment of information. This illusion is facilitated by push algorithms and increasingly, AI-generated recommendations and posts (Narayanan, 2023). The increasing prowess of AI tools to parse through large datasets and the increasing inability of users in discerning between AI-generated content and human-generated content is increasing our reliance on AI tools as 'experts.' This is a troubling trend. More generally, the belief in authority when it is convenient for political reasons is itself one of the most dangerous aspects of the modern world. The belief in experts can be misguided, especially when the expertise is limited, when the issues are contested, and when trade-offs in public policy will be required decisions. Interjecting AI tools into this kind of situation will only create more confusion.

Online social spaces such as Instagram, X (Twitter), Threads, YouTube, and TikTok are actively pushing content into your feed, producing a kind of passive acceptance of what comes up on the feed as trustworthy information. People who distrust a platform's feed will tend to leave that platform and find one in which they at least convince themselves is trustworthy. Tracking the source of particular posts can be very difficult as they get spread or are pushed into someone's social media feed, and so, unless the content triggers a negative response little effort is expended in making some judgment about the trustworthiness of the platform.

This has the effect of diminishing the sense that anyone in particular is responsible for the information offered. This is one of the central characteristics of gossip as hearsay: no one is responsible for its content. This conforms to our first pattern of **irresponsible speech** (see Section "Pattern I: Irresponsible Speech" in Chapter 12). We see a similar situation in the exchange of online information, encouraged by the 'Like button' (and negatively by trolling). People naturally want other people to like their posts. Liking a post might express agreement, but its primary effect is to mark an exchange or investment—an investment of social capital through a transaction of praise (or in other contexts, of blame). People collect positive (or negative) transactions. Such simplified interpersonal transactions mimic gossip's social function of establishing and maintaining allies and communities, creating an immediate and vast means of establishing social value (monetized in what are called 'influencers') (see Section "Pattern III: Exclusion of Target of Gossip (Community)" in Chapter 12).

We can see further evidence of this tendency toward group conformity in studies of the emotional responses evoked by misinformation. Zollo et al. (2015), for example, found that with an increase in the length of online discussions tended to encourage negative comments and sentiments. This fits with **the fourth pattern** characterizing gossip as tending toward masked implication and import (see Section "Pattern IV: Masked Implication and Import" in Chapter 12).

5. MOTIVES FOR INFORMATION SPREAD

Truth and falsity are not the primary drivers for information spread, but rather personal and group investment in certain kinds of information drive the spread of information. We have discussed in Part 1 how research into the spread of misinformation by Vosoughi et al. (2018), Goel et al. (2012, 2016), and Juul et al. (2021), in effect, support the critical role of social dynamics in information diffusion. The value of information is often not epistemological but social (see Section "Pattern III: Exclusion of Target of Gossip" in Chapter 12).

The motives for sharing misinformation on social media have been investigated by Chen et al. (2015). They have also found that social factors play a primary role in the spread of information. For example, provocative information that prompted online conversations spread more easily than less catchy information. Similarly, social and interpersonal motives play a critical role in misinformation diffusion. Laato et al. (2020) studied these social factors in the spread of COVID-19 misinformation, including the belief that 5G network towers facilitated the contagion. They found evidence of what others have called cyberchondria: the "unfounded escalation of concerns about common symptomology based on review of online content" (Starcevic and Berle, 2015). We have surveyed in Chapter 9 the wide range of social and psychological motives behind the spread of information and misinformation. All of this fits with the general description of gossip defined above: gossip is more expressive of the community of gossipers than it is about the target of the gossip (see Section "Pattern IV: Masked Implication and Import" in Chapter 12).

Even when veracity is at issue, this is evaluated relative to who else seems to believe the information. In particular, "[n]ews-seekers depend on friends, contacts and individuals followed as trusted news sources as much as or more than they depend on the media outlets themselves" (Knight Foundation, 2016). Interpersonal networks matter the most in the sharing and believing of information.

6. FORMATION OF COMMUNITIES

The primary effect, if not purpose, of such gossip is the building and confirmation of a community of gossip-friends, often in relation to social ene-
mies or outliers. What is shared or produced by such gossip-friends are
rumors, and not information modeled on knowledge. It does not count as
justified true belief. Justification is lacking and its truth is often irrelevant.
Again, this conforms to the general characteristic of gossip as expressive *of*
the community of gossipers (see Section "Pattern III: Exclusion of Target
(Community)" in Chapter 12).

7. THE IMPORTANCE OF GOSSIP-FRIENDSHIP

What we are calling gossip-friendship characterizes the communities of
diffusion in OSNs. Gossip-friends share a propensity to exchange gossip online about certain topics. Such online friendships will in general be
contingent and limited (although they need not be). Online relationships,
while they follow the basic degrees of intimacy we see in offline relationships, are far more replaceable and labile (Arnaboldi, 2015). Twitter networks, in particular, involve a high turnover of connection when compared
to offline networks. Arnaboldi (2015) explains this as both a consequence
of fewer family connections in online networks and social opportunism,
encouraging a "social butterfly" attitude toward social friendships (see
Section "Pattern III: Exclusion of Target (Friendship)" in Chapter 12).

Gossip-friendship creates the possibility for a new kind of Word-of-
Mouth (WOM) model of information diffusion. Online gossip diffusion
often follows a pattern like WOM diffusion, but with an important difference. WOM "communication takes place within a social relationship
that may be categorized according to the closeness of the relationship
between information seeker and the source, represented by the construct
tie strength" (Money et al., 1998; Duhan et al., 1997; Bristor, 1990). Online
gossip follows similar patterns, but it is less dependent on "the relationship
between information seeker and the source." Or rather that relationship
need not be of any particular intimacy, either emotionally or as reflected
in frequent communications. What is required is trust. Trust is personal,
and thus, often given for inadequate reasons. It can be motivated by an
attraction to fame and personality or by ideology. Celebrities are prime
figures in this, since they are not part of a network of reciprocal communication. Their influence is asymmetric, but the disproportionate level of
trust afforded to them allows their statements to spread in similar ways
to other WOM diffusions. (There are variations in the stability of online

relationships depending on the users' commitment and interest in using a particular platform. There are, for example, aficionados of Twitter, as well as regular and casual users.)

In WOM networks trust and intimacy are correlated. Information in such networks flows through such correlated ties. Research suggests that the tie strength between people (or nodes of information distribution, like certain sites or channels) affects information flows. Brown and Reingen (1987) found that "Individuals in a strong tie relationship tend to interact more frequently and exchange more information, compared to those in a weak tie relationship." The Brown and Reingen study predates the internet. Its conclusion is not surprising. Its conclusions remain true of OSNs. OSNs distort our ways of gossiping (which is what takes place in a WOM network). The natural correlation between trust and intimacy in our everyday lives gets disconnected online. Intimacy online is often fragile and factitious. People easily disappear, and we lack the details of face-to-face interactions. Social sharing still requires trust, and so intimacy and trust are likely to become less correlated, less intertwined online than offline. Brown et al. (2007) offer some evidence for exactly this effect. OSNs in effect become parodies of offline social interactions, highlighting the most volatile aspects of our social relationships. This would be a fruitful psychological arena to investigate.

Gossip-friends exist within the specific possibilities enabled by OSNs. One can see this in the interactions facilitated by TikTok and Instagram. Both of these platforms highlight the power and effects of celebrities and so-called influencers. Their power of influence, however, has been absorbed into the gossip structure of these platforms. These platforms simultaneously reward fame and flatten the difference between these influencers and everyone else. (The network is flattened because hierarchical differences between nodes are diminished; one can have a greater degree of connection and closeness online with influencers than one can have offline, for example.) On both platforms, these influencers respond to their fans. People compete for attention. On TikTok, in particular, the difference between a regular user and someone influential is simply an effect of popularity and marketing effects. Celebrities in the traditional sense of famous people who seem somehow separate and well-known, however, still retain their power. They have huge followings. But the putative intimacy of the internet, so much greater than that produced in earlier forms of media propaganda, allows such figures to function not as intimate friends of any kind, but as gossip-friends, fitting within a network of influencers and various other kinds of online friendships. What this means is that celebrities and influencers, who would not be part of any real friendship network, expressive of real mutual connection or as manifest in a high rate of communication, function online as gossip-friends. (This is not a democratization of the social order, but a false intimacy that gives celebrities and influencers greater power of effect.)

One new quality of these kinds of gossip-friendships is that they need not be reciprocal and can be asymmetrical. On TikTok, influencers (or their handlers) can respond to comments. Anyone is a potential celebrity. With more global celebrities, their influence is all toward consumers, but the relationship is much less emotionally distant than was likely in pre-internet media.

8. ONLINE AND OFFLINE INTERMIXING

Gossip online and offline is guided by personal psycho-social motivations. Our responses, from sharing to rejection, depend, as we have discussed, on personal and emotional concerns, sometimes taking the form of public agreement or contempt. It is less the truth or falsity of information and more the emotional and personal investment, concern, and sensitivity to that information that motives our sharing, reaction, and sometimes belief. These emotional reactions are situated relative to friends (online gossip-friends, often), and this is the means by which people online enter into a community organized around that which is shared (see Section "Pattern III: Exclusion of Target" in Chapter 12). This is very much how gossip works. Given the lack of face-to-face contact online, however, this community is partially built through imagined understandings and presumptions. We, of course, gossip online with people we also know offline. Consequently, many of our online attitudes are shaped by offline commitments (Dunbar et al., 2015; Mesch and Talmud, 2006; Nadkarni and Hoffman, 2012; Lieberman and Schroeder, 2020).

These eight points suggest that our OSN behavior should often, although not always, be described as a form of gossiping. There are multiple and legitimate ways we can use online resources to learn many different things—from how to fix a dishwasher to how to solve differential equations. Nevertheless, much of the information spread through online social networks is best understood relative to the communities it helps form and maintain. Online exchanges might ultimately lead to our acceptance of information as knowledge, but often the factual questions are absorbed in social dynamics. Information must be understood not simply relative to its content, but relative to its role in a social economy. News feeds, like on Facebook, for example, since they are themselves filters reinforcing the interests and beliefs of a particular user, are always in danger of becoming rumor-mongering channels. The exchange of gossip has social significance, a mix of competition and cooperation for social advantage. The truth or falsity of what is exchanged matters primarily relative to social advantage (or disadvantage). The truth value of the gossip will often be irrelevant to this social value. The upshot of this is that when we model information (or misinformation) diffusion we are not modeling (or trying to explain) something called information. We are attempting to model the actions and behavior of people through the effects and traces of that behavior on OSNs.

DREAM COMMUNITIES

The logical characteristics of gossip, therefore, match some of the logical characteristics of dreams. For the moment we will look at two aspects of gossip and dreams that we described at the end of the previous chapter.

Dreams, whatever relationship they might have with the dreamer, and however expressive of the dreamer, are not dreamed on purpose, and it is strange to speak of a dreamer being responsible for the dream in the way he might be responsible for a statement. Instead, dreams seem to happen to us, as if from elsewhere. We engage with others within a dream space within which we act and experience these others. Of course, this seemingly public space is our private dream experience, which we recognize usually only after we awake. These others, however, are unstable and diffuse, and we can at any time shift into them and become other. Our online experience involves elements of this dream structure. But this dream structure is in the form of public discourse that defines our gossiping.

The speech within dreams is like the speech shared in gossip—no one is responsible for it in a direct way: we do not treat such speech as speech in anyone's own voice. In a dream, there is the further oddity that if I am dreaming, the speech is in some sense me, and yet it is not me. It is mediated speech, expressive of my psychology in some unspecified way. And yet in my dream and afterwards, I react to this mediated speech as if it were unmediated, with often intense emotional and visceral reactions.

We see all of these elements in our involvement with the web. Information on the web often follows the pattern of gossip in being speech for no one's voice or beliefs in particular. The messages and images shared may express someone's belief, but they are often still shared just as gossip is: *'have you heard about this . . .'* The common sense of information, especially as it is shared online is that it exists and means somehow separate from anyone in particular. This is misleading, as we have argued, but it is nevertheless common. Like with public gossip and rumor, this shared, and therefore public information gets offered in a half-public, half-private way.

One element of this dream logic is the sense of personal connection and involvement with what is public. For example, studies have shown that the content and knowledge discovered online, or even just searching for information, produces an inflated sense of personal knowledge. The online engagement and involvement with public information are felt or understood as personal. This is an example not only of the dissolution of the difference between what is personal (private) and what is public (shared), but also a confusion about what is mediated, and thus constructed by others, and what is unmediated, as if one were just perceiving, remembering, feeling, or thinking something.

This response to what is mediated as if unmediated is a defining attitude of online experience. The attitude is not ignorance, but rather part of the dream-like fantasy that can absorb us in our scrolling through quasi-personal publicly shared images, videos, and conversations on Instagram and TikTok, for example. But this attitude is not only an effect of our viewing. The ease with which anyone can become a creator of content involves the construction of public selves presented as personal communications. This is shown through the kind of implied friendships offered if you follow someone.

But also, people construct themselves through face modifying applications made available on platforms like TikTok, but easily available from many sources online. The most extreme form of the mediated as unmediated is offered by AI-generated stories and voices as well as images and videos, distributed and available on easily accessible platforms, including YouTube and Instagram.

Dreams are not like sentences or propositions that can be about some state of affairs, nor can they be evaluated as true or false. They are neither. A dream, of course, can involve situations, people, and actions that demand a response. But once we awake we have left the dream; it has become a memory. We can no longer make judgments or even understand the states of affairs we experienced without some radical interpretation about what dreams are and mean (or can mean). Nevertheless, dreams grip us, when they do, not because it is true or false, but by how it troubles our beliefs or confirms them.

The dream space can feel unmediated but it is in fact highly mediated. Nothing is actually happening. We are not face to face with anyone. Nevertheless, we feel panic, desire, and many other things. These feelings, especially if they were shocking or disturbing can continue to unsettle us after we awake and have escaped the dream.

CONCLUSION

Our interactions with others over the web are also very mediated in ways we have described above. But again, they can feel visceral and unmediated. The way messaging and posting work online allows for either an immediate reply and reaction, even if not face to face, or a delayed response (or no response). The web records and displays, and only functions as a direct and immediate communication device when we so desire (in conjunction with the wishes of our interlocutor). This makes the web a kind of memory chamber, but it also highlights its mediated nature. This mix of mediated content seeming visceral and unmediated matches again our dream experience.

The relative anonymity of users and the way that information becomes gossip, foregrounding emotional and interpersonal motives and concerns, combined with lack of face-to-face interactions (or their easy management and dismissal) makes our experience of the web highly imaginary, encouraging fantasies and projections. Rumors parody our offline communities, as we discussed in Chapter 9. The web and OSNs are also parodies, simplifications of aspects of our offline concerns and interests. Our interface and involvement with these are akin to our own ways of dreaming, with the logical form of our dreaming. The web is never just one thing. But one thing it encourages and reveals is our dreaming together in a mix of personal confession and public display.

REFERENCES

Arnaboldi, V. *Online social networks: Human cognitive constraints in Facebook and Twitter personal graphs.* Elsevier, 2015.

Bessi, Alessandro, et al. "Users polarization on Facebook and YouTube." *PloS One* 11.8 (2016): e0159641.

Bristor, J. M. "Enhanced Explanations of Word of Mouth Communications: The Power of Relationships," Research in Consumer Behavior, Vol. 4 (pp. 51–83), 1990.

Brown, Jacqueline Johnson, and Peter H. Reingen. "Social ties and word-of-mouth referral behavior." *Journal of Consumer Research* 14.3 (1987): 350–362.

Brown, Jo, Amanda J. Broderick, and Nick Lee. "Word of mouth communication within online communities: Conceptualizing the online social network." *Journal of Interactive Marketing* 21.3 (2007): 2–20.

Chen, Xinran, et al. "Why students share misinformation on social media: Motivation, gender, and study-level differences." *The Journal of Academic Librarianship* 41.5 (2015): 583–592.

Duhan, Dale F., et al. "Influences on consumer use of word-of-mouth recommendation sources." *Journal of the Academy of Marketing Science* 25 (1997): 283–295.

Dunbar, Robin IM, et al. "The structure of online social networks mirrors those in the offline world." *Social Networks* 43 (2015): 39–47.

Gettier, Edmund L. "Is justified true belief knowledge?" *Analysis* 23.6 (1963): 121–123.

Goel, Sharad, et al. "The structural virality of online diffusion." *Management Science* 62.1 (2016): 180–196.

Goel, Sharad, Duncan J. Watts, and Daniel G. Goldstein. "The structure of online diffusion networks." *Proceedings of the 13th ACM Conference on Electronic Commerce*. Valencia, Spain, 2012.

Juul, Jonas L., and Johan Ugander. "Comparing information diffusion mechanisms by matching on cascade size." *Proceedings of the National Academy of Sciences* 118.46 (2021): e2100786118.

Laato, Samuli, et al. "Why do people share misinformation during the COVID-19 pandemic?." *arXiv preprint arXiv:2004.09600* (2020).

Laslett, Peter. "The face to face society." In Peter Laslett (Ed.), *Philosophy, politics and society* (pp. 157–184). Basil Blackwell, 1956.

Lieberman, Alicea, and Juliana Schroeder. "Two social lives: How differences between online and offline interaction influence social outcomes." *Current Opinion in Psychology* 31 (2020): 16–21.

Mesch, Gustavo S., and Ilan Talmud. "Online friendship formation, communication channels, and social closeness." *International Journal of Internet Science* 1.1 (2006): 29–44.

Metzger, Miriam J., et al. "From dark to light: The many shades of sharing misinformation online." *Media and Communication* 9.1 (2021): 134–143.

Money, R. Bruce, Mary C. Gilly, and John L. Graham. "Explorations of national culture and word-of-mouth referral behavior in the purchase of industrial services in the United States and Japan." *Journal of Marketing* 62.4 (1998): 76–87.

Nadkarni, Ashwini, and Stefan G. Hofmann. "Why do people use Facebook?" *Personality and Individual Differences* 52.3 (2012): 243–249.

O'Connor, Cailin, and James Owen Weatherall. *The misinformation age: How false beliefs spread*. Yale University Press, 2019.

Knight Foundation. "Mobile-first news: how people use smartphones to access information." (2016). https://knightfoundation.org/reports/mobile-first-news-how-people-use-smartphones-acces/

Narayanan, A. "Understanding social media recommendation algorithms". (2023). Knight Foundation. https://knightcolumbia.org/content/understanding-social-media-recommendation-algorithms

Reinhart, Alex. *Statistics done wrong: The woefully complete guide.* No Starch Press, 2015.

Spirer, Herbert, and Louise Spirer. *Misused statistics.* CRC Press, 1998.

Starcevic, Vladan, and David Berle. "Cyberchondria: An old phenomenon in a new guise." In E. Aboujaoude & V. Starcevic (Eds.), *Mental health in the digital age: Grave dangers, great promise* (pp. 106–117). Oxford Academic, 2015.

Vitak, Jessica, Nicole B. Ellison, and Charles Steinfield. "The ties that bond: Re-examining the relationship between Facebook use and bonding social capital." *2011 44th Hawaii International Conference on System Sciences.* Kuaui, Hawaii, USA, IEEE, 2011.

Vosoughi, Soroush, Deb Roy, and Sinan Aral. "The spread of true and false news online." *science* 359.6380 (2018): 1146–1151.

Zollo, Fabiana, et al. "Emotional dynamics in the age of misinformation." *PloS one* 10.9 (2015): e0138740.

CHAPTER **14**

The Grammar of Online Self-Gossip

INTRODUCTION

As we discussed in Chapter 12, gossip normally requires that the target of gossip be absent or silent, and so self-gossip should be impossible. In practice, however, we actually can and do gossip about ourselves. We will describe the particular grammar of this behavior and offer some examples of this kind of gossip-behavior. Then, we will use the grammar of self-gossip to describe and analyze some patterns of our online behavior and interactions. In so doing, we will integrate patterns of online self-display with our notion of social-discursive grammar.

SELF-GOSSIP

Novels, like life, are filled with self-gossipers. We will derive the concept of self-gossip from an account of our everyday social practices, using one of the most sophisticated and careful linguistic explorations of these practices: the writings of Jane Austen.

Austen's (2006) *Pride and Prejudice* provides a very clear example of self-gossip. Toward the end of that novel, the protagonist Elizabeth Bennet finds herself confronted by Lady Catherine, who wants to compel Elizabeth to renounce any interest in marrying Darcy. Lady Catherine wants to establish her authority and virtue as a lever with which to manipulate Elizabeth. Consequently, Lady Catherine mentions what other people say about her, claiming that she is known as frank and sincere, by which she

DOI: 10.1201/9781003401674-19

means honest and forthright. Lady Catherine invokes what she claims is other people's gossip about her in order to then confirm her frankness. In so doing, she, in effect, gossips about herself, as if she were simply reporting on herself. This is all in bad faith, of course. She simply wants to establish her claim on a moral privilege that she thinks she can use to impress Elizabeth, and compel her to refuse to marry Darcy. Lady Catherine's self-gossip is a kind of self-making, using re-description or paradiastole, the form of manipulative redescription that we discussed in Chapter 3. She reports what she has heard others say about her, and uses these reports to suggest that her own statements are, therefore, unbiased and legitimate.

We can describe the basic discursive grammar of this kind of self-gossip in the following way. You pretend to be silent by repeating what others have said about you. This is a kind of self-masking. Once in your mask of silence, you can repeat other people's hearsay about you. You pretend to let them speak through you about you. In effect, you disguise your own voice using the voices of others (you might call this a form of self-curating). Quoting others like this protects you from the charge of self-aggrandizement, since you can say 'I am not offering my own opinion of myself, but simply reporting other people's opinion.' As in all gossip, you are abrogating any direct responsibility for what is said, and displacing the authority and veracity of what you repeat to 'what you have heard.' In effect, Lady Catherine quotes what she has heard about herself as a way of presenting those comments as a rumor about her, so that these statements become the voice of public opinion. Of course, this kind of self-gossip is completely self-serving and, even if the statements she repeats were said, they were not meant.

Elizabeth is not taken in by Lady Catherine's self-propaganda. She responds ironically, almost sarcastically: if she cannot pretend to be as frank as Lady Catherine, she is more frank in *not* pretending to be frank. The irony here is not that Elizabeth is saying one thing and meaning another. She is rather saying one thing and meaning it and implying another and meaning that as well: what she says is not all she means. She is being frank by admitting that she is not being frank. In saying she is not frank she is denying what she really is—that is she is not being frank, but the point is to show that she is more frank (honest) than Lady Catherine.

It is natural at this point to imagine that the issue here is about the meaning of the word 'frank,' as if Lady Catherine and Elizabeth are both being honest in their self-descriptions because they have different definitions of these words. This is not the case. Their understanding of what the words mean is more or less the same. What they disagree about is what counts as an example of being frank and sincere. But there is something more subtle going on as well. Lady Catherine pretends that what she says is what she means, that saying she is frank in effect means she is frank. This is clearly not true. Elizabeth does not imagine that things are that simple, hence her ironic claim that she is not as frank. She describes herself relative to Lady Catherine, using Lady Catherine's words (their meaning intact), but with different import. Elizabeth is able to state that she is honest by not claiming a false honesty. This honesty, however, requires the recognition of a disjunction between what someone says and what someone means. She is honest about this disjunction, while Lady Catherine pretends that it does not exist.

Elizabeth, however, shows that frankness and sincerity are not simply something you can be by virtue of saying that you are. We can only judge if someone is frank and sincere by attending to the complexity of the relationship between how things seem (what is said) and how things are (in this case, what Elizabeth means); thus Elizabeth says and means 'I am not as frank as you, thus I am more frank.'

Lady Catherine, on the other hand, understands her own tactless aggressive display and assertion of personal desires, under the description of "frank" and "sincere." And so, as honest and forthright expressions. She is not honest, however, and her frankness is deceptive and her sincerity is tendentious. Lady Catherine asserts something about herself as if it were obviously true. Her desire that it be true is enough for her to believe that it is true, supported by the quoted voices of others, which she herself reports.

In an online situation, people collect likes, followers, and friends. And if these likes and followers are not your real friends, then it counts for more, because it shows your public scope and power, and thus within the internet economy it increases your value. The likes and followers lack the content of the descriptions Lady Catherine quotes, but they have the same purpose of revealing someone's value under the authority of public opinion, given now a kind of quantitative measure—as numbers of likes or followers.

We have to remember that the target of gossip is always in some sense obscure, blank, partial, silent, and in ways absent, and we can always become, even to ourselves, this kind of target, since we too are obscure, blank, partial, silent, and in ways absent. We can discover ourselves through how others describe us. To prove our work is good, we sometimes repeat the praise others have given us. And our relationship to our own lives, mind, and understanding is often a kind of hearsay. We self-gossip about our dreams, about what drives and motivates us, about our past, about our relationships, about our actions and behavior. In these cases, we are absent in some sense. Our dream self, for example, is not there to disagree with our descriptions of our dreams. We might even understand rationalization, the backwards reasoning by which we justify what we have already decided or think, as a form of self-gossip. We provide reasons for our actions and beliefs that may be true or they may not be; it is hard to say. We often have no direct way of determining why we do things. We are mysterious to ourselves, so we borrow phrases, ideas, and whatever reasoning and linguistic means we can to fill in the mystery. We are often rumors to ourselves.

ONLINE SELF-GOSSIP

Social media platforms allow us to vicariously comment (gossip) about strangers, who often become quasi-friends to the degree that we know something about them. Because those we watch—and anyone else, including ourselves—can publish self-created and focused content, we can directly and easily gossip about ourselves online. What we post and share on our various social media accounts are all displayed in an online virtual public space, creating a predefined context for self-gossip. OSNs provide spaces in which we can construct ourselves using manipulated images, text found online, and whatever else we can post or share messages sent by others to us. No one is directly present to anyone else (unless someone is live streaming). People brand themselves, turning their mediated self-image into a commodity that they sell themselves. In effect, we are all in danger of becoming Lady Catherines.

Online platforms allow us to participate in visual gossip, including visual self-gossip. If I am watching various Instagram or TikTok posts the person visible in the post is absent, and I am absent from them. Although we can comment and in a mediated way communicate with those whom we watch, but we need not. Similarly, I can share what I watch with whomever I want, just as in any normal gossip situation. In sharing a post, of course, I am not speaking in my own voice; and if I am the creator of a post, I am sharing a mediated performance. This sharing can also be a form of self-display, part of my online persona. Such a display, unless it is a live stream, is fully mediated, where no one is present in front of anyone else. These patterns of online communication, of course, match the same discursive pattern of both gossip and self-gossip.

TikToks and Instagram videos are pushed into my feed, based on my past viewing habits. If the algorithm or AI is effective this content will match my interests, if not always my desires. This is analogous to my quoting others about myself, although the feedback loop is built into the program, by which means my behavior is tracked and reinforcing by my reactions and interactions with the contents of my feed. This is further emphasized by my liking or sharing content. When I share this content with friends and family, it becomes part of my relationship with these people: we become gossip-friends.

The online situation, however, allows and encourages building new relationships with other users. Such sharing builds a relationship with the people with which I share this content. My behavior online helps create my public profile, affecting my status and value as an online voice. People who strive to become influencers share and create content in order to build these online relationships (Marwick and boyd, 2011). Marwick and boyd, using the term micro-celebrity developed by T. Senft (2008), describe this upbuilding through self-display an audience as a community: "Micro-celebrity implies that all individuals have an audience that they can strategically maintain through ongoing communication and interaction" (2011). Online sharing with strangers is by definition a form of self-display, since initially the relationship is asymmetrical: I show, others watch. I show myself as a kind of open offering to whomever will respond or watch. As I gather watchers and followers, a community forms around my sharing and the persona this sharing creates. Through social media I can become a self-mediated avatar constructed through my own self-gossip. Again, this is Lady Catherine's great desire.

The ease with which content can be created on some platforms (TikTok and Instagram, for example) further encourages the kind of self-making that Lady Catherine performs through her self-gossip. TikTok provides easy access to apps that allow people to modify their appearance in pictures and videos. Such appearance-modifying applications are readily available elsewhere on the web and are widely used. As always there are counter-movements to this kind of self-constructed display, so that some people will post or share 'ugly' pictures and videos. Variations abound.

The self-gossip functions and affordances of OSNs are extensions of the now long-developing selfie culture spawned by the camera function available in smartphones. These cameras have easy-to-use settings that allow for manipulation and alterations of our physical appearance in the endless digital photographs many people take of themselves. Such digital manipulation has encouraged a desire to recreate these effects in the flesh through plastic surgery. A recent study of 175 participants (of whom 80% were women) at a dermatology clinic found that using smartphone applications such as filter effects and photo manipulations influenced their desires to "emulate filtered and edited versions of themselves" using cosmetic surgery (Khan et al., 2024). These desires were an outcome of several factors, including following celebrities or influencers online, filtering photos before sharing them on OSNs such as Snapchat and Instagram, use of filtering applications such as FaceTune, and the tendency to take and share selfies on an everyday basis.

Other studies have explored the effects of increased social media usage and photo-editing applications on self-esteem and attitudes toward cosmetic surgery (Chen et al., 2019, Tremblay et al., 2021, Seekis and Barker, 2022; Hermans et al., 2022). People's sense of self is increasingly shaped by their involvement with these photo-editing applications. A 2023 article in MedEsthetics found that younger generations were more likely to get information about cosmetic procedures from social media (41% of 18–29-year-olds and 28% of 30–44-year-olds). A 2018 BBC article cited another statistic: 55% of facial plastic surgeons in 2017 saw patients who wanted surgery to help them look better in selfies, compared to just 13% in 2013.

A CNN article on this topic found similar patterns. Whereas previously patients would request cosmetic surgery procedures that recreated a certain feature of a celebrity such as their nose or chin, there is now an increasing trend where patients are requesting procedures that recreate photo-edited versions of themselves. Examples of such cosmetic surgery procedures include facials that attempt to reduce the size of skin pores to give the skin an airbrushed effect, use of fillers for airbrush facelifts, eyelid surgery and brow lifts, as well as minimally invasive procedures such as laser resurfacing. Users of photo-editing application have an endless stream of inspiration in how to achieve different kinds of "looks." An article about TikTok's AI-based filters illustrated how these filters conjure up entire new looks based on fashion and lifestyle trends such as "bold glamour" or "teenage look," while offering ways to address everyday annoyances such as moles and blemishes (Dazed Digital). Meanwhile, a 2022 article in the MIT Tech Review examining the adverse effects of filters on body image issues for girls and women stated the surrealistic requirements of the Instagram face: "ethnically ambiguous and featuring the flawless skin, big eyes, full lips, small nose, and perfectly contoured curves made accessible in large part by filters." These desires expressed here are akin to attempting to merge oneself with one's self-gossip: to become in actuality the self-constructed image one has presented to an audience of strangers.

The new medical term for this desire is Snapchat dysmorphia. The term was coined by Dr. Tijion Esho, a cosmetic surgeon in the UK, to document a shift in patients' fantasies from wanting to resemble celebrities to now wanting to resemble their photo-edited selves. Rajanala et al. (2018) examined how the obsessions with making eyes and lips look bigger and fuller and other similar facial alterations were an outcome of people losing touch with reality. Surgeons express their exasperation at being asked to create perfectly seemingly symmetrical and regular features, since they are realistically unattainable (Guardian).

THE CULTURE OF NARCISSISM

The online culture of self-display continues a trend of cultural self-involvement that Lasch (2019) characterized in the 1970s as a culture of narcissism in America. The culture of online self-display, however, is also found in China, where building personal brands through selfie videos is very popular. Applications for modifying physical appearance are readily available and used almost universally. By all indications there are important differences between the habits and tendencies which characterize Chinese online culture and those which characterize Western cultures, but the prevalence of self-display and the attempt to build communities of factitious intimacy through online videos is striking. (In China, Douyin is the sister application of TikTok; Weibo is the dominant microblogging platform, akin to X (Twitter).) It could very well be that modern mass society of whatever form encourages the narcissistic modes of self-gossip and self-performance. We will not explore the anthropology of cultural narcissism, nor will we attempt to add to the already extensive literature on the psychology of narcissistic behavior and personalities. Rather, the basic structure of narcissism provides us with a clarifying conceptual schema that we can use to illuminate the peculiarities of online self-gossip.

It is important to understand that narcissism is not simply a focus on the self. The key structural element is that the narcissist is full of self-focus and display as part of a performance for others. As Lasch (2019) describes it: "Notwithstanding his occasional illusions of omnipotence, the narcissist depends on others to validate his self-esteem. He cannot live without an admiring audience." In their self-focus, a narcissist is neither independent nor self-sufficient. Standing out is not standing alone. Narcissism is egotism in a culture that pretends to value egalitarianism.

The viral celebrities of online culture are not pursuing any real singularity, but rather simply trying to keep people attracted and attached. The web provides an audience with diminished personal investment, only encouraging superficial narcissistic displays in pursuit of fame and a grandiose virtual self. This audience is fickle, however. Online fame, like much of the fame that is gained through performance, is often short-lived. Fame of any kind brings counter-attacks. These attacks online can be very extreme and vile.

An influencer called nintendo.grl, who has 9 million followers, describes the consequences of becoming internet famous:

> There is this power TikTok has: "It's just so, so popular, and that can be a scary thing.... You have to be constantly fighting against other content creators to be seen," she said. "You don't realize the impact of having so many eyes on you," she added. "Those people who've chosen not to like you, they're going to see you, right there on their screen, and nothing you do is going to make a difference. You've got to learn to deal with the hate."
>
> (Harwell and Lorenz, 2022)

There is nothing surprising in this. Like any kind of fame leveraged for money, people who become influencers have a dependent relationship on their audience. This dependence creates anxiety, while the fame spawns adulation, envy, and resentment. As Lasch comments, the narcissist imagines that his interpersonal insecurity and anxiety can be "overcome only by seeing his 'grandiose self.'" This grandiose self, dependent on a fickle audience, remains insecure which only encouraging more grandiose self-display. The narcissist cannot help but try to conform to some image that will win approval from the audience. Narcissism always involves some form of conformity. The need for an audience insures this.

We are not suggesting that everyone that posts online videos is a narcissist, but rather that the structures of these social media platforms facilitate a narcissistic logic. One can use them for other ends in some cases. Certainly, with Instagram and YouTube one can create educational videos the purpose of which is to lead people to longer online discussions or blogs about various issues. Nevertheless, the production of videos, especially on platforms like TikTok, and the attraction of becoming an influencer, or simply gaining likes and followers, creates a cultural and economic impetus toward self-branding. This branding is the creation of an image, expressed through online recorded performances, that is particular in a way that attracts and audience. Value is attained through measurable popularity, the focus of which is the displayed, half-constructed self. We are offered an intimacy with a stranger, posing as a friend, in which our interest is a confession of our own interests and desires. Our desires are reflected back in the virtual and never to be obtained reality; the influencer gives themselves over to our view, mediated by online technology.

CONCLUSION

Self-gossip is a kind of discursive practice in which we use statements of others about ourselves as a means of gossiping about and usually praising ourselves. It is a kind of performance. The self-display performed on social media, on TikTok, for example, which is recorded and then distributed as message (as content), is an attempt to create a rumor: to go viral. Lady Catherine quotes others to prove she is like what she says she is like. She reports gossip, again pretending it is public rumor, and, therefore, both accepted opinion and a true characterization. It is a self-serving unverified report, invoking a virtual community, at least as far as Elizabeth is concerned, in support of Lady Catherine's view of herself. It is a form of self-display by quoting others. It is as if she were saying: this is what my followers say about me, because this is how I appear (or so she imagines and wishes). Lady Catherine is a precursor to the online aspiring influencer.

The key factors in online self-display rest on the gossip structure of online social platforms. The fact that recordings are distributed, offered to an audience of strangers who are not present, who are not face to face with the creator of the video, creates the exclusion pattern; the target of gossip is absent (see Section "Pattern III: Exclusion of the Target of Gossip" in Chapter 12). In this case, the gossiper, quoting herself, is absent from the audience; and the audience is absent from the creator. Mediation goes in both directions.

There is no warrant for the veracity of what is offered other than the fact that it is offered by the person making the content or displaying themselves (see Section "Pattern II: Unwarranted Assertion" in Chapter 12). Since so many of these videos are filtered, manipulated, and doctored using various kinds of production software, what is offered is more like quoted speech than ordinary speech. The influencer makes himself or herself into an image, and then suggests that he or she is that image in some sense (see Section "Pattern I: Irresponsible Speech" in Chapter 12). The first pattern characterizing gossip that we identified was that no one is responsible directly for the gossip speech—it is as if quoted. Or it is reported in a way to deny any commitment to its veracity: "This is just what I saw." It is interesting how common it is to share other people's content on platforms like TikTok as part of one's own self-display. On YouTube reaction videos are very popular: someone films themselves, for example, reacting to a music performance video. Such videos are useful advertising for the musicians, but the content of the reaction video is often very thin. The content is sometimes nothing more than —"Hey, look at me looking and listening to this other thing." Even without this explicit quoting, online self-displays, especially if highly mediated through manipulative applications, is to turn the self into their image. The popularity of plastic surgery to reproduce in flesh the look one achieves online is a perverse example of this.

OSNs encourage and facilitate an unstable mixture of private and public online. Voyeuristic followers can turn against someone who posts online photographs of their vacation, because the influencer posts photoshopped and edited photographs of their vacation. The private is not really private, and the public interest is motivated by a voyeuristic desire to see what is private. Self-display, because of the threat of rejection, criticism, or indifference, takes a form that is both acceptable and interesting to a target subset of the potential audience. This kind of reaction, while grounded in an unfortunate psychology of resentment common with human beings, is also a common gossip behavior. People love to criticize others when they are absent, and such criticism is encouraged by the way we can misinterpret what others say and do. This fits with what we called Pattern IV, the way that gossip can be a mask encouraging various interpretations. In the next chapter, we will examine the technological affordances organizing the TikTok platform as an example of the grammar of narcissistic self-gossip.

REFERENCES

Austen, Jane. *Pride and prejudice*. Pat Rogers (Ed.). Cambridge University Press, 2006.

Chen, Jonlin, et al. "Association between the use of social media and photograph editing applications, self-esteem, and cosmetic surgery acceptance." *JAMA Facial Plastic Surgery* 21.5 (2019): 361–367.

Harwell, Drew, and Taylor Lorenz. "Sorry you went viral". *Washington Post* (2022).

Hermans, Anne-Mette, Sophie C. Boerman, and Jolanda Veldhuis. "Follow, filter, filler? Social media usage and cosmetic procedure intention, acceptance, and normalization among young adults." *Body Image* 43 (2022): 440–449.

Khan, Iman F., et al. "Effects of the COVID-19 pandemic on patient social media use and acceptance of cosmetic procedures." *The Journal of Clinical and Aesthetic Dermatology* 17.3 (2024): 42.

Lasch, Christopher. "The culture of narcissism." In Rupert Wilkinson (Ed.), *American Social Character* (pp. 241–267). Routledge, 2019.

Marwick, Alice, and danah boyd. "To see and be seen: Celebrity practice on Twitter." *Convergence* 17.2 (2011): 139–158.

Senft, T. "Camgirls: Celebrity and community in the age of social networks." *International Journal of Performance Arts and Digital Media* 4.2–3 (2008): 189–193.

Tremblay, S. C., S. Essafi Tremblay, and P. Poirier. From filters to fillers: An active inference approach to body image distortion in the selfie era. *AI & Society*, 36 (2021): 33–48.

Rajanala, S., M. B. Maymone, and N. A. Vashi. Selfies—living in the era of filtered photographs. *JAMA Facial Plastic Surgery* 20.6 (2018): 443–444.

Seekis, Veya, and Grace Barker. "Does# beauty have a dark side? Testing mediating pathways between engagement with beauty content on social media and cosmetic surgery consideration." *Body Image* 42 (2022): 268–275.

CHAPTER 15

The 'Information Ecosystem' and Gossiping AIs

INTRODUCTION

Throughout this book, we have been exploring the multifarious uses of the concepts (and words) of *information* and *misinformation*. We extended our discussion of the normative form of ways of knowing into our analysis of information and then into gossip and rumor, which offer the best models for what we share and exchange through social media and through the web. We will draw together a few of our previous arguments and analyses in this chapter by examining the conceptual implications that undergird two very attractive ways of describing our involvement with online information. The first way is the idea that information is polluted in various ways and by various agents. The second way is the idea that information functions as an ecosystem. These descriptions form a picture that on the surface looks compelling. Our modern lives can seem noisy with information, polluted with false and misleading messages, images, videos, stories, news, and so forth. This pollution is seemingly part of a disordered information ecosystem. So, we imagine that we need to clean up our informational ecosystem. As tempting as this metaphorical picture is to explain what Wardle et al. call "information disorder," it encourages a factitious understanding of information and misinformation and mischaracterizes how we think and live amidst information and knowledge, both online and offline.

DOI: 10.1201/9781003401674-20

THE DISORDER OF 'INFORMATION ECOSYSTEM'

We agree with Claire Wardle and others who argue that 'fake news' is too narrow of a concept and has become an overly politicized term. Wardle and Derakhshan (2017) recharacterize what they call "information disorder" using three terms: misinformation, disinformation, and malinformation, the last being the use of true information in misleading and tendentious ways. These distinctions are useful and capture real differences, but they nevertheless disguise a deeper and critical confusion about how all three relate to our general practices of knowing and communicating. This confusion fits with the more general description of what Wardle et al. call "information pollution." Pollution can be cleaned up, and polluted information implies the possibility of clean information, suggesting further that such cleanliness would be more natural. We think this is both false and misleading.

Wardle and Derakhshan (2017) define their three information disorder terms in the following way:

- Misinformation is when false information is shared, but no harm is meant.

- Disinformation is when false information is knowingly shared to cause harm.

- Malinformation is when genuine information is shared to cause harm, often by moving information designed to stay private into the public sphere.

Each of these types of information is defined relative to the intention of the person(s) sharing this information. Intentions and consequences are both difficult to determine. Reducing these intentions to either the intention to cause harm or the intention not to cause harm is both tendentious and radically simplifying, as we will illustrate below.

In addition, 'misinformation' describes a vast ill-defined domain of phenomena. We cannot be informed of anything if we cannot also be misinformed. Misinformation is a natural element of our ways of knowing, which, as we have argued, are guided by norms and dependent on descriptions or formulations. Harm or the lack of harm is neither here nor there in many cases of misinformation. Doctors and researchers often draw false conclusions about disease, developing treatments that in retrospect hurt patients rather than cure them. This false medical understanding can lead to counter-productive and even dangerous treatments. There were no bad intentions. Nevertheless, such faulty information and understanding remains a form of misinformation. The typology fails to properly describe this kind of case, since it characterizes these kinds of information relative to intention and not content.

We should also remember that misinformation can be used for propagandistic purposes, just as information can be used to mislead people. And since malinforming as a practice utilizes putatively genuine information, genuine information should also be included in this typology if misinformation is. The point is that information and misinformation can be used in many ways, two of which are described as disinformation and malinformation. But there are many other ways.

Malinformation as it is characterized is a real problem. Sharing private information in a public way is abusive and a violation of trust. Journalists have a long history of this kind of behavior. They might defend themselves by saying they do not intend harm when they share such private information and only intend to inform the public or even to increase circulation; any harm is accidental and maybe even deserved, they could plead. This is one problem that follows from defining discourse relative to moral intentions; such intentions are not only hard to fathom and determine, but they are nested and open to many redescriptions. (This power of redescription is, of course, our old friend, paradiastole).

Disinformation might look more straightforward. Certainly, there will be many cases of propaganda whose intent is to harm others. But that reveals one immediate problem. False information used to purposively harm others is a fancy way of describing the activity and practice of lying. But not all cases of misinformation are lies, as we have already discussed. 'False information' is actually an equivocal phrase and concept. Characterizing both misinformation and disinformation using 'false information' implies a misleading parallel.

The idea that disinformation is defined by the use of false information to cause harm is wide-spread. But there are variations. A European Commission report on fake news also includes profit as a motive. The report states that disinformation "includes all forms of false, inaccurate, or misleading information designed, presented and promoted to intentionally cause public harm or for profit" (de Cock Buning, 2018). We assume someone might even intend both to harm others and to profit from either the information sharing itself or the harm. But as it is phrased, the definition is too vague and misleading: whose harm and whose profit? It depends. But the moralizing tone of the definition seems directed at supposedly bad misinformation distributed by bad people with bad intentions. Disinformation is not as morally simple as this. During World War II, the Allies organized a successful disinformation campaign to fool the Germans about the site of the coming invasion of France. The goal was to misdirect the attention of the Germans away from the Normandy coast. Ultimately, the goal was to harm the Germans in order to benefit the Allied strategic goals; so, what was harm to one was a benefit to the other. This could be called a profit. But this is to judge the goal, rather than to understand the specific disinformation relative to this goal. The goal was to mislead the Germans. The effects of the disinformation were bad for the Germans and good for the Allies. In this case, the disinformation was a kind of fake-out. As in dribbling a soccer ball, one acts to get your opponent to think you are doing one thing, when in fact you will do something else. To understand disinformation, how it works and why it works when it does, you will need to know the specific point of the disinformation and not simply that it would harm someone.

INFORMATION IS CONTESTED

The problem with using these terms (misinformation, disinformation, and malinformation) as ways of characterizing information disorder lies not just with the equivocation and tendentiousness of the notion of harm or the oversimplification of questions of intention. The concept of information cannot be easily defined as either ordered or disordered. Let us return to our more general point. As we have argued, both knowledge and information are contested and nebulous concepts. Knowledge varies in kind. We rely on various and different criteria in order to establish the veracity and credibility of these different kinds of knowledge. There is no absolute knowledge or certainty. Knowledge is evaluated relative to normative criteria, and what we claim to know will be contingent on how it is described, manifested, or formulated.

Information is in many cases, although not in all, a species of knowledge. And thus, it is normative and contingent in the same way. It cannot be absolutely true. We can be informed in many different ways. Information can take a variety of forms, all of which are case-specific. Information can be expressed in a proposition or a list. We can be informed by blood stains and by feeling the wind on our faces. Because information often involves some kind of abstraction from a statement, situation, interaction, or experiment and is often recorded, it can seem to stand separate from us. But it is separate in the way the alphabet is separate from the particular languages that give it sense. Without those languages, the alphabet would just be marks. The same is true of information; our understanding remains an essential factor.

We can say, therefore, that information is content abstracted into various forms of representation: tally marks, data, images, statements, and so on. Information is not a bare fact; it is a derived content. It is extracted from various contexts relative to a particular set of social and cognitive concerns. Misinformation is information that we discover or believe is false (we could be wrong about that). The sense, implications, coherence, and validity of some bit of information, whether that information is understood as data or as consisting of propositions, will be determined at some point by our judgment. As we have argued earlier, information (and hence misinformation) cannot exist in itself, but only for us. The ecosystem analogy fails to bring any of this complexity into view.

Wardle (2023) appeals to the information ecosystem when she argues that online posts and messages need to be understood within a social context and not simply relative to whether they are true or false. In some sense, the claim she makes is correct. Communication always takes place within a social context. If we do not focus on the social realities manifest online we will certainly not understand the world revealed on the web. But then she adds something to the notion of an information ecosystem that confuses things:

> Academics are not going to effectively strengthen the information
> ecosystem until we shift our perspective from classifying every
> post to understanding the social contexts of this information, how
> it fits into narratives and identities, and its short-term impacts and
> long-term harms.

She imagines that academics can strengthen the information ecosystem. It is not clear how understanding social contexts will strengthen the ecosystem. How are we to understand the relationship between an information ecosystem and a social context, in any case? Is the social context part of the ecosystem? If so, then Wardle's suggestion is highly condescending. Are we to track these social contexts in order to correct what people say in order, therefore, to correct their thoughts and thinking? Not only would that be a great abuse of power, but do we really want to shape the ecosystem to produce the beliefs we think are true? Who will decide on what these are? And why should we give anyone that kind of power? But luckily the whole idea is impossible to accomplish.

Maybe the social context uses the information ecosystem as a tool, or maybe as an extension of the offline or online social context. It is not clear, of course, how one would use an ecosystem as a tool. But you can certainly use sources of information as tools. In any case, if this is what Wardle means, then the information ecosystem is just a collection of information sources to which someone has access. The ecosystem analogy, again, adds very little to our understanding.[1]

The deeper problem remains: there is no real information disorder, since there can be no ordered information within any social community. This is true of scientists, as well. It is not the community of scientists that pursues trustworthy claims and accounts of various things, but the practices of science pursued within these communities. Scientists, like everyone else, act out of self-interest, and sometimes cut corners, manipulate, lie, and distort. If there is no real information order within the community of scientists, then we are unlikely to find it elsewhere.

Wardle concludes her comment above with the idea that we should evaluate how posts fit within social contexts, which include narratives and so-called identities. The evaluation of these social uses of web posts is characterized as "short-term impacts and long-term harms." This is a return to the moral politics of harm. We are again encouraged to be moral policemen, and to evaluate the exchange of information relative to its consequences (or imagined consequences). In particular, we should, she suggests, value exchanges relative to "long-term harms." Who decides what counts as harm and if these harms will manifest or lead to long-term consequences? The complexity of social life and social systems make long-term predictions foolish, in any case. The speculation about these consequences will necessarily rest on political assumptions. Pursuing this kind of evaluation of the so-called ecosystem is an example of social engineering, and as such should not be disguised under some scientific pretense. It is politics, plain, and simple.

Can the problems with these specific uses of the information ecosystem metaphor be overcome? There have been a few attempts to specify and conceptualize the metaphor of an information ecosystem. Evan F. Kuehn (2023), for example, analyzes various versions of the information ecosystem metaphor, and then offers his own more analytic definition. He writes relative to the discipline of Library Information Sciences (LIS), but his definition is also focused on the internet and captures the essential elements of the metaphor:

> In the context of academic research, an information ecosystem refers to "all structures, entities, and agents related to the flow of semantic information relevant to a research domain, as well as the information itself."

The gesture here is holistic; it is a system. Kuehn characterizes the system as having three main parts: "its possible constituents (structures, entities, agents), a relation requirement (relatedness to semantic information and its flow) and a scope of interest (research domain)." He admits that different disciplines will determine an information structure, entity, and agent in a variety of different ways. There are a number of problematic elements in this definition. He talks, for example, of "a flow of semantic information." There is no actual flow in a system in which information can be found and retrieved. He also includes the information found and retrieved, which would be the content of whatever is retrieved. Thus, one of the agents would be the person who reads that information. Such a library information system has a clearly defined retrieval function. The retrieval of a book, for example, must be efficient and trustworthy, but this is not to guarantee that the book is trustworthy or true in whatever sense one imagines. The search engines and the content resources of the web, while more open-ended, have certain similarities with a library. But as we have mentioned there is no guarantee that the book or content retrieved in a library is true or false (unless the library is defined as a library of only true things; or alternatively of false things; but still, there would likely be disagreements about what to include in such libraries). The worry about misinformation on the web, therefore, cannot be assuaged by the library version of the analogy.

A more attractive analogy for the web might be to construe it as some kind of virtual and networked encyclopedia: an encyclopedia as an information ecosystem. As tempting as this is, we think that in general this analogy is also misleading. The encyclopedia analogy encourages the idea that web pages should offer true information, and be a source of knowledge. As we have argued earlier, knowledge is not just a collection of facts. A web page represents something we can know or communicate. The web in many ways acts like an external memory device, so that it offers us memories of what might or might not be knowledge, that then we can take up in various ways. The content stored on the web is in some ways a kind of collective memory or recording, and thus cannot have the purported authority of an encyclopedia. We do use it and especially some platforms (e.g., YouTube) as repositories of knowledge and know-how, and we can learn from these. But our relationship to even these instructional videos is only sometimes like our attitudes toward encyclopedias. The internet is many things at once.[2]

INTERNET, WORLD WIDE WEB, AND ONLINE SOCIAL NETWORKS

The ecosystem metaphor captures important elements of the web and our interactions with it. In particular, it highlights the way elements of the web and OSNs seem to the user to be a systemic part of an environment, which they can manipulate in various ways. In the rest of this chapter, we would like to describe the complex systems of the technology and our interface with it in order to highlight important features that affect how we are involved with its epistemological and informational potential.

We begin by returning to a comment by Tim Berners-Lee, the software engineering inventor of the World Wide Web. In a 2014 interview with Harry Halpin and Alexandre Monnin, he comments that:

> . . . the design of the Web is not just the design of one thing but the design of two things: a social and technological protocol. For example, in e-mail, there's a general technological protocol like SMTP and there's a social protocol. In e-mail, the social protocol that states that everyone involved is ready to run a machine that has the space to store e-mail messages while they are en route to their destination, that people will send e-mail to each other on perfectly reasonable topics, and that people will read e-mail that they receive.

The design and redesign of the web required that engineers attend to both technological and social protocols. The social protocol about email was faulty, since the designers failed to imagine the possibility that unwanted, unreasonable, and irrelevant email messages would be sent to people. This is what we now call spam. The social problem spawning spam remains an issue to this day, since there is no easy way to constrain human social behavior by technological design.

What are the fundamental technological protocols organizing and defining the internet and the World Wide Web? The internet at a basic technological level is a distributed packet-switching network that includes other networks. It is a network of networks. The internet is technically the machine and computing infrastructure through which information flows. The dominant software network that functions through and on the internet is the World Wide Web, a collection of web pages organized through URIs (Uniform Resource Identifiers), linked by hypertext protocols (e.g., Hyper Text Transfer Protocol) and software languages (for example, Hyper Text Markup Language). In addition to the web, the internet hosts email, instant messaging services, File Transfer Protocol (FTP), and other transfer protocols.

In other words, the internet hosts a complex collection of infrastructural software tools that allow for the transfer of information between various points. These transfers can be between human beings by means of various interface devices. Computers can also send and receive messages and information. Online, we operate using virtual sites of various kinds. These are transactional spaces in which different kinds of exchange can take place, and can be tracked, stored, and analyzed.

Social media, in particular, has become not only a mode of communication, but also a mode of forming communities and of gossiping. The activity of gossip mirrors the structural capabilities and limitations of the internet. For example, fast and highly mediated communication with people physically distant and not involved in face-to-face life creates a natural fragility to online communities. People can easily disappear. The very tenuousness of these online communities requires social reinforcement, and hence gossip and rumor become a recurrent way in which such communities define themselves and interact.

Online interfaces simplify and delimit the ways we can interact with content and with other online users, as well as with networked computers. An interface is designed with a set of particular capabilities, which are exploited in various ways by users (sometimes beyond the intentions of the designers). The most general kind of interface is the search engine. The success of these search engines, in particular the ascendancy of Google, rests on their success in providing access to the relevant information searched for by users. Google's successful page-ranking algorithm combines the indexing of content with a tracking and prioritizing of those pages, which are indexed by topic or content, that were most popular. In effect, they utilize a measure of social importance in order to find relevant sites for a particular search. This is a kind of abstract measure of the gossip about web pages.

The emergence of online platforms like Facebook, YouTube, and Instagram, added two further dimensions to the basic online interface modalities. What we are calling the first dimension describes the online platforms and their interface affordances. As online platforms and their interfaces became more seamless and powerful, these interfaces incorporated in direct ways the kind of content a user might be interested on their interface pages. Users became consumers of information that was pushed or recommended to them using particular algorithms, such that the interface becomes a dynamic profile of the user. The second interface dimension arising from social media platforms concerns human behavior. These dominant social platforms, building on the individual way we interface with the web, encouraged users to mix self-display and self-mirroring.

It is easy to forget that these interfaces are fundamentally social discursive structures, even though they are designed and dependent on software development and computational power. Discursive structures and modes are aspects of what Berners-Lee calls social protocols. Platform interfaces provide ways for us to communicate with others and with the network (and its computing power). Communication through and with internet-based networks is bound up with what Norbert Wiener called feedback and control (Wiener, 1988). An interface is a system of feedback and control by means of which we communicate and access other users and devices linked to the web.

It has become a common practice to describe the capabilities and possible uses of programs and interfaces and networks as affordances. This term has its legitimate technological uses, but we want to extend its sense to include the interaction of agent and computer network. This means, however, that one must see the agent as already a part of many social networks, and as utilizing and embedded within linguistic practices that are shaped, facilitated, and restricted by the online interface. We use the notions of grammar and syntax to describe these structural relationships because in effect we are examining OSNs as extensions and developments of our general social discursive practices (and not simply as technological affordances).

The easy proliferation of information and the speed and superficiality of our online interactions encourages often highly prejudicial and unthoughtful transfers of information. These immediate and emotional-driven responses are further encouraged by the fact that most online interactions are not face to face. Even when using video, we can easily disappear, hide, or become anonymous. Or we can use an avatar or another account to mask our face and identity. Social media, in particular, becomes a mode not simply of communication, but of forming communities and of gossiping. The activity of gossip mirrors the structural capabilities and limitations of the internet. For example, fast and highly mediated communication with people physically distant and not involved in our face-to-face life creates a natural fragility to online communities. People can easily disappear. The very tenuousness of these online communities requires social reinforcement, and hence gossip and rumor become basic ways in which such communities define themselves and interact.

While users remain reactive and complex in their processing and uses of online information, their role in the information network encourages a greater passivity relative to what they read, and tends to facilitate simplified attitudes toward information. We like the information or do not; we share it; we sometimes make comments. But these reactions need not indicate belief or any kind of commitment in what a user shares or about which someone comments. There is little motive, time, or resources to determine the warrant or validity of online statements, many of which are strictly speaking not simple facts, but complex claims of various kinds. This allows for the proliferation of one-sided claims, since counter-statements are diminished or silenced. It also encourages the expression and sharing of statements with little warrant. Here again, we see the ways online interface and web capabilities encourage gossip; these online interfaces create the grammar of gossip in their very organization and in their specific affordances. The online simplification of the conversational situation to short bursts of information from various and different contexts encourages us to understand online information as content for which no one is fully responsible. No one need take full responsibility for these statements, beyond approval and disapproval.

While only human beings gossip, Large Language Model (LLM) Artificial Intelligences have a number of gossip-affiliated characteristics. LLMs learn through neural net processes, utilizing large databases through which they are trained. They learn not through controlled inputs but by sifting through data whose status is no more guaranteed than gossip. These AIs build up pictures and textual outputs based on probabilities. There is no clear warrant for what such an AI learns; no one is responsible for the speech and images it produces. Nevertheless, we treat what they produce as intelligible. Optics researcher Janelle Shane describes in a 2024 Scientific American article that what LLMs produce is more or less gossip, although she does not use that word:

The way that we're trying to use these algorithms now as a way of retrieving information is not going to lead us to correct information, because their goal during training is to *sound correct* and be probable, and there's not really anything fundamentally tied back to real-world accuracy or to exactly retrieving and quoting the correct source material.

An AI is not responsible for what it produces. It has learned through a combination of processing vast amounts of data, none of which is guaranteed to be true, accurate, or meaningful. And the process of this learning is facilitated by the corrections and weightings that direct it. There is no clear warrant for what it learns; no one is responsible for the speech and images it produces. In effect, LLMs learn by means of gossip and then facilitate online gossip by spreading what they have learned. They are gossip machines.

AIs are being used increasingly as search engines. But the peculiarities of the online interface can best be described using the structural effects of the recommendation algorithms used by networks like Facebook and TikTok.

A number of social network platforms such as Facebook and LinkedIn populate a user's feed with content derived from the content and activities of the user's friends. So, if user X has two friends (user Y and user Z), the bulk of the content on X's feed will mimic the activities of Y and Z. For example: Y posted this, or Z liked that, or W is a friend of Y and hence is a recommended friend for X, and so on. On these social networks, most of the time people engage with other users whom they already follow. Such networks are uninteresting if you do not have many friends, or if you do not follow popular accounts. Consider the case of user X with two friends Y and Z. If X has not followed any of the larger popular accounts, the feed on X's page will consist of activities that only Y or Z have performed on the network. Such content is unlikely to motivate a user to spend much time on the platform.

Facebook's recommendation algorithm, therefore, produces a model of our interests through assuming we are like our friends, in effect, reinforcing this online community. We become the silent target of our friends' interests. We are treated as a target at the center of a community of similar people (defined simply by their connection with us). The algorithm is akin to Virgil's monster Rumor—a head with many eyes and tongues—but what it produces is not rumor, but a feed of information determined by our networks of friends.

The TikTok algorithm operates quite differently. It is more of a mechanism that generates self-gossip, rather than gossip among friends. TikTok users spend most of their time on what is called the For You Page (FYP), on which content endlessly appears. This content is algorithmically selected for its combination of novelty and potential for addiction. Unlike other social network algorithms, TikTok's FYP is not based on the follower count or history of high-performing videos on the platform. So, while an account with zero followers might not be of much value to the algorithms of other social networks, on TikTok that is not the case. Every video has a probability of being featured on someone else's FYP feed. Depending on the engagement metrics of the video, it gets plugged into larger and larger communities by appearing on the feeds of more and more users. This offers every video the chance to achieve wide visibility, regardless of the number of followers of the user who created the video.

The TikTok algorithm utilizes three primary factors. The first factor utilizes context information derived from settings set on the user's interface device (mobile phone), as well as account data that the user has provided. More importantly, the algorithm monitors and evaluates two other factors: a user's interaction with content on the app and information about the videos watched.

A user's interaction is defined by two categories of activity. The first category of activity tracks what we might call positive engagements with content. The algorithm monitors and evaluates, for some user X, the accounts that X follows, the videos for which X has posted comments, the video completion rate, the videos that X has posted, the videos that X has liked, shared, or marked as favorites, and also X's interaction with the ads presented by TikTok. The second category of activity monitored determines what kind of content X dislikes (that is, content toward which X is disinclined). This is determined through the evaluation of the accounts or sounds that X has chosen to "hide" from the feed, and videos that X has marked as being not appropriate or not interested.

Another factor that influences the TikTok algorithm is information about the videos that a user watches. The algorithm collects and classifies the information that a user searches (using what is called the Discover feature). In addition, the algorithm tracks a user's interaction and responses to captions, sounds, hashtags, video editing effects, and trending topic categories of videos that a user watches. From this information, TikTok's FYP algorithm develops a complex profile of the types of videos that a user might be inclined to watch.

As a video sharing platform, TikTok has also made it easy for users to create videos, apply video editing effects, and share these videos with others. Videos can be anywhere from five seconds to ten minutes long, although longer videos are not recommended since the video completion rate is an important factor in determining the video content of a user's video feed. The shorter length of videos and algorithms also makes it possible for a user to watch more videos per hour than any other video platforms, including YouTube. This brings us to an important, even if obvious, network structure observation. TikTok relies on a large subset of its network of users to produce content. This content is uploaded and then redistributed by the algorithm, which is continually modified through its feedback protocol. The content just appears. Like in all good gossip, the source of the content is mediated, and often the content is copied from others. In effect, the FYP feed is a stream of rumors.

It should be acknowledged that TikTok's FYP algorithm is responsible for TikTok's amazing success. As of 2023, TikTok had 50 million daily active users, and was the most downloaded app in several countries. With more than 1 billion active global accounts, TikTok's user base accounts for little less than a fifth of all Internet users worldwide. A TikTok user spends an average of 90 minutes every day on the platform, which takes top honors for the most time spent by users on any social networking or video platform.

All social media platforms function as gossip economies. We have highlighted the ways in which recommendation algorithms perpetuate the grammar of gossip, even though these algorithms in some ways replace the person-to-person gossip of users. These algorithms, however, are parasitic on network relations among "friends" in the Facebook case, and on the logic of self-gossip within the mediated environment of posted videos in the TikTok case. These algorithms should be understood as fundamental constituents of the user interface with the online environment. This interface should be conceptualized.

Online environments are interactive and dynamic—a mix of structure and content, which is why the algorithms are constitutive of the interface. Our relationship with the interface affordances as well as the content has a dynamic, structural form that involves feedback and control, like any cybernetic device (information device). The relationship is also discursive, since it is a form of interactive communication, even if mediated by software and hardware. With these observations in mind, how should we understand the interfaces of these specific social media platforms? And what can this reveal to us about our relationship with the various forms of online information and content?

THE INTERFACE TRANSDUCER

The interface between ourselves and the online environment structures our ways of interacting with online content. When we understand the available applications, network affordances, and monitoring algorithms as part of this interface, then we can easily recognize the Janus-faced nature of these interfaces. Janus is a Roman god who faces in two directions: a god of doors, transitions, and beginnings. These OSN interfaces have evolved such that they are doors for us into the online environment, but they are also doors into our interests and behavior for those who have control of these interfaces. We interface with the web and the web interfaces with us. In saying this, we are personifying the interface. Given the dynamic intelligence with which our behaviors are tracked and used to push content onto our online feeds, we feel fully justified in that personification.

This Janus-faced interface, however, might even more accurately be analogized as a bidirectional transducer. A transducer converts one kind of energy into another, like quartz can convert mechanical pressure into electrical impulses. A bidirectional transducer can do this in two direction, like an antenna, which can convert radio waves into electrical impulses and can also convert electrical impulses into radio waves.

We have focused on the TikTok- and Facebook-type of recommendation algorithms, but we are tracked and analyzed in various ways by online applications. The general point is that my online interactions with online content gets converted into information about me, which produces reactions by various software applications. More generally, my interactions with online resources produces virtual consequences, and those consequences are often available to others to see, use, and comment upon: a simple online posting can have this effect. Because we are tracked online and through our phones, we can also see that by using current phone and computer technology, we are giving access to our lives through the same interface devices that give us access to online resources. The use of smart phones, with their GPS capabilities, only extends this access of whoever controls these applications into our lives. This is all well known, if poorly attended to.

The algorithmic interfaces of particular OSNs convert my engagement with online content (even if this is just passive watching in the case of TikTok) into a model (a representation) of my interests that then leads to my exposure to new and similar content. This content populates a virtual environment with which I engage, producing more content. The online environment is a highly mediated construct. The continuous responsiveness of algorithms and AIs to my behavior partially hides this mediation. My interactions with that environment and its content is immediate. The mediated online presentation of images, videos, and information produce a visceral reaction, and thus a kind of experience of immediacy, exacerbated by the quick replacement of one video with another, one message with another, one story by another. Our experience of this mediated (and curated content) does not require social effort: I watch whatever is shown to me. Voyeurism becomes emotionally and socially easy.

The computer/online interface has evolved into a bidirectional transducer that facilitates and allows for our conversion into a matrix of information, which becomes the means for feeding us with other examples of information and content. An OSN interface is a looking glass, which is also a door, a portal through which we can interact with online content in a variety of ways. Through the looking glass we find many a queen of hearts (influencers and stars of self-display: all versions of Lady Catherine). This wonderland operates in ways that we can only half see. The wonderland of the online environment is structured and directed by algorithms and AIs that track and evaluate us in order to create virtual communities that mimic the discursive grammar of gossip and self-gossip. This is the kingdom of gossip.

Consider the illustration of the online interface in Figure 15.1. The interface is like a distorting window that both reflects like a mirror but also lets images through. The interface allows individuals to create and manipulate online versions of themselves, which they can then send to others. Such manipulations include each individual's own online behavior, their observations of the online behavior of other individuals, and thereby the corresponding mutual influence of individuals on each other. Thus, the interface is a bidirectional transducer, which includes a continual generative feedback loop.

Nodes A, C, F, P, T, and Z represent actual individuals. Of these nodes, A, C, F, P, and T are users of some OSN. Their online identities are represented by an apostrophe. So, A' is the online profile of A, F' is the online profile of F, and so on. These connections between individuals and their online profiles are indicated by dotted lines. Nodes Q, E, and J have a single arrow pointing out, representing that they are connected to other individuals in the real world (not necessarily to A, C, F, P, and T).

Connections between individuals in the real world are represented by straight arrows, and connections between online profiles are represented by curved arrows. The directionality of the arrow indicates either friendship

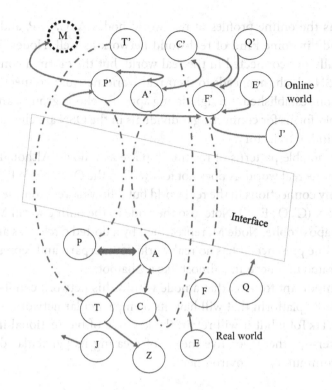

FIGURE 15.1   An online gossip community.

or followership. For example, nodes A and C are friends with each other in the real world, but node A follows node T in the real world. Here, the terms 'follow' and 'followership' refer to the phenomenon where the activities and lifestyles of public figures (entertainers, athletes, politicians, celebrities, and other widely reported-about individuals) are covered extensively in print, broadcast, and internet media for public consumption.

Thus, Node T represents a figure in the public domain, a celebrity of some sort, about whom much is written and published in different kinds of media). Node T in turn follows Z, another public figure. The diagram thus shows a hierarchical ordering of individuals and their social dynamics. Note also that Z does not have an online profile. Z represents an individual who does not have an online account in this particular OSN, but is connected to other individuals in the real world who have online accounts on this OSN.

There is also another important kind of link between nodes, represented by the link in the real world between A and P. But before we explore that link, let us look at the online world. As mentioned above, the online world has the online profiles of real-world nodes A, C, F, P, and T who are already in some kind of real-world network as well. Nodes A and P are initially not connected in the real world, but they form a connection in the OSN which then leads to their real-world network connection. The connections established through dating apps, Facebook groups, and other similar platforms for connecting individuals in the OSN are characterized by this kind of trajectory.

Other notable patterns of relationship are as follows: Although A follows T in the real world, A does not follow T' in the OSN. Node F does not have many connections in the real world but follows several online profiles in the OSN (C', Q', E', J'). Note also the node in the online world M which lacks an apostrophe. Node M, represented by a dotted circle, has an exclusively online presence. It has no real-world counterpart, and represents an AI-generated user account, almost like a Chatbot.

It is important to note, that a node within this network can itself be a social media platform that will have its own particular network structure (as does TikTok); but it will retain the key role of bidirectional interface transducer—as the generative means of creating its particular dynamic virtual community or environment.

CONCLUSION

The information ecosystem picture construes information (and in many ways knowledge) to be understood as a kind of resource like water, and that users interact with it as animals might in a natural environment. We have been arguing that this is not how information exists and is used in our lives. Knowledge is not something that can flow or that circulates in some environment, as if all we had to do in order to know something was to drink it, wash with it, and consume it. To understand something is not to consume it. We need not understand what we eat.

Again, we do understand the attractiveness of such a metaphor. Information, given its complex status and form in our lives, does not exist as information separate from our own uses of it. It fits with our own cognitive understandings, and our social worlds offline as well as with those online, embedded as those latter are in the infrastructure of the web and OSNs. As Narayanan (2023), argues in his excellent article titled *Understanding Social Media Recommendation Algorithms*, social media platforms are complex non-linear systems. Such non-linear systems are not controllable by the linear means that are often suggested by academic researchers. Despite any appearances to the contrary, our comments here are not directed against Wardle, whose work has been of great significance in our attempts to understand the emergent social technology of the internet. Rather, we want to suggest that while there are ecosystem aspects to online platforms and networks, it is misleading to treat the ecosystem metaphor as the prevailing figure for an understanding of how these networks work and how we interact with them. It also oversimplifies and distorts the complex and multiplicitous forms of information.

Our discussion in this chapter has led us to a further refinement of the two problems with which it began. Firstly, misinformation and other related concepts should not be understood as polluting clean information. These distinctions, which do matter, are always contingent and normative in a contested way. Secondly, describing the web as an information ecosystem is at best misleading and worst nonsensical. Our metaphors for the web and the role of information in it should not be neat and tidy; they should be overlapping, somewhat conflicting and multiple.

NOTES

1 Maybe some CEO or designer could strengthen the information ecosystem by altering OSNs such that they offer different capabilities—alter the medium in order to change the message, as Marshall McLuhan might suggest. Even if there were some possible alteration that would diminish the information disorder, there is no incentive to do this, since the economic imperative of OSNs is to attract and retain users.

2 The internet is, of course, also a communications system. This fact naturally encourages us to want to trust and believe what we are told. The communication is not only between people, but with sites and sources, including now with AI sources and created videos, texts, and postings. Even when we use the internet to communicate by text, instant messaging, or some other means and method, the ability to record and store what we send to each other creates a mediating buffer. We can respond immediately to a text message, but we might not, or might see it or respond to it only hours or even days later. This diminishes the social friction that is always a part of face-to-face interactions. We can say something and not be present when it is read or we can ignore any response to what we say that we do not like. We take up the role of a broadcast, although one directed to those with whom we correspond. Or we can become broadcasters and content creators for a broader public by making, for example, Instagram or TikTok videos.

REFERENCES

de Cock Buning, Madeleine. *A multi-dimensional approach to disinformation: Report of the independent high-level group (HLEG) on fake news and online disinformation.* Publications Office of the European Union, 2018.

Halpin, Harry, and Alexandre Monnin. "Interview with Tim Berners-Lee." In Harry Halpin & Alexandre Monnin (Eds.), *Philosophical engineering: Toward a philosophy of the web* (pp. 181–186). Wiley-Blackwell, 2014.

Kuehn, Evan F. "The information ecosystem concept in information literacy: A theoretical approach and definition." *Journal of the Association for Information Science and Technology* 74.4 (2023): 434–443.

Narayanan, Arvind. *Understanding social media recommendation algorithms.* Knight First Amendment Institute, 2023.

Shane, Janelle. "Please don't ask AI if something is poisonous," Scientific American (2024) https://www.scientificamerican.com/article/has-generative-ai-lost-its-strange-charm/

Wardle, Claire. "Misunderstanding misinformation." *Issues in Science and Technology* 39.3 (2023): 38–40.

Wardle, Claire, and Hossein Derakhshan. *Information disorder: Toward an interdisciplinary framework for research and policymaking.* Vol. 27. Council of Europe, 2017.

Wiener, Norbert. *The human use of human beings: Cybernetics and society.* No. 320. Da capo Press, 1988.

PART V

Conclusion

DOI: 10.1201/9781003401674-21

CHAPTER 16

The Dynamo and the Internet

INTRODUCTION

Samuel Coleridge described his goals as a poet in a letter to William Godwin [22 Sept. 1800]:

> ... I would endeavour to destroy the old antithesis of Words and Things; elevating, as it were, Words into Things and living things too.

(Prickett 1986, 134–138)

Coleridge's dream for poetry has also been the dream of philosophers, scientists, and information theorists, although what counts as a thing has expanded to include numbers, computation, radio signals, causes, and much else. This dream is at the core of the dominant ideas of information, misinformation, and data, ideas that are of concern in computational social sciences, media studies, and the various information and data sciences. In all of these cases, the vector of transformation tends to be directed in one direction—from words to things, or rather the drive is to dissolve judgment into cause; concepts into things in the world; humans into machines, and then with a twist to reconstitute machines as minds. The central concept in all of this attempted dissolution is *information*. The goal of many is to demonstrate how information can in effect be both thing and word, although this is to speak loosely. More precisely information is seen as

DOI: 10.1201/9781003401674-22

meaningful data or facts, and thus partly of matter (thing-like) and partly meaningful.

John Michael Dunn does not follow this trend, but formulates the underlying issue as a question. As we have discussed earlier, he comments that "the fundamental philosophical question regarding the representation of information is: how much "lies in the eye of the beholder?" (Dunn, 2008). In other words, how much of the content of information is in the signal and how much is derived and developed by us, through our understanding? Again, this is akin to Terrence Deacon's observation that we can calculate "the information-conveying capacity of any given communications medium, and yet we cannot give an account of how this relates to the content that this signal may or may not represent" (2010, 2014).

These technical questions about information are actually part of broader cultural anxieties about how to understand ourselves as human beings relative to the world revealed by modern science, and the conditions of life infused and shaped by technology. The 19th-century historian Henry Adams, the great grandson of John Adams, in his idiosyncratic autobiography tells the story of what he calls his education, or rather his failed education. He has failed to understand what the world has become under the pressures and successes of science. As an historian of the mind and of culture, Adams suggests that he is a Branly coherer, a detector of radio waves (Adams, 1918, 1946, 1973). In his alienated confusion, Adams confesses that he sees the world described by physics as real, but himself (and all human beings) as unreal; "I am a projection, fantasy, dream," he seems to say: "The world exists, but do I?"[1]

Adams describes a human being "as the sum of all the forces that attract him." Such a creature is bound to the world and its historical form by these attractions. If a person is a particularized set of attractions, then the mind of a culture describes the center of gravity of those forces that organize persons within it. For the 20th century, Adams claims, this center of gravity is the dynamo, which describes the non-intentional extreme as opposed to an intentional world epitomized by the Virgin Mary in the 14th century. This is not a simple opposition between a mechanical universe and an organic, divinely infused one, but rather between different senses of mind expressed through a way of symbolizing the order of forces that would organize a life in relation to our possible fates delimited by the historical moment. The Virgin is a transducer of human thought and desires, of human forces, and the forces of the natural world, embodied in Mont Saint Michel and Chartres (Adams, 1987). The relation between divinity and humanity exemplified in Christ is further humanized in this characterization, making the Virgin more a part of this world, in the way the dynamo also is, than a part of a transcendent realm.[2]

The Virgin and the dynamo exemplify what Blackmur (1980) calls "the force of symbol and the symbol of force." What is the "force of symbol"? Our exchanges of gossip are replete with this kind of force. Rumor embodies it. Any battle over ideals, revenge for insults, or act of sacrifice demonstrate this force. It is also utilized in thinking, understanding, writing, and reading. One aspect of the force of symbols would be shown by the symbol of force: the dynamo. Adams imagines we are constrained and directed by forces. While the force of symbols might be shown by the symbol of force, Adams' goal is to invert this and to understand how the force of symbols would be itself a symbol of force. Through such an inversion, symbols would themselves be a manifestation of force. Since the modern symbol of force for Adams is the dynamo, the force of symbols should be understood to be on par with the dynamo, with the work it does and the electric field it produces.

The Virgin exemplifies this idea that the force of symbols, how and what they mean, can become the same as force itself; people act through and relative to their understanding of this force in their existence made manifest by symbolic means. The force of the Virgin can be the symbol of the Virgin only if all symbols, like icons in the Eastern orthodox tradition, participate in the divinity of the Virgin as a kind of fact.[3] Divinity, in this case, becomes the means of characterizing the world as what Adams calls a Unity, within which a unit (the symbol of the Virgin) necessarily refers. He claims that we moderns have lost that kind of unity, and thus that kind of meaning. While mechanical force is expressive and symbolic of power, Adams believes that we lack the means of understanding our human lives as expressive of this in the ways made possible when the Virgin was the dynamo of the world and a symbol of humanity.

We are all made from forces that we ourselves do not understand, since these forces are not simply ideas, but the manifestation of the world, of nature, grasped in and by our limited scientific understanding. An education does not simply consist of surviving the assault by the indifference of nature, but requires that one understand one's understanding as part of that indifferent and mechanical nature. The modern sciences might describe that indifference, but they do not domesticate it, as Lucretius, for example, imagined ancient philosophy and science might. Adams seems to agree with Spencer when he claims that the hard problem Darwin had bequeathed to us was how to explain consciousness. Adams, however, will not assume that we even understand how to describe what we are such that it could be explained. Science, Adams claims, does not offer "any scheme of reconciliation between thought and mechanics."[4] These forces have vectors that the historian must learn to read. His learning is his education.

The Virgin as the intercessor between human beings and God incorporates symbols of our humanity with symbols of divinity. This incorporate force constitutes the condition and form of life in Adams' account of the 14th-century Mind, as he calls it. Without this intercessor, our sense of the world, the sense through which we live and history is made, falls into what Adams calls Multiplicity. Science produces this fall of the world into Multiplicity. If we are to fit into this new world spawned by science, then we must find a way of using this multiplicity to unify our relation to it. Adams translates physics, specifically the kinetic theory of gases, into a metaphysical allegory describing the fundamental unit of the modern universe as this Multiplicity, by which he means the movement and particularity of atoms. This Unity of Multiplicity, as he formulates it, while fine for science, results in "chaos for man." Science describes reality, and this reality lacks any teleological order. It is hostile to human beings. We have become aliens to the universe in which we live. Through science and the evolution of our culture through time, thought (mind) has separated from the social order, and so we live amidst disorder: "Without thought in the unit, there could be no unity; without unity no orderly sequence or ordered society. Thought alone was Form. Mind and Unity flourished or perished together." This is one of the ways Adams has of characterizing the desacralization of our world: "[m]odern science guaranteed no unity." This unity is not the unity of a grand unified theory, but rather the unity of the moral and intellectual sense of ourselves with our understanding of the world. This unity is manifest in the action of building a monument to the force of the Virgin at Chartres, for example.

Adams translates concepts from physics—force, energy, unity—into mental terms which are simultaneously terms of culture and history. He comments for example that "Adams never knew why, knowing nothing of Faraday, he began to mimic Faraday's trick of seeing lines of force all about him, where he had always seen lines of will." (426). He admits that this "trick of seeing lines of force all about him" is metaphoric, an effect of his ignorance of mathematics resulting in a counter tendency "to leave the mind to imagine figures—images—phantoms." [427]. But it is through these figures, images, and phantoms that the mind enters into the mechanical universe. He continues:

> one's mind is a watery mirror at best; but, once conceived, the image became rapidly simple, and the lines of force presented themselves as lines of attraction. By this path, the mind stepped into the mechanical theory of the universe before knowing it, and entered a distinct new phase of education.

By 'mind,' Adams partially means to describe both the seat of our personhood, broadly understood, and those psychological contents that affect the world and cause us to act, primarily beliefs. Underlying this fusion of physics talk into mind and cultural history talk is the sense that the world of physics has a coherence that our understanding of our human selves and our human being does not.

What Adams attempts with the words and concepts of 'force,' 'unity,' 'mind,' 'dynamo,' 'virgin' is equivalent to what theorists attempt with words and concepts of 'information,' 'misinformation,' 'data,' and even in a different way with the concept of knowledge. We will focus on information as the most critical of these attempted transformations. Matter is mindless, despite the fantasies of pan-psychism. But, unlike matter, the idea of information seems to have a kind of content that is more than matter but less than meaning, although it promises to be meaningful— somehow. This is the temptation that the concept of information offers. Mingers' and Standings' theory of information, for example, reveals that temptation. They argue that information is both objective and veridical. Its objectivity means that it exists separate from us as something substantive and causally efficacious: "information has causal effect whether or not humans are involved and if it can be shown that something has causal efficacy, then that is an argument for its existence." This is to give information magical powers. In so doing our human role in perceiving, knowing, and understanding gets simplified and dissolved in these magical powers of information.

This information magic promises to solve the general problem of how to link or integrate the physical with the mental. David Chalmers (1996) makes this specific when speculating about the relationship between brain and mind:

> We need some sort of construct to make the link, and information seems as good a construct as any. It may be that the principles

> concerning the double realization of information could be fleshed out into a system of basic laws connecting the physical and phenomenal domains.
>
> We might put this suggestion as a basic principle that information (in the actual world) has two aspects, a physical and a phenomenal aspect. Whenever there is a phenomenal state, it realizes an information state, an information state that is also realized in the cognitive system of the brain. Conversely, for at least some physically realized information spaces, whenever an information state in that space is realized physically, it is also realized phenomenally.
>
> David Chalmers, *The Conscious Mind.*

Information is cast as Janus-faced. It has a physical aspect and it has a phenomenological, and thus mental, aspect. Chalmers imagines information is seemingly an emergent kind of thing that has this dual aspect. And if so, then the mind/ matter dualism is resolved. The universe has something that is already both: information.

This idea may be attractive, but we have argued that it is false and confused. Our concern, however, has not been with the theoretical attempts in the philosophy of mind or physics to construe information in this way. Our goals have been more modest. The idea that information is somehow self-sufficient and independent of our human involvement leads to the conclusion that misinformation cannot be a species of information; it must be a kind of pollution. We have argued that this is a mistaken understanding of information and misinformation. The concepts of information and misinformation are entangled with ideas about knowledge. Because of this entanglement, people begin to imagine that we can know more than we can. We lose the sense that our knowledge is contingent and normative, not absolute and certain. Again, this is a mistake. Janus-faced information is the new modern dynamo, promising to heal the conceptual wounds that separate the world of physics from the world of the mind.

SOCIAL DYNAMICS AS THE DRIVER OF INFORMATION

A focus on the putative truth and falsity of information masks the fundamental social dynamics that determine information diffusion. Information and misinformation spread as gossip. The truth will not cure, prevent, or even mitigate the spread of misinformation. Instead, online social networks mirror, augment, and feed into the human propensity to gossip. We have argued while gossip has for basic discursive patterns, these collect around two fundamental characteristics:

a. Gossip is more expressive *of* the community of gossipers than it is *about* the target of the gossip.

b. What is said in gossip, because of the irresponsibility in which it is exchanged, and its accepted lack of warrant, and because of the way gossip is dispersed and held within the community of gossip exchange, floats free from responsible counter-statement.

Gossip has no foundation or warrant that can be readily examined. It is irresponsible speech. A rumor may be true and you may believe it, but your belief is no justification of its truth. But in gossip, truth is not important; gossiping is defined not by the contrast between true- and false-beliefs, but by social dynamics. It is constrained only by its means of transmission and the dispositions of individuals within a community to accept it.

Online information diffusion matches the conceptual patterns that define gossip. If online information diffusion is understood as a form of gossip, then we can understand that diffusion as a function of various social imperatives, which variously shape, reinforce, undermine, and exploit communities and individuals. The veracity of the information is often beside the point. Online social networks have become kingdoms of gossip, not of fact or truth, nor even of misinformation and falsity. This confusion of gossip, information, and knowledge is a new form of the Multiplicity that threatens chaos, as Adams describes it.

CONCLUSION

Our point in highlighting and exploring the discursive practices of gossip has not been to argue that people gossip about each other on the internet; of course, they do. It is that much of what we call information and mis-information online is itself a form of gossip—or a sibling of gossip. And as a consequence, our understanding of the differences between gossip, information, and knowledge have become muddied, confused, entangled, and uncertain. The uncertainty cannot be escaped or corrected by the institution of theoretical fiats, like the proclamation that truth is a neces-sary property of information or of any scientific claim. These theoretical proclamations feed into ideas about public censorship and information management, under the guise of defending the truth. What counts as a fact, as information, and as knowledge should be explored and argued, but it should not be legislated. We are reminded of an observation Hayek (2011) makes in *The Constitution of Liberty*: "[I]ndividual freedom rests chiefly on the recognition of the inevitable ignorance of all of us concerning a great many of the factors on which the achievement of our ends and welfare depends." We could not agree more.

NOTES

1 A more elaborate discussion of Adams relative to cognitive philosophy can be found in Bourbon (2004).
2 See Chapter 10 of Mont Saint Michel and Chartes.
3 For an excellent investigation of the philosophical meaning of icons see Miguel Tamen (2001).
4 He assumes erroneously that thought and consciousness are more or less the same.

REFERENCES

Bourbon, Brett. *Finding a replacement for the soul: Meaning and mind in literature and philosophy*. Harvard University Press, 2004.

Adams, Henry. *The education of Henry Adams*. Ernest Samuels (Ed.). Houghton Mifflin Co., 1918, 1946, 1973.

Adams, Henry. *Mont St. Michel and Chartres*. Penguin Books, 1987.

Blackmur, R.P. *Henry Adams*. De Capo P, 1980.

Chalmers, David J. *The conscious mind: In search of a fundamental theory*. Oxford University Press, 1996.

Deacon, Terrence W. "What is missing from theories of information?" In Paul Davies and Niels Henrik Gregersen (Eds.), *Information and the nature of reality: From physics to metaphysics (Canto Classics)*. Cambridge University Press, 2010, 2014.

Dunn, J. Michael. "Information in computer science." *Philosophy of Information* 8 (2008): 581–608.

Hayek, F.A. *The constitution of liberty (Definitive Edition)*. University of Chicago Press, 2011.

Prickett, Stephen. *Words and the word: Language, poetics and biblical interpretation*. Cambridge University Press, 1986.

Tamen, Miguel. *Friends of interpretable objects*. Harvard University Press, 2001.

Index

Printed in the United States
by Baker & Taylor Publisher Services